South Africa's Labor Empire

South Africa's Labor Empire

A History of Black Migrancy to the Gold Mines

Jonathan Crush, Alan Jeeves,
and David Yudelman

Westview Press

BOULDER • SAN FRANCISCO • OXFORD

David Philip

CAPE TOWN

HD
8039
M74
S63
1991

This book is included in Westview's African Modernization and Development Series.

Published in 1991 in the United States of America by Westview Press, Inc., 5500 Central Avenue, Boulder, Colorado 80301, and in the United Kingdom by Westview Press, 36 Lonsdale Road, Summertown, Oxford OX2 7EW

Published in 1991 in southern Africa by David Philip Publishers (Pty) Ltd, P O Box 23408, Claremont 7735, South Africa

Library of Congress Cataloging-in-Publication Data
Crush, J. S.
    South Africa's labor empire : a history of Black migrancy to the
gold mines / Jonathan Crush, Alan Jeeves, and David Yudelman.
        p.   cm. — (African modernization and development series)
    Includes bibliographical references (p.   ) and index.
    ISBN 0-8133-7417-0 (Westview, cloth)
    ISBN 0-86486-200-8 (David Philip, paper)
    1. Gold miners—South Africa.   2. Blacks—South Africa.
3. Apartheid—South Africa.   I. Jeeves, Alan.   II. Yudelman, David.
III. Title.   IV. Series.
HD8039.M74S63   1991
331.6'9968—dc20   91-14141
                                                            CIP

Printed and bound in the United States of America

The paper used in this publication meets the requirements
of the American National Standard for Permanence of Paper
for Printed Library Materials Z39.48-1984.

10   9   8   7   6   5   4   3   2   1

Contents

Tables and Illustrations

Figures

Photos, following page 150

Crown Mines, Johannesburg, South Africa's largest
producer of gold before the 1950s.

Black miners drilling gold reef in narrow underground
stope, ca. 1920s.

Black miners with white supervisor in stope, ca. 1920s.

Miner at stope face.

Turn-of-the-century mine compound on the Witwatersrand.

Inside a mine compound, ca. 1920s.

William Gemmill, the Chamber's "labor czar."

Beginning in the 1950s, a fleet of WLNA DC-3s was used
to maintain a regular service for picking up migrants
from throughout the northern zones.

Mine compound at Harmony Mine, Orange Free State,
built in the early 1950s; the distinctive panopticon
characterizes many compounds of the period.

Modern mine hostel complex, Elandsrand Mine, built in the 1970s.

Modern Johannesburg, with mine headgear in foreground.

Life President Hastings Banda of Malawi addresses five thousand Malawian miners at Western Deep Levels Mine on a visit to South Africa in 1971.

Unemployed workers wait for mine jobs outside a fortified recruiting office in rural Natal.

Part of a crowd of fifteen thousand miners gathered at the Jabulani Amphitheatre, Soweto, for the 1987 Annual Congress of the National Union of Mineworkers.

A delegate to the 1987 Congress remembers the 1946 mine strike.

Defiant miners dismissed during the last days of the 1987 strike.

NUM leaders Marcel Golding, Cyril Ramaphosa, and James Motlatsi at a press conference during the 1987 strike.

Acronyms and Abbreviations

AMWU	African Mine Workers' Union
ANC	African National Congress
ARB	Department of Labour Archive
AV	Anglovaal
AVS	Assisted Voluntary Scheme
BAB	Bantu Administration Board
BLS	Botswana, Lesotho, and Swaziland
BNA S	Botswana National Archives, Gaborone, Secretariat Series
BSA	British South Africa Company
CAD	Central Archives Depot, Pretoria Archives
CM	Chamber of Mines
CMAR	Chamber of Mines of South Africa, Annual Report
CNC	Chief Native Commissioner
CO	Colonial Office
COSATU	Congress of South African Trade Unions
CUSA	Council of Unions of South Africa
DNL	Director of Native Labour
DO	Dominions Office
ERPM	East Rand Proprietary Mines
FM	Financial Mail
GFSA	Goldfields of South Africa
GNLB	Government Native Labour Bureau
HNP	Herstigte Nasionale Partie
HRL	Human Resources Laboratory
ILO	International Labour Office (before 1946); International Labour Organization (after 1946)
JCI	Johannesburg Consolidated Investment
MNW	Secretary for Mines and Industries Archive
MWU	Mine Workers' Union
NRC	Native Recruiting Corporation, Johannesburg
NTS	Native Affairs Department Archive
NUM	National Union of Mineworkers
OB	*Ossewa Brandwag*

OFS	Orange Free State
PM	Prime Minister
PRO	Public Record Office
QA	Queen's Archives, Kingston
R	rand*
RM	Rand Mines
SAAU	South African Agricultural Union
SADCC	Southern African Development Co-ordination Conference
SAIRR	South African Institute of Race Relations
SALB	*South African Labour Bulletin*
SALC	Southern African Labour Commission
SALP	Southern African Labour Papers
SAP	South African Police
SNA	Secretary of Native Affairs
TEBA	The Employment Bureau of Africa
TNB	Tropical Northern Bechuana
UNISA	University of South Africa
UW	University of the Witwatersrand
VRG	Valid Reengagement Guarantee
WNLA	Witwatersrand Native Labour Association
ZA	Zimbabwe National Archives, Harare

---

*Particularly in the early chapters, references to currency are usually in pounds. Until 1961, South African currency was the South African pound, distinct from sterling but linked to it because of South Africa's membership in the sterling monetary area and earlier because of its adherence to the gold standard. In 1961, the currency became the rand (R) at the rate of one rand to ten South African shillings.

Preface

This book has three main objectives. First, it provides a historical account of the growth and consolidation of black migrancy to the South African gold mines between 1920 and 1970. Second, it documents and tries to explain the changes that have occurred in the migrant labor system since 1970. Finally, it assesses the prospects for the continuing transformation of subcontinental labor migrancy in the future.

The role of labor migrancy in the development of modern South Africa is a story that highlights the country's uniqueness, including its unrivaled endowments of gold and other resources and its social and political structures, manifested in the policies of segregation and apartheid. Although South Africa's peculiar labor systems are a distinctive feature of its development, in other respects it shares many of the characteristics of contemporary industrial society. Modern South Africa is recognizable by its developed transport and communications systems, centralized administration, and diversified manufacturing sector. At its core, there is the centrality of the state, its commitment to economic growth, and its symbiotic relationship with big business. Growing state and bureaucratic power mediates between national and international business and between business and organized labor. Modern South Africa is also characterized, however, by the development of a migrant labor system unequaled in scale and longevity. In other industrializing societies, labor migration was a transitory phenomenon, marking a one-time shift from an agrarian to an urban-industrial order. In South Africa the movement between rural and urban areas became entrenched at the center of the economic system and a permanent feature of life for millions of workers. Subcontinental labor migration was necessary to mine the gold that paid for (and was part of) the process of South African industrialization.

For eighty years, a highly organized migrant labor system took full advantage of subcontinental poverty and unemployment to deliver low-wage black labor to the mines. During most of this period, the gold price was tightly controlled, and this meant that the South African gold mining industry could not pass on higher costs to the buyers of its gold. The industry therefore had to keep costs stable or go out of business. Black labor, a major component of total costs and doubly vulnerable because it was migrant and politically rightless, bore the brunt of this unrelenting pressure. Without the almost complete containment of the costs of black labor, the extraordinary levels of gold production achieved since 1886 would not have been possible. Periodic crises, in the form of labor shortages or worker protest, occurred but were neutralized by the constant strengthening of the recruiting system and, where deemed necessary, by force. On the moving frontier of the industry's subcontinental labor empire, there were always workers whose lack of alternative opportunities made them available for mine work at prevailing wages. The imperatives of cost containment drove the mining industry to seek its labor in ever more distant, undeveloped, and impoverished recruiting zones.

For decades a central element of capitalist development and white prosperity, migrancy is now increasingly problematic. Pressure toward transformation comes not only from chronic internal crises but also from national and international political and technological forces that are restructuring labor relations and global markets. Today, employer and employee confront fundamentally new choices and relationships shaped by volatile and uncertain forces in the international gold market, in the regional and domestic politics and demography of southern Africa, and in the unstable diplomatic and economic position of the South African state.

As a result of mounting domestic and international pressures since 1970, basic changes are underway in the migrant labor system. They will not be completed quickly or easily. Although we argue that the cumulative effect must eventually transform the mining industry, we consider that the industry is only just embarking on what will be a halting and uncertain course away from the racial division of labor, dependence on long-distance oscillating migration, and the compound system that are the core of the present system. "Transformation" involves no guarantee of progress to a better world. Nor does it preclude delays or even partial reversals of direction. But whatever the eventual outcome, the future is likely to be shaped by many of the same forces that have molded the recent past. Mine migrancy's development over the next decade will play a crucial role in shaping the new society that is emerging.

* * *

The research for this book began when all three authors were at Queen's University, Kingston, Ontario. Following several years of work on South African labor history before 1940, Alan Jeeves and David Yudelman turned in 1984 to the more recent period. Simultaneously, Jonathan Crush began research on the mine labor market in rural South Africa. Our initial findings were published in several single- or jointly authored articles (see Bibliography). In 1985, we agreed to pool our research materials and research findings and to work collaboratively. The difficulties of long-distance collaboration once two of the authors had left Queen's slowed our progress. We greatly appreciate the patience of the series editor, Paul Lovejoy, and of Dean Birkenkamp, Barbara Ellington, and Martha Leggett at Westview Press as we brought the manuscript to completion.

With the initial direction of the project agreed upon, we each pursued those topics that interested us, using shared source material. The result was that Jonathan Crush wrote the first draft of the chapters on labor stabilization and domestic recruiting in the 1970s and 1980s (Chapters 6 and 7), Alan Jeeves drafted the two historical chapters (Chapters 2 and 3) and the chapter on white labor (Chapter 4), and David Yudelman drafted the chapter on migrancy in context (Chapter 1). Crush and Jeeves jointly drafted the chapter on the National Union of Mineworkers (Chapter 8), and Crush and Yudelman the chapter on foreign labor (Chapter 5). The Conclusion was written jointly. We circulated the initial chapter drafts among ourselves for comment and revision. Although we all contributed to each chapter in some way, we agreed to leave the final decisions about content to the original author(s).

Our thematic arguments on the historical development, contemporary transformation, and future of mine migrancy are laid out in Chapter 1. The remainder of the book explores these themes chronologically and in greater depth. Inevitably there are gaps, and as we approached the present, our sources necessarily became fewer and more selective. Much of the evidence we collected for the period after 1970 came from widely scattered sources as well as from extensive interviewing. To enable interested scholars to trace the documentation in more detail we have deposited relevant material with the Archives at Queen's University.

The long gestation period of this book meant that earlier drafts of individual chapters, and the manuscript as a whole, have enjoyed fairly wide circulation since 1986. In some cases, our arguments have already been absorbed into publications by others on the subject. We would like to thank those scholars who responded to our request for comments on the manuscript, particularly Wiseman Chirwa, Bill Freund, Wilmot James, Rick Johnstone, Jean Leger, Jeff Lever, Dunbar Moodie, Randall Packard, and Philip Steenkamp. We are also grateful to those who commented critically when individual chapters were presented at various academic conferences and seminars. The venues included the Southern African Research Program at Yale and Wesleyan universities in 1986, the 1986 African Studies Association Annual Meeting in New Orleans, the 1987 History Workshop at the University of the Witwatersrand, the 1987 Canadian Association of Geographers Annual Meeting in Hamilton, and the 1988 Annual Meeting of the Canadian Association of African Studies in Kingston.

We wish to thank all of those who assisted with the research. A large number of individuals in government, management, and the work force consented to be interviewed for this study. The list is too long to be reproduced here but includes NUM officials Cyril Ramaphosa and Marcel Golding; senior mining executives Harry Oppenheimer, Robin Plumbridge, and Bobby Godsell; and the former minister of mineral and energy affairs Danie Steyn, his director general, Louw Alberts, and the head of the Reserve Bank, Jan Lombard. Archivists and librarians at the following institutions were particularly helpful: the Public Record Office, United Kingdom; the Transvaal and Central Archives Depot, Pretoria; the University of the Witwatersrand; the Southern African Labour and Development Research Unit at the University of Cape Town; the National Archives of Botswana, Swaziland, and Zimbabwe; Barlow Rand Archives; and the Chamber of Mines. James Gemmill, Tony Fleischer, Tom Main, Errol Holmes, and Dennis Gordon were particularly helpful on the activities of the Chamber of Mines and its recruiting organization. Hylton Davis gave permission to consult the records of the NRC/WNLA in Johannesburg, and Trevor Nel and Ted Larkan provided access to mine recruiting material in Natal. Cyril Ramaphosa, Marcel Golding, and Jean Leger kindly provided material on the National Union of Mineworkers. Jonathan Crush wishes to acknowledge the assistance of the research staff (particularly Paul Wellings, Zamankosi Mpanza, Nkrumah Mazibuko, Alan Peters, and the late Jill Nattrass) of the former Development Studies Unit of the University of Natal. We would also like to thank Stephen Giles at York University and Stephen Haenel at Westview Press for their editorial work on the manuscript. Alan Jeeves is especially indebted to Mary Bentley, whose editorial skill caught many problems and inconsistencies. The artwork was prepared by Jonathan Crush and Alan Jeeves and drawn by Ross Hough and David Crush. The Graphic Design Unit at Queen's University prepared camera-ready copy of the artwork and tables.

Finally, our research was made possible by generous financial support from a number of organizations. We are indebted to the Social Sciences and Humanities Research Council of Canada (SSHRC). Jonathan Crush was also supported (from 1983 to 1985) by an SSHRC Post-Doctoral Fellowship and, since 1987, by an SSHRC Canada Research Fellowship. Supplemental funding for this project came from the Advisory Research Committee of Queen's University, the Central Research Fund of the University of Alberta, and the Centre for Resource Studies at Queen's University.

Jonathan Crush
Alan Jeeves
David Yudelman

South Africa's Labor Empire

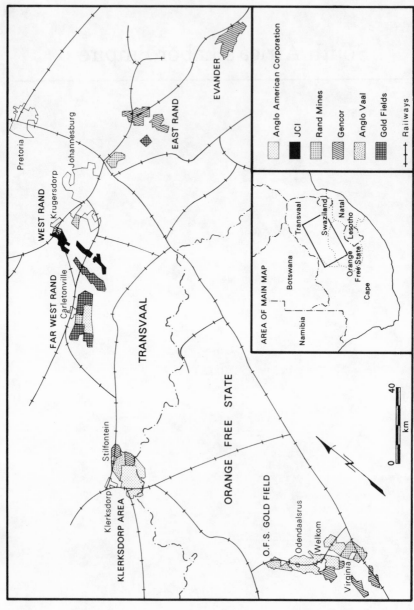

Location map of major South African mines. *Source:* TEBA Regional Map, compiled and produced by Map Studio, Wendywood, South Africa, 1982.

1

Migrancy in Context,
1890–1990

The development of modern South Africa, by far the richest, most powerful, and industrialized country in Africa, has for most of the twentieth century been based on the exploitation of its mineral wealth, particularly its vast reserves of low-grade gold-bearing ore.[1] But there is little doubt that if large numbers of low-wage, unskilled migrant miners had not been recruited from throughout the subcontinent, there would never have been a deep-level gold mining industry in South Africa. The world's largest supplier of gold (Figure 1.1) would have been, at best, a minor producer pecking away at the surface outcrops of enormous deep-lying reefs. If an ore body similar to South Africa's had been discovered in Australia, Canada, or the United States, it would almost certainly have been left in the ground because of an inability to mobilize the right type of work force. Even today, after great technological advance and dramatic change in the cost structure of gold mining, this remains true.

Gold has consistently been and remains South Africa's most important industry, one of its biggest employers, and the driving force of its industrial economy. More than anything else, the large-scale use of foreign mine labor subordinated the entire subcontinent to the South African economy. In search of labor, the controllers of the gold mines constructed a recruiting empire that at its zenith extended throughout southern Africa and north into southern Tanzania. From the first discoveries on the Witwatersrand in 1886, the continuous migration of black workers back and forth between rural reserves and the mines was central to profitable gold production. This pattern of oscillating migration developed much earlier on the Kimberley diamond mines but became entrenched on a much larger scale in gold mining and in this way was established as one of the key distinguishing features of South African industrialization. The migrants' repatriated wages became a major contributor to the income of the supplying areas. At the beginning of the 1990s, over half of Lesotho's national

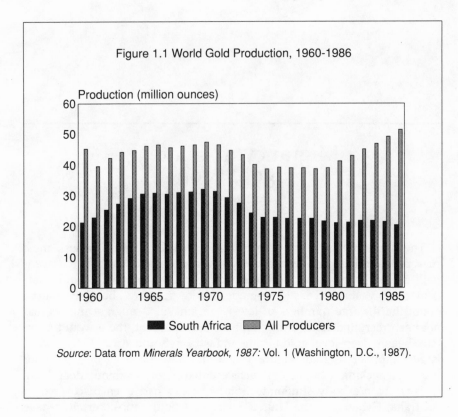

Figure 1.1 World Gold Production, 1960-1986

Production (million ounces)

■ South Africa   ▨ All Producers

Source: Data from *Minerals Yearbook, 1987:* Vol. 1 (Washington, D.C., 1987).

income derived from migrant miners working in South Africa; in Mozambique the figure was almost a third.

The migrant labor system has shaped southern Africa's political history as much as its economic history. The origins of institutionalized racism in South Africa are bound up with it. Apartheid cannot be understood merely as the product of Afrikaner nationalism, Calvinist prejudice, and frontier wars. It is as much, or more, the legacy of English and German financiers, Scots and American engineers, British and Australian trade unionists, and British civil servants. Together they created the most enduring and far-flung oscillating migrant labor system in history and laid the foundations of a particularly ruthless system of racial discrimination.

Many labor systems around the world were more draconian, coercive, and brutal than South Africa's. Plantation slavery in the New World and Soviet forced labor in the Siberian gold mines made the harsh conditions in the South African gold mines pale by comparison.[2] But most of these systems never aspired to be voluntary labor systems operating under the norms of modern industrial capitalism. The story of South African mine migrancy is not a pleasant one. Much of the blood and sweat will never be chronicled because the remarkably comprehensive data and statistics kept by the industry throughout its history have focused on production rather than the producers.

Outsiders have frequently remarked on a major contradiction in the mining industry's use of black labor. The development of gold mining in South Africa represented a triumph of sophisticated ore-extraction technology, corporate organization, and financial arrangements. By contrast, the industry's management of its workers for most of its history was characterized not only by a lack of compassion but also by gross inefficiency and wastefulness. The constant ability to expand the geographic pool from which the migrants came enabled employers to keep blacks' wages low and almost static in real terms between 1897 and 1970.[3] Operating in the belief that this open frontier and the conditions that sustained it would never change, managers saw little need to improve the way they organized and used migrant labor over this long period.

The story of migrancy is only now beginning to be told from the migrant's point of view. The traditional rosy view of the migrant portrayed him as a raw but willing peasant, attracted by city lights, eager to prove himself, save enough money to acquire cattle and land, and, on his return, marry and start a family. Although containing a germ of truth, this view concealed a darker reality of dispossession, social dislocation, disease, and death. This story is only now beginning to be fully documented.[4]

The destructive impact of migrancy on black rural society was noted by most contemporary commentators. But recent research also indicates that, at times, migrancy performed a vital role in preserving the rural household by the transfer of income to the countryside. Although the destructiveness is plain for all to see, the system succeeded in part because it was sometimes the best of the few alternatives open to rural blacks.[5] This is not to suggest that the overall impact of migrancy was positive; rather, it is to point out that, although many rural households were destroyed by the periodic absence of their young, able-bodied men, some were saved by the money sent home by the migrants. Young men frequently left the rural homestead to escape dependency relationships with their elders, and although many of them eventually returned to the rural household with injuries and infectious diseases contracted in the mines, some returned in better health than when they initially migrated. Migrancy's varied causes and ambiguous impacts help explain why the migrants kept going and why so many of them were unrecruited "voluntaries" who made their own way to the mines. The migrants were not rushing blindly to self-destruction like lemmings but were in most cases making a rational decision in a situation of unattractive alternatives.

Migration served many interests other than the mining industry; though individual wages were meager, the total was large and meant substantial income to impoverished supplying areas. The supplier states, local traders, and officials all benefited from the revenues generated and the income repatriated by the migrants. Chiefs and homestead heads were drawn in by the lure of additional revenue to purchase land and cattle or merely to survive. Mine migrancy survived then—as is does today—partly because of the extent and diversity of the interests that benefited from it.

Overall, however, this study is not so much the story of the migrant as an examination of the centrality of the black miner to the gold mining industry and to South Africa itself.[6] Modern South Africa cannot be fully understood without first understanding the dynamics of the migrant labor system that bestrides the subcontinent. Nor can South Africa's potential for fundamental change be grasped without first assessing the subtle but undeniable transformation that is now beginning to occur within the migrant labor system. This study is therefore both a history and a contemporary analysis. It examines the role of mine migrancy in the development of modern South Africa and attempts to suggest how changes in both migrancy and mining are interacting to transform the political economy of South Africa.

The Historical Context

If there is one generalization about the history of gold mining in South Africa that commands agreement, it is that the country's labor policies have been extraordinarily stable. By 1920, the mining companies had refined their low-wage system of oscillating migration and authoritarian control into a rigidly hierarchical racial division of labor. Yet its essential features were not foreordained. They emerged from a long struggle between contending interests in the ranks of mining capital, labor, and the state. With the main elements of the system in place by 1920, it remained stable for half a century, despite agricultural deterioration in the countryside and rounds of unrest in the mines, particularly in the early 1920s and late 1940s. What began as a transitional phenomenon, not uncommon in industrializing societies, became entrenched as a central feature of South African society and the regional economy. In the period after 1970, however, deep-seated domestic and international forces have thrown the mining industry's longstanding labor system into turmoil.

The Formative Phase, 1890–1920

Our story does not cover in detail the early years of the migratory labor system from 1890 to 1920, on which there is a growing literature.[7]

Initially, the mining industry had little alternative to a system of migrant labor. The pattern established earlier in the Kimberley diamond fields saw forces largely internal to African societies and homestead production push workers on to the labor market.[8] Striving to maintain their rural base and independence, Africans tried to protect themselves by using migrancy as a form of limited wage employment. Slowly but inexorably, however, migration became unavoidable rather than discretionary for many. Under the pressures of colonial taxation, land dispossession, population increase, and ecological decay, increasing numbers sought work in cities and mines and on plantations. Even so, patterns of participation in migrancy were highly variable and uneven. In many places, independent peasant producers or sharecropping tenants became sufficiently successful in the expanded produce markets to avoid labor migration even when, as in the first decade of the century, the mines were desperate for labor.[9]

The mine owners competed among themselves and with other employers to draw these workers into their labor system. Beginning in the 1890s, the employers' association, the Chamber of Mines, began to recruit for the industry as a whole. The Chamber's recruiters and their black and white assistants, called "runners," invaded the rural areas in search of labor. An army of independent agents, styled "touts," accompanied them and recruited for the highest bidder. Many of the independents had organized themselves into companies and competed with each other and with the Chamber for contracts with the big mining houses. By 1910, most of the country traders had also been swept into the system. Fathers contracted their children; chiefs their followers; traders their indebted customers; while brigands connived with the mine companies to hijack migrants bound for other employment. Competitive recruiting and the accompanying large cash payments in the rural areas through the "advance system"—the payment of a cash advance in exchange for a future obligation (a debt lien) to work in the mines—delivered the labor but at a price. This system crucially raised the participation rate in the migrant system (the proportion of the male population recruited) and greatly expanded the geographic size of the pool from which the mines drew their labor.[10]

With recruits flowing freely by 1910, the mining industry set out to rationalize its recruiting organization and to reduce costs under the discipline of an industry-regulated system, bringing together the major producers. The objective was to incorporate or drive out the independent recruiting companies and to eliminate competition among the mines themselves. Earlier efforts to achieve this goal had always foundered on the competition that persisted while the labor supply was uncertain. The development of important new labor sources after 1905, particularly the eastern Cape and the tropical areas of Central Africa, was instrumental in overcoming supply problems. At this point, the industry turned to refining internal administrative control. The second of the two organizations that eventually achieved increased efficiency and stability emerged in 1912. Through the Native Recruiting Corporation (NRC), operating mainly in South Africa, and the already-established Witwatersrand Native Labour Association (WNLA) operating elsewhere, the Chamber of Mines overcame chaos in the labor market and exerted centralized control. A full-scale employers' monopoly (technically, a monopsony) under WNLA and the NRC forced the independent recruiting companies out of business (some switched to recruiting for white farmers). It ensured uniform recruiting policies for the mines, sharply reduced the number of recruiters employed, controlled wage levels, and eliminated the use of runners.[11]

Blacks in rural homesteads continued to try to use the system to their own advantage, but growing poverty and land shortage undermined their efforts. After 1914, particularly, black families were increasingly squeezed off the land and began settling in the cities. The mining industry worried about this development because city dwellers were generally lost to mine employment. Permanent urbanization also threatened the various interests in the supply areas, which depended on the flow of labor to and from the mines. Most migrants came from outside the Transvaal. The supplying governments had no intention of allowing them to move permanently to the Rand. Continually short of funds, neighboring colonial governments depended on the income from migrancy and viewed the workers as a commodity, but one to be rented rather than sold. The governments charged the mine companies fees for every employee sent and, even more important, insisted that a large part of workers' wages be deferred and repatriated to await them in their home country. In this way, the governments ensured that a large part of migrants' earnings would be spent at their homes outside South Africa—much to the annoyance of local merchants in South Africa.

Similarly, chiefs and other notables encouraged their followers to participate in wage labor but insisted on their continued allegiance to traditional leadership structures. Colonial state and rural chief shared an interest with the mining companies in perpetuating migrancy, though they often fought over the spoils.[12] The restraining of one-way urban migration—later known as "influx control"—was therefore an interest that the mining industry shared with governments in the supplying areas, chiefs, and even the heads of families whose sons constituted the bulk of the labor force.

The labor system also emerged out of a protracted conflict with white farmers.[13] Coercive labor practices in late nineteenth-century South Africa enabled many white farmers and pastoralists to protect their resident labor against the predatory activities of mine recruiters, touts, and labor thieves. Because productivity was low, farm labor needs were far higher than on an equivalent farm in, for example, North America. However, the lack of cheap and reliable transport to the urban markets and of adequate capitalization constricted farm production and resulted in rather modest labor requirements compared to later periods. Increasing state subsidies and protectionist measures gradually transformed white farming beginning in the 1910s and 1920s. Always wasteful of labor, the farmers began to need much more of it and to demand the state's protection from other employers, particularly the gold mines. In one of its first legislative acts, the Union government prohibited recruiting for the mines over much of rural white South Africa, forcing the mines to expand recruiting outside South Africa.

Just as government actions guaranteed farmers' labor supplies, so the Mines and Works Act (known as the Color Bar) of 1911 and its subsequent amendments helped to protect the white miners' monopoly of all the higher paying jobs (see Chapter 4).[14] A product of an uneasy compromise between white trade unions, the Chamber of Mines, and the government, the different elements of the Color Bar protected the jobs of semiskilled, white supervisors (the customary Color Bar) and skilled artisans (the statutory Color Bar).[15] Though distinct from the migratory system, the Color Bar evolved together with, and remained complementary to, migrant labor. It sheltered whites from competition from the low-paid and increasingly skilled black workers and therefore imposed higher wage costs on management.[16] In a low-grade industry where the margin of profit was slight, the wage bill could threaten the profitability of the marginal producers. Because the white miner vote was crucial in several key constituencies, the government generally pressed the mines to give their white employees special treatment. It was, therefore, far more common to hold down or decrease black wages. The best way to do this was to rationalize the recruiting system to minimize the number of recruiters competing for black workers.

Although largely rightless and unorganized, black miners resisted with a long series of strikes, work stoppages, go-slows (work slowdowns), and riots that showed they were far from passive or oblivious to the erosion of their position. Management, which shared many of the racist attitudes of the white workers, learned to live with the higher wage bill imposed by the Color Bar and to ensure that the black work force paid much of its costs. There were, of course, concrete advantages for management in a racially hierarchical labor system. Common cause between white and black labor was unlikely under such a structure. Second, the logistics involved in getting hundreds of thousands of black workers underground daily as well as feeding or housing them required an authoritarian pattern of control. The customary Color Bar, which encouraged most of the white miners to become overseers rather than artisans, reinforced that pattern of control.

The emergence of modern South Africa can be dated from the first two decades of the twentieth century. The growth of interventionist government was an international phenomenon and certainly not unique to South Africa. Everywhere states got involved in new activities and strengthened their administrative and coercive capacity through greatly enlarged civil services, judiciaries, and police forces. The modern state comprises a network of bureaucratic, coercive legal systems, and other institutions to make and enforce public policy. Governments are merely one element (albeit a key element) in the modern state, and when they are thrown out of office the state is generally left largely intact. Modern states developed greatly increased roles as producers of wealth, employment, and industrial peace. The formation of the International Labour Office (ILO) in 1919, for example, was symptomatic of the greatly increased cooperation between capitalist states and large private-sector employers that resulted from World War I, the Bolshevik revolution, and the waves of militancy that swept the international working class at the time.

A similar process occurred in South Africa. The alliance between the Transvaal state and industry, put into place in the first decade of this century, provided a basis for equally close cooperation after unification in 1910. What distinguished South Africa from other modern states was the unusually sharp racial, ethnic, and class divisions that characterized the working class and the wider social order. Other distinguishing features included the centrality of gold mining in the economy and the highly organized system of oscillating migrant labor which sustained that industry.

From the first, labor regulation was a major task of the state, whatever the political complexion of the regime in power. The gold mines depended on the state for the development, policing, and everyday running of their migratory labor system.[17] During periods of crisis, mining executives invariably looked to government to suppress labor militancy and to insulate them against competition from other employers. The authorities rarely disappointed them. Fearful of large concentrations of young migrant black males in close proximity to Johannesburg and its satellite white communities, the state implemented rigorous controls over black mobility and the labor market through the pass laws, which first became really effective in the early years of the century. Legislation passed in the first few years after the unification of South Africa in 1910 enabled the state and the Chamber of Mines to solve supply problems, deal with the security issues, regulate competition, and manage labor relations in a way that confirmed both the Color Bar and long-distance oscillating labor migration as the central supports of the system. Enshrined in law and

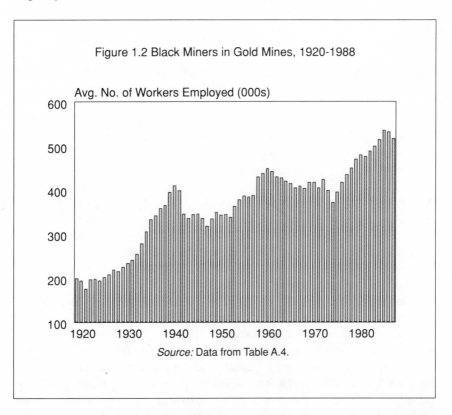

Figure 1.2 Black Miners in Gold Mines, 1920-1988

Source: Data from Table A.4.

social practice by the 1920s, they have underwritten profitable gold production ever since.[18] After 1948, they were adapted and extended by the National party government far beyond the gold mines to South Africa as a whole, becoming the lynchpin of the apartheid state.

The Expansionary Phase, 1920–1970

By 1920, the construction of a centralized recruiting system under the control of the Chamber of Mines was complete. The fifty years after 1920 constituted the mature phase of the system (see Chapters 2 and 3). This expansionary period saw recruiting levels soar from about 200,000 in 1920 to a peak of 427,000 in 1961 (Figure 1.2). Most of this growth was orchestrated for the industry by a relatively unknown visionary of ruthless genius, William Gemmill.[19] Gemmill became Chamber general manager in the early 1920s and served in that capacity until 1940, when he moved north to Salisbury to assume control of tropical recruiting operations. His organizational achievements were basic to the industry's success in meeting its expanding labor needs when production began to grow rapidly in the 1930s and 1940s. However, expansion on this scale could never have occurred without the growing hunger for work among displaced peasants and for hard currency among governments that had nothing better to export than their labor. Other governments assisted the growth and maintenance of the system in the tropical regions of the subcontinent just as the South African state did at home.[20]

The modern state's growing role in economic planning and industrial relations was crucial to this expansionary phase. The expansion and entrenchment of migrancy depended not only on the active assistance of the South African government but also on the British and Portuguese imperial connections. State support sometimes faltered. In 1913, the British and South African governments imposed a ban on "tropical" migration from north of 22° south latitude because pneumonia was decimating this group of workers. The restrictions threatened further expansion and jeopardized the mining companies' ability to meet their labor needs. Overall, however, the trend in industry-state relations was toward more cooperation and interdependence.

Over this long period, few mining executives seriously questioned industry reliance on oscillating labor migration. Although there were intervals of serious shortage, most of the time the recruiters delivered the workers with gratifying regularity. Apparent predictability, however, masked important elements of instability, the result of sometimes severe regional fluctuations in the flow of labor. The recruiters found that they could not depend on the reliability of individual sources of labor. Even traditionally important suppliers, such as southern Mozambique, the eastern Cape, and Basutoland (Lesotho), experienced sharp fluctuations in recruiting levels. Whether as a result of state intervention or changes in local conditions, the mining industry frequently could not control particular labor markets. Yet the recruiters adapted to these shifts while maintaining the basic elements of their labor system. Fluctuations in the supply from particular territories never led to serious proposals to abandon the migrant labor system as a whole.

The reason for this was simple. Shifts in the sources of supply, however dramatic and unsettling, never meant that the mines had to do with less labor for long. Their recruiters were consistently able to find and exploit new sources. The migrant labor system, like mining itself, expanded consistently. Though more expensive to obtain, foreign workers accepted longer contracts, tended to return more readily, and could be directed toward less popular mines, where the conditions were harsher and more dangerous. The persistence of the system certainly owed much to the cost constraints of low-grade mining and the political rigidities of the Color Bar. Yet it was also a result of the possibilities for growth which persisted on the outer labor frontiers. The mines' labor system endured because it could expand.

In the effort to control mining costs, management turned early to the problem of white labor. Although this cadre of supervisors and artisans was small in numbers, its wage bill in 1910 almost equaled that of the much larger black component. Originally, the scarcity of the skills provided by the white immigrant miners to some extent justified their higher wages, but in the two decades after 1902, the character of white mine labor changed radically. Local whites, often Afrikaners (descendants of the original, mostly Dutch-speaking white settlers) fleeing rural poverty, replaced the immigrants as they died or left. The new miners came largely from the "Poor White" class, generally lacked the expertise of their predecessors and functioned as overseers of gangs of black miners.

The defeat of the white miners in the Rand Rebellion of 1922 was followed two years later with the election of a "Pact Government" of the National and Labour parties. Contrary to most conventional interpretations, the change in government did not reverse the weakening position of white labor in the increasingly interventionist South African state. The policies of the Pact did preserve and entrench the legislative Color Bar with the enactment of new legislation in 1926. The relatively small group of skilled, artisan miners benefited most. However, the majority of white miners, particularly the unskilled and semiskilled group, were hard hit by the aftermath of the 1922 strike. As a result, the ratio of black to white labor increased substantially, while the total white wage bill fell significantly. Even the new industrial conciliation legislation, introduced before the 1924 election but retained by the Pact, cannot be taken as evidence of the power of white labor, since its actual effect under the Pact was to eliminate the strike weapon, taming and co-opting the white unions.[21]

With white labor beaten into submission after 1922, the Chamber of Mines turned to removing the uncertainties that made the migrant labor supply liable to frequent unpredictable fluctuations. The migrants remained only partially proletarianized and integrated into urban life. Still involved in the rural economy, many could find part or all of their family subsistence there, although this was becoming more difficult as peasant agriculture gradually succumbed to loss of land, population increase, and restrictive government measures.[22] As long as the migrants could still order their lives around the rural areas, and as long as they could find more rewarding or less onerous employment, the mines were vulnerable to fluctuations in the overall supply of labor.

The flow of labor from any one area could fluctuate markedly from year-to-year and from month-to-month. Workers interspersed variable spells on the mines with equally variable spells at home. Most moved out of mine work as they got older. And they constantly sought better alternatives to the mines. To deal with this situation, the Chamber of Mines made sustained efforts to open new territories for recruitment. In the two decades after 1932, the Chamber implemented a strategy masterminded by its general manager, William Gemmill, to exploit the labor resources of Central Africa.

The 1940s, not unlike the 1970s, posed several challenges to the mines' labor system (see Chapter 3). First, there was the beginning of a long-term movement of more-proletarianized (though still rural) South African workers away from mining toward better-paid employment. The wage increases that might have resulted (as they did in the 1970s) were vigorously resisted by the Chamber of Mines. It met the immediate pressures for higher wages with force and a renewed push northwards for less-proletarianized labor. This happened again in the 1960s, when the mines used their far-flung empire to defuse pressure for higher wages at home. Second, drought in the countryside, and increasing responsibilities in the absence of many white miners who were serving with the Allied armies in North Africa, led black miners to push their demands more actively. At the same time, a profitability crisis on some mines produced severe cost-cutting by management and a deterioration in working conditions. The employers rejected most of the improvements, including wage increases, recommended by the Lansdown Commission in 1943.

The resulting grievances prompted the formation in 1941 of the African Mine Workers' Union (AMWU) by the Transvaal African Congress. As the AMWU grew in strength under the tutelage of the South African Communist party, the attitude of Chamber and state shifted from watchful tolerance to outright suppression. The AMWU nevertheless was a prime mover in the 1946 strike, when over 70,000 workers came out in support of work-place demands and wage increases. The state and the Chamber ruthlessly suppressed the strike. By refusing to deal with the AMWU, and encouraging the use of force against it, the mining companies successfully defended their coercive industrial relations practices and the migrant labor system.[23]

The major Orange Free State gold discoveries in the 1940s provided the mining houses with an opportunity to develop a new model of labor mobilization and control. But, as the new mines opened, the companies simply replicated the old system, particularly the single-sex compounds in which workers were housed. When the Fagan Commission recommended limited recognition of black unions in 1948, the mining industry mounted the strongest opposition of all employer groups, arguing that unions for migrant workers were unthinkable.

The National party's victory later that year ensured that there would be no major changes in the way labor was mobilized and controlled. The Anglo American group did develop plans to settle a small cadre of more skilled black workers permanently on some mine properties. There was no support for this elsewhere in the industry and no major protest when the Nationalist government blocked the proposal. Committed to reversing permanent black urbanization, the government of D. F. Malan restricted the number of workers in family housing on mine properties to 3 percent. In pursuit of its apartheid doctrines, the government erased the tepid and erratic reformism of the pre-1948 period, when the government under Jan Smuts had temporarily eased the pass laws, toyed with black trade union recognition, and briefly considered some accommodation to the realities of black urbanization.[24] Far from resisting the state's enforcement of oscillating migrancy, the mine owners readily fell into line and turned again to expanding migrancy. In the thirty-five years that followed, no large gold mine came close to placing 3 percent of its black miners in family housing, even though they were specifically permitted to do so.

The Contemporary Context

From about 1970, mine migrancy began to enter a new phase, just as South Africa itself, its neighbors, and the world gold market began to move into a new era. The bulk of this book, Chapters 4 to 8, will focus specifically on the contemporary period. This section merely outlines some of the major developments and the context essential to understanding their significance.

At one level, today's mine labor system shows great continuity with the past. The search for work among displaced peasants and for revenue among impoverished governments in the region remains as acute as it was fifty years ago. The black labor force is still overwhelmingly migrant. Not only has the compound system survived, but also the mining companies have invested heavily in it by upgrading and providing additional facilities. The quality of life in the compounds has undoubtedly improved but remains regimented and barren, condemned by the workers themselves in interviews with independent researchers.[25] Production changes underground have been slow, despite large investment by the mining industry in research and development. The racial hierarchy is little changed, with white supervisors maintaining their privileges and dominant position.

While the continuities with the past are overwhelming, nothing about the recruitment and use of mine labor is as certain as it once seemed. Today, it is the discontinuities and differences that attract most attention. Many of the changes would have been unthinkable even twenty years ago. Their scope and scale are still unfolding. The form they eventually take will depend partly on external factors but crucially on an intense struggle for control between workers and management in the mines themselves.

There were many indicators of change: In the early 1970s the fixed international price of gold was abolished; steep price increases followed but in turbulent, unstable gold markets; internally, growing violence caused major damage and production disruptions; large labor shortages began to appear, resulting from political developments in neighboring countries; and there were dramatic increases in the real wages of black miners from the very low base of the 1960s.

These uncertainties in the migrant labor system called for a new approach at the Chamber of Mines. William Gemmill's son, James, his somewhat pale successor as the czar of the migrant labor system, went into forced retirement, to be replaced by a different kind of visionary. His successor was a managerial technocrat named Tony Fleischer. Within the mining groups, new industrial relations divisions began to formulate and determine labor policy. Nevertheless, except perhaps rhetorically, acceptance of change came slowly to the inner circles of mining management. In the compounds and mineshafts, by contrast, militant black miners organized and pressed for basic improvements.

Underlying these changes were more fundamental forces affecting South Africa and the entire region. The British and the Portuguese relinquished control over their southern African dependencies, which included some of the most important suppliers of mine labor. The regimes that succeeded them remained ambivalent about their dependence on mine migrancy. Their public hostility frequently concealed self-serving collaboration that was little different from that of their colonial predecessors.

The South African government is increasingly hostile to labor migration from outside South Africa. Even more important, it has also become ambivalent about long-distance labor migrancy within the country. In the last two decades, its preference has been for a type of "commuter migrancy," which allows daily or weekly return to a home base within traveling distance of the place of employment. In 1986, however, it formally acknowledged the futility of its existing controls over black urbanization and abolished influx controls and the pass laws, intending to replace them with a new system geared to the availability of housing and employment in the urban areas.[26]

These policy shifts are no minor matter. Long-distance, contractual migrancy has been at the core of government policy since 1948. It is the essence of grand apartheid, the policy of the creation of nominally independent black bantustans, or homelands, based on territorial segregation. Any move away from it implies potentially profound changes to the migrant labor system. Together with other forces, it must eventually transform race relations in the wider society. Black labor, most of it recruited from a distance and still housed in the bachelor compounds, remains central to the gold mines, and therefore to the prosperity of the economy and state. Mine migrancy will not disappear overnight, but a pivotal process of transformation has now begun. Just as the development of modern South Africa in the first decades of the twentieth century was inextricably tied to the entrenchment of migratory labor, this new phase of migrancy is bound up with structural change in South Africa as a whole.

In this study we suggest that the conditions that have entrenched and sustained traditional migratory labor to the gold mines have now begun to erode. Behind this process are five closely linked developments. First and most basic, Western governments unshackled the price of gold on international markets; second, the mining industry's northern labor empire broke up; third, the industry faced a major crisis of control in the mines themselves; fourth, the National Union of Mineworkers (NUM) emerged and the white Mine Workers' Union (MWU) declined; and fifth, new forms of migrancy emerged.

The International Gold Market

The central importance of gold to the South African economy is well known.[27] Even during the 1960s when the artificially fixed price of US$35 an ounce threatened mining profits, and manufacturing boomed in response to import substitution policies, gold continued to sustain the economy. Because gold mining has always been internationally competititive and did not require the level of direct subsidies doled out by the state to farming and, later, manufacturing, it was never a mere supplicant of the South African state but coexisted with it symbiotically. The state depended on the gold mining industry as an employer, but more importantly as a source of revenue and foreign exchange. The industry depended on the state to create the necessary social and economic environment required by its low-wage, coercive labor system and to ensure that industrial strife did not get in the way of low-cost gold production.

Both industry and state continue to depend on an international market that they do not control. In spite of South Africa's dominance as a producer, it has never been able to exercise significant control over a price that was once controlled by the United States government and is now driven by complex and heterogeneous patterns of international demand. This situation is in marked contrast with the diamond market. Despite its waning dominance in diamond production, De Beers continues to control sales and prices in cooperation with the South African government through the Central Selling Organization in London. The Anglo American Corporation, which, like De Beers, is controlled by the Oppenheimer family, is the world's largest corporate producer of gold, but its influence over the gold price is negligible.

At the end of the 1960s, the United States government succumbed to international and domestic pressures and began to free the gold price.[28] Once demonetized, gold increasingly became a commodity. Yet it was a commodity unlike any other. To many, it remained a unique store of value and in the minds of investors an important hedge against inflation. Private citizens in the United States were once again allowed to hoard gold, and the price, artificially restricted for decades, soared. Prior to this, the fixed gold price had remained unchanged since 1949 and was actually declining in real terms. This forced the mines to absorb cost increases and discouraged any thought of radical change in labor policy, because labor was by far the largest single element in costs.

The gold price rose sharply through the 1970s, peaking at US$800 an ounce in a speculative frenzy in 1980, then rapidly falling back to US$600, and fluctuating between US$300 and US$500 for most of the 1980s (Figure 1.3). The price increase swept aside many of the mining industry's most cherished certainties. As on earlier occasions, a surge in the dollar value of gold stimulated investment in new mining ventures. More than in any previous growth phase, however, expansion resulted not from new discoveries but simply from economic changes that suddenly made millions of tons of previously unpayable ore profitable to mine. Dying mines surviving on state subsidies sprang back to life; others reopened abandoned shafts and drives. Mining groups that had been declining suddenly found their marginal mines revitalized. Even minute traces of gold left in the ubiquitous and disfiguring mine dumps of the Witwatersrand could now be profitably extracted.

Very large profits meant that the mines could afford to increase blacks' wages in real and substantial terms for the first time in decades (Tables 1.1 and 1.2). This was a necessary condition for any radical improvement in the condition of the black migrant miner. But it was not a sufficient condition. A similar windfall in the 1930s also put the industry in a position to afford a major improvement in wages or conditions, or both, but did not result in any significant changes. The mining industry failed to see any compelling reason for making significant changes in the 1930s. While the "necessary" conditions for change existed, there was no "sufficient" condition. Some of the windfall proceeds went to shareholders but most went on creating new mines and opening up entirely new gold fields.

In the 1970s, shareholders also profited, and the groups expanded existing mines. But there were important differences. Only a handful of major new mines were opened up in the 1970s and 1980s and, for a

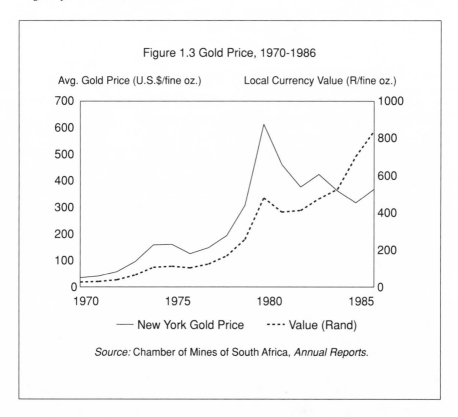

Figure 1.3 Gold Price, 1970-1986

Avg. Gold Price (U.S.$/fine oz.)   Local Currency Value (R/fine oz.)

— New York Gold Price   ···· Value (Rand)

Source: Chamber of Mines of South Africa, *Annual Reports.*

number of interrelated reasons (none of which had anything to do with altruism), significant amounts of the windfall funds were at last diverted to the black miners in the form of dramatic increases in cash wages (Table 1.2).

Additional pressure grew for better conditions and changes in the system of migrancy itself. Beginning with the Durban strikes of 1973, black labor militancy increased generally throughout South Africa. At the same time, violence and riots in the mine compounds threatened to become a major problem. The threat of the spread of this militancy was a powerful incentive to employers to implement modest increases in black miners' wages (see Chapter 8). The higher gold price made these increases feasible. The result was modest but significant wage gains for the miners, though the really major increases in wages had to wait for the supply squeeze of 1974. The mine companies, which had always contained labor costs with ruthless efficiency, allowed the cost of producing gold to escalate far faster than the rate of inflation (which was itself running at much higher levels than in the 1960s). As a result, by the end of the 1980s

Table 1.1 South African Gold Output, 1970-1989

	Gold Ore Treated (000s metric tons)	Fine Gold Produced (metric tons)	Gold Revenue (R bil)	Working Profit (R bil)
1970	79,965	1,000.4	0.83	0.31
1971	78,659	976.3	0.89	0.35
1972	73,245	909.6	1.16	0.55
1973	76,018	855.2	1.79	1.02
1974	76,000	758.6	2.62	1.64
1975	75,126	713.4	2.56	1.33
1976	77,870	713.4	2.38	0.95
1977	76,712	699.9	2.81	1.23
1978	83,016	704.4	3.90	2.12
1979	86,246	703.5	5.84	3.61
1980	93,263	672.9	10.37	7.93
1981	95,873	655.8	8.56	5.15
1982	103,061	662.6	8.78	4.68
1983	104,813	677.9	10.18	5.38
1984	110,675	679.9	11.57	5.87
1985	114,124	670.8	15.29	8.04
1986	118,137	638.0	17.28	9.17
1987	117,999	601.8	17.49	7.72
1988	119,450	617.7	19.69	7.69
1989	119,207	605.5	20.10	5.31

Source: Data from Chamber of Mines of South Africa, *Annual Reports* (Johannesburg, 1970-1989).

South Africa had lost its previously undisputed ability to produce an ounce of gold more cheaply than any of the other major producing countries.

Besides the changes in the international gold market, the early 1970s brought major international commodity price booms, the product partly of the Club of Rome forecast of long-term resource shortages. The South African mining industry responded by undertaking major expansions in iron ore, ferro-metals, and coal. The state played its part through an extremely ambitious program of infrastructural expansion. It constructed two deep-water ports, expanded others, and introduced associated services, such as high-volume railway lines and containerization.

In the 1970s and early 1980s, South Africa remained true to the dictum that its progress occurs politically by disasters and economically by windfalls. Despite recurrent political upheaval and chronic mayhem in the townships, South Africa avoided many of the woes of the other

Table 1.2 Average Wages of Black Mineworkers, 1970-1987

| | Cash Wages | | Real Wage |
	Rands	Index	Index
1970	207.80	100.0	100.0
1971	221.20	106.4	100.6
1972	256.70	123.5	109.3
1973	349.70	168.3	135.5
1974	564.80	271.8	196.2
1975	947.90	456.1	289.6
1976	1,102.80	530.7	303.4
1977	1,235.00	594.2	305.2
1978	1,420.50	683.5	314.5
1979	1,668.60	802.9	324.9
1980	2,037.40	980.3	347.0
1981	2,520.00	1,212.7	369.3
1982	2,985.10	1,437.0	384.4
1983	3,425.80	1,653.4	393.5
1984	3,975.00	1,912.9	407.6
1985	4,452.00	2,142.4	392.9
1986	5,127.00	2,467.3	381.5
1987	6,218.00	2,992.3	403.4

Source: Adapted from P. Hirschsohn, "Management Ideology and Environmental Turbulence: Understanding Labour Policies in the South African Gold Mining Industry" (unpublished M.Sc. thesis, Oxford University, 1988), Appendix 3.

commodity producers. Though its venture into iron ore exports through Saldanha Bay on the west coast was disastrous, the inflation of the 1970s and OPEC's radical increases in the price of oil continually buoyed up the price of gold. While South African consumers felt the impact of sharply increased oil prices and shortages, the mining companies benefited as gold and coal prices rose in response to the oil situation. But eventually the terms of trade turned against both oil and coal. More important, the gold price has been in gradual decline since its peaks of the early 1980s (Figure 1.3). It averaged about US$437 in 1988. Gold revenues accounted for about 40 percent of South African export earnings compared with around 50 percent at the beginning of the decade.

With many new mines about to come into production around the world, an oversupply of gold is possible in the early 1990s. In any case, South Africa's dominance as a producer has steadily lessened, although it remains the largest supplier (Table 1.3). When sanctions loomed and the world's bankers withdrew most credit facilities, gold sales underwrote

Table 1.3 Major Gold Producers, 1983-1986

	1983		1984		1985		1986		Totals	
	Production (million ounces)	% of Total	Production (million ounces)	% of Total	Production (million ounces)	% of Total	Production (million ounces)	% of Total	Production (million ounces)	%
South Africa	21.85	48.4	21.86	46.7	21.57	43.9	20.51	39.7	85.79	44.5
Soviet Union	8.60	19.0	8.65	18.5	8.70	17.7	8.85	17.1	34.80	18.0
Canada	2.36	5.2	2.68	5.7	2.82	5.7	3.36	6.5	11.22	5.8
United States	2.00	4.4	2.08	4.4	2.43	4.9	3.74	7.2	10.25	5.3
Brazil	1.85	4.1	1.90	4.0	2.20	4.5	2.30	4.5	8.25	4.3
China	1.85	4.1	1.90	4.0	1.95	4.0	2.10	4.1	7.80	4.0
Australia	0.98	2.2	1.30	2.8	1.88	3.8	2.41	4.7	6.57	3.4
Philippines	0.82	1.9	0.83	1.8	1.06	2.2	1.30	2.5	4.01	2.1
Papua N. Guinea	0.58	1.3	0.83	1.8	1.19	2.4	1.13	2.2	3.73	1.9
Chile	0.57	1.3	0.54	1.2	0.55	1.1	0.58	1.1	2.24	1.2
Zimbabwe	0.45	1.0	0.48	1.0	0.47	0.9	0.48	0.9	1.88	1.0
Colombia	0.43	0.9	0.73	1.6	1.14	2.3	1.28	2.5	3.58	1.9
Others	2.82	6.2	3.05	6.5	3.22	6.6	3.58	7.0	12.67	6.6
Total	45.16	100.0	46.83	100.0	49.18	100.0	51.62	100.0	192.79	100.0

Source: Compiled from Minerals Yearbook 1987: Vol. 1 (Washington, D.C., 1989), p. 433.

the balance of payments. Since 1980, gold output has contributed between 10 and 16 percent of gross domestic product (GDP). Mining taxes underwrite the national budget, ensuring that the state remains sensitive to mining industry needs.

Gold mining as a whole, of course, has continually benefited from the government's exchange-rate policy. The policy is designed to ensure that South African rand receipts from gold sales stay high by allowing the rand to fall against the U.S. dollar, the currency in which gold is priced internationally. In the mid-1980s, the government considered making major changes to the mining taxation system with the objective of raising more revenue. Typically, the outcome was the appointment of a government commission on general taxation (the Margo Commission) followed by a technical committee (the Marais Committee), which recommended a more lenient tax regime for the gold mines. The government accepted the Marais Committee's proposals, which followed the fifty-year policy of the South African state: underwriting mining profits in bad times, while taxing them fairly heavily in good times. The only unusual aspect of the changes was the favoring of high-grade over low-grade mines. This change went counter to an even longer tradition of sheltering the low-grade mines. If the policy of protecting the marginal producers is ending, it will be at least partly because migrant labor costs have risen so much since the early 1970s that the government in many cases no longer sees the point in subsidizing the low-grade mines and the employment of foreign black nationals.

In spite of their problems in the 1980s, gold and mining in general are more important to the South African economy entering the 1990s than they were in the 1960s. They will remain fundamental into the next century. Most of the larger high-grade mines, worked by tens of thousands of migrant miners, will continue to be major producers for many years, unless a falling gold price should make them unprofitable. More than ever before, the gold industry will depend on future developments in the world gold market.

South Africa, in common with other developing countries and resource exporters, has found it extremely difficult to shift its major exports from natural resources to manufactured goods, while international sanctions have made such a goal even more than usually unattainable. South Africa continues to be able to sell all of the gold it produces, and this will remain its major source of foreign exchange. Thus, developments in the international gold market—over which the industry, the South African state, and the miners themselves have little influence—will continue to be central to the future of migrancy, to the South African economy, and to the southern African region.

The Decline of the Northern Labor Empire

In the 1960s, the mining industry's dependence on non–South African sources of labor deepened at precisely the time that these sources were becoming much less assured. Some mining groups began to press for a new, higher-cost wage policy that would draw South African workers back to the mines. The more cost-sensitive producers resisted, however, and domestic sourcing did not increase markedly until 1974. In that year, unexpected events forced the mines suddenly to substitute domestic for foreign labor on a large scale. This in turn required much more attention to improving working conditions and wages, as South African blacks had more employment options than others in the subcontinent and were more resistant to working under the arduous conditions typical of the gold mines.

The mining industry's northern labor empire was under threat beginning in the early 1960s, when newly independent Tanzania and Zambia disengaged from the migrant labor system. While Portuguese rule held in Mozambique, and Malawi remained stable under Hastings Banda, himself a former mine migrant, the mine managers believed they had little to fear from their two main foreign suppliers. This complacency changed in response to the traumas of 1974. With little warning, colonial rule in Mozambique collapsed following revolution in Portugal, and, in an apparently unconnected development, the Malawian government ordered the return of its 120,000 miners. The occasion, though not the main cause, was an air disaster that killed over seventy Malawian miners (see Chapter 5).

On previous occasions of shortage, the industry's recruiters were able to open more distant recruiting zones and to avoid wage increases. Once again they pressed for access to Angola and Rhodesia and intensified their efforts in the BLS countries (Botswana, Lesotho, and Swaziland). But demand still far exceeded supply, and they were forced to fall back as rarely before on some of their oldest domestic labor markets. Recession, rural impoverishment, mass retrenchment throughout other sectors, and the resulting black unemployment in manufacturing industries meant that the mines could now compete effectively for labor at home. The emergence of a large and growing domestic labor surplus initially permitted the migrant labor system to survive intact, though somewhat battered. Within a short time, the proportion of foreign to domestic black miners had been reversed from 70:30 to 40:60. If one regards labor from Lesotho as essentially domestic, because of its landlocked proximity to the mines and economic dependency on them, the decline of the northern labor empire was even more striking.

In the period after 1977, the individual mining groups and companies tended to pursue slightly different policies on foreign labor and to prefer different foreign sources.[29] Officially, the industry remained wedded to foreign sourcing, stating now that it expected to maintain about 40 percent of the complement from these areas. Strategic lessons learned earlier underlined the importance of avoiding reliance on a few sources or becoming too dependent on either domestic or foreign labor. Governments could never be trusted, and workers were always liable by their sudden departure to demonstrate that the mines were nobody's preferred employer. Efficiency considerations also explained the continued preference for foreign workers, who were more experienced, tended to dominate the upper skill categories, and were less militant. With few employment alternatives at home, their migrant behavior was easier to regulate, although this also began to apply increasingly to the South African miners. Although important, none of these considerations meant that foreign labor would be irreplaceable in the long run.

During the crisis of the 1970s, the state acted quickly to aid industry access to new external and internal labor reservoirs. Thereafter, certain policy contradictions began to surface. The large revenues received by the supplier countries from migrant labor, and the possibility of mass repatriation of otherwise unemployable foreign miners, provided South Africa with a potent political weapon against the supplier states. The foreign-affairs bureaucracy, therefore, tended to support the industry's arguments for foreign labor, viewing them as useful hostages in an increasingly hostile region. On the other hand, unemployment and growing poverty in the bantustans made influx-control administrators anxious to get rid of foreign workers and replace them with South Africans.

In the mid-1980s, South African President P. W. Botha reacted to a number of disputes with Mozambique unrelated to migrancy by announcing that the Mozambican miners would be repatriated, even though this move was in direct contravention of international treaties. Disputes between elements in the South African government and the mine owners over Mozambican labor stretch back to the 1920s and earlier. None of the differences disrupted the flow for long, and the 1980s were no exception. Whatever the Mozambican and South African governments want, or say they want, the workers keep coming. The bureaucratic cleavages on the issue within the South African state undoubtedly account for some of the reasons the Chamber of Mines has been able to maintain its longstanding independence and privileged position in importing migrant labor from foreign countries. But there are a number of fundamental economic and social needs fulfilled by migrancy which are often obscured by political rhetoric on all sides and which are more often than not overriding. Even the International Labour Organization, for decades a leading opponent of migration to South Africa, has failed to suggest alternative avenues of employment for the supplier countries (see Chapter 5).

The Crisis of Control

As the geographical composition of the work force shifted in the 1970s toward domestic labor, the mining compounds and hostels exploded. Mostly quiet over the previous decade, the mines now experienced almost continuous outbreaks of violence and rioting, illegal strikes, work stoppages, and go-slows. Attacks on property and company officials intensified. The riots came in spite of increases in wages and significant improvements in living conditions. Although many of the targets of violence were the agents and symbols of management, miners more often vented their frustrations on each other. The employers blamed age-old ethnic rivalries and outside agitators, while liberal and radical critics focused on low wages and the unnatural confinement imposed by life in austere, single-sex work dormitories.

The scale and persistence of the violence eventually convinced both government and the employers of the need to find spokesmen among the miners with whom they could discuss grievances and negotiate and enforce agreements. Some understanding of the need for dialogue developed alongside—but did not replace—reliance on repression. To start with, new forms of co-option and control, in the guise of half-measures such as works committees, were unsuccessfully tried. More realistic voices began to emerge in management, stressing the advantages of collective bargaining with black trade unions. Union leaders, they argued, would give early warning of grievances, provide a means for conflict resolution, and forestall violence.

Despite a seventy-five-year tradition of consensus in labor policy, the industry divided in its response to the unionization issue. More conservative thinkers argued for the certainties of the past, for traditional mechanisms of control, and, where these failed, for greater doses of coercion. Others, especially the dominant Anglo American Corporation, argued that coercion should be increasingly replaced by negotiation to move the black work force into a new corporatist industrial-relations system. This division was reflected in the important majority and minority submissions of the mining industry to the government's Commission of Inquiry into Labour Legislation (the Wiehahn Commission). Between 1977 and 1981, the Wiehahn Commission produced six reports, the last of them on "Industrial Relations in the Mining Industry." Together, they had a major impact on labor relations in South Africa and the legal rights of black workers and trade unions (see Chapter 8).[30]

Although important, policy differences between the mining houses have not threatened basic agreement among the employers on a wide range of issues. Their industry association, the Chamber of Mines, makes for efficiency and saves money. It provides common services, administrative support, and research facilities on a wide range of technical matters and health and safety issues. Everyone benefits by having a neutral umbrella organization run day-to-day labor policy, the one area where competition, if it became significant, could seriously threaten profits. While Anglo American, for instance, increasingly went its own way on wage rates in the period after 1982, the variation from agreed Chamber rates always remained modest (see Appendix, Table A.2). The monopsonistic system of recruitment (an employers' monopoly) has not been overturned, particularly for the less-skilled workers (most of the labor force). Moreover, the other policy differences are mostly of degree rather than kind. None of the companies, including the most progressive, has abandoned coercion as an instrument of labor relations, as Anglo American forcibly demonstrated with mass dismissals during the last days of the 1987 strike.

Just as the state had been forced to mediate in the dispute between industry and white labor between 1910 and 1924 to protect jobs, revenue, and its own stability, it interceded between black labor and white employer in the late 1970s and early 1980s. Labor relations specialists such as N. E. Wiehahn who chaired the State President's Commission on Labour Legislation, 1977–1982, and P. J. Van der Merwe, director general of the Department of Manpower and a Wiehahn commission member, played a major role in persuading the state and big business to accept the need for black labor organizations and black unions. These were not traditional bureaucrats but academics brought into government service at the most senior levels. They were not part of the old order or resistant to its transformation. This process of promoting from outside the bureaucracy started with the Department of Manpower and later spread to other departments, such as Constitutional Development and Mineral and Energy Affairs. Although the government's intervention was no more disinterested and evenhanded than it had been sixty years before, it was crucial to providing the conditions for the recognition and growth of black unions. The authorities wanted, as before with the white miners, to deal with labor issues by administrative rather than political means and to encourage the emergence of credible labor leaders who could negotiate binding agreements with employers.

Van der Merwe, a university professor who became the most senior bureaucrat behind the state's concerted and successful program that resulted in official recognition of black trade unions, says there were three main reasons for the state initiative. First, by 1979, economic and workplace changes had made industrial law an anachronism that failed to recognize that blacks were dominating skilled, as well as semiskilled and unskilled, labor categories. Second, many employers, particularly large companies with foreign ownership or exposure, were becoming increasingly aware of the urgency of accommodating black labor. Third, there

were already about fifty black unions operating outside the ambit of the
legislation, and they were growing. The government wanted to keep labor
relations from becoming an overtly political issue, and it attempted to do
this by incorporating black labor into the official system of industrial
relations. "We succeeded just in time," claims Van der Merwe. "The black
unions would otherwise have rejected the system altogether."[31]

The Rise of the NUM and the Decline of the MWU

In 1982, after several years of debate and hesitation, a majority of the
mining groups that ran the Chamber of Mines advised member companies
to permit the new unions to organize. The National Union of Mineworkers
(NUM), an offshoot of the Council of Unions of South Africa (CUSA),
was formed in 1982. Under its first general secretary, Cyril Ramaphosa,
the NUM successfully exploited this new opportunity. While the Chamber's concession was crucial to the immediate success of union organizing
efforts, the causes of unionization lay deeper. Conventional wisdom had
long held that migrant mineworkers would be difficult, if not impossible,
to organize, a view that was refuted by the rapid progress of the NUM.
In the five years to 1987, no union in South Africa, or probably in the
world, grew faster.

From the outset, the NUM received very different treatment from the
individual mines and the controlling houses. In general, the giant Anglo
American group quietly encouraged the union by providing selective
access to the hostels and relaxing qualifications for recognition. By contrast,
the Goldfields group, in which the U.K. parent had a large stake, stren-
uously opposed unionization. The degree of management cooperation
was vital to the NUM, whose membership even now remains heavily
concentrated on Anglo American mines. Thus, though the NUM is undoubtedly a dynamic, independent organization and certainly not the
stereotypical sweetheart union, it is to some degree a foster child of and
dependent on both industry and government. In theory, what the state
and employer give, they can also take away, and in an extreme situation
the NUM could still be broken. The failure of the 1987 strike suggests
this. Conversely, the relatively restrained response of both employers and
officials to the strike suggests that they remain convinced that such a
course would be more dangerous to mining interests than the continuing
and combative existence of a strong union. The NUM had felt strong
enough to call for the industry-wide strike on the issue of wages and
conditions. There was also a wider agenda to demonstrate worker support
for international economic sanctions against South Africa and the seizure
of control of the national economy. Lasting more than three weeks, the
strike was the largest coordinated industrial action by black miners since

1946 and constituted an impressive demonstration of the depth of NUM's organizational structure and the loyalty of its members. The Chamber of Mines seemed to welcome the test of strength, concerned perhaps that the growing power of the union needed restraining lest it become still harder to deal with in the future. About 300,000 workers (40 percent of the black labor force in the gold and coal mines) came out in support of the union. The NUM had come a long way since 1982, but in the end it was the employers who came out on top, and the union won no substantial concessions for its members.

Nearly 50,000 Anglo American workers were dismissed in the last days of the strike, and the NUM's leadership in many mines was decimated. Within three months, 25,000 miners were reemployed. The NUM went to the Industrial Court to ask for the reinstatement of a further 13,000. In April 1988, Anglo American agreed to rehire a further 9,500 and to provide the 6,000 who would not be rehired with at least eighteen weeks' back pay. Some saw this as a victory for the NUM, but many shaft stewards and union officials were among those who lost their jobs permanently. James Motlatsi, for example, the president of the NUM, was not reemployed by Anglo American. In the aftermath of the strike, the mining houses drastically curtailed the freedom of access of union organizers to mine property and withdrew recognition agreements on some mines. On the defensive, the NUM began a painful process of rebuilding grassroots confidence and support.

Nonetheless, the NUM, unlike the increasingly beleaguered white Mine Workers' Union (MWU), seems to have an assured place as the industrial representative of South Africa's miners. What is less certain is the NUM's future as a wider political organization. It has been compared to the Polish union Solidarity, and some in the NUM and its associated federation, the Congress of South African Trade Unions (COSATU), sought to achieve a comprehensive social and political mandate. The suppression of most mass-based political organizations put enormous pressure on the black trade unions from at least the late 1970s to fill the vacuum by pursuing wider social and political goals. A heated debate ensued within many of the unions, including the NUM, between populists with radical political goals and trade unionists who wanted to confine the agenda to worker issues.[32]

Despite the changes in the last two decades following 1970, white labor remained wedded to the apartheid institutions sheltering it. Elsewhere in the economy, beginning in the 1960s, white labor shortages created demands for a more-skilled, better-educated black work force. This led to the gradual erosion of the Color Bar in manufacturing. It survived in the mines virtually intact, however. The white Mine Workers' Union resisted all but the most minor adjustments in the legislative and customary protection of its members. Faced with their continuing intransigence, the government vacillated for twenty years, but finally passed legislation to phase out the mine Color Bar in 1987. Even then, political timidity led to further delays in proclaiming the bill. The law went into force in 1988 and cleared the way for the formal introduction of black workers into the more skilled job categories. By the end of the 1980s, more than 100 blacks were employed as supervisory miners with blasting certificates. However, the industry, despite its depressed state, was still short of an estimated 750 blasting-certificate holders. A speedy end to the racial hierarchy in the mines is unlikely. While whites will continue to dominate management and supervisory positions into the future, the legal basis on which they do so has changed.

Beneath the surface, a creeping erosion of the Color Bar began in the 1960s and 1970s with many black miners performing "white" jobs.[33] Though they have not been receiving white workers' wages for doing this, and the wage gap remains huge, blacks' wages have increased many times faster in real terms than whites' wages since 1973. Black miners now have a large and dynamic union recognized by the employers. And the statutory Color Bar has been dismantled, the first step toward institutionalizing the training of artisan and managerial black miners and destroying the still-pervasive customary Color Bar.

Computerized Migrancy and Stabilization

The dramatic events of 1987 are closely connected with another less obvious but equally important transformation in the geographical and social composition of black mine labor over the last two decades. In contrast to the pattern of the past, workers now return regularly and repeatedly to the same mine, work gang, and job. They no longer intersperse periods of mine work with extended and irregular stays in the countryside. Periods of employment (they no longer sign legal contracts) have been standardized. After working for about eleven months, migrants return home for a fixed leave period of several weeks before returning on a date fixed by management. Failure to return at the agreed time often (though not always) leads to forfeiture of the job.

The limited flexibility that accompanied the traditional system of migrancy—which gave migrants some choice of the mines they would work at while not committing the employer to take back the migrant—has gradually, and then more rapidly, given way after 1970 to a much less arbitrary form of administrative migrancy made possible by the extensive application on a truly massive scale of the computer. The role of the computer in the modernization of South African migrancy has been little commented on, but it is the single crucial variable in making possible the modernized form of migrancy that is taking shape in the gold mines.[34]

Computerized migrancy is a hybrid that incorporates some features of traditional oscillating migrancy and some features of stabilized, proletarian employment. On the one hand, the migrants still move back and forth between their place of residence and their place of employment and are not allowed to develop permanent residential rights at the place of employment. On the other hand, the workers are increasingly becoming "career miners" who work eleven or so months a year for the same employer, year after year, continually upgrading their skills and productivity. Computerized migrancy relates to old-style migrancy in the same way that the industrial conciliation system relates to old-style adversarial trade unionism. In both cases ostensibly impersonal regulation and administration supplant coercion and overt confrontation. The major difference is that computerized migrancy is administered by the private sector, not the state, and it makes possible the instantaneous "on-line" regulation of hundreds of thousands of workers.

In its computer files, the Chamber of Mines has millions of finger prints of workers throughout the subcontinent. It also uses photo-recognition systems. The Chamber tailored the data base to its needs, and its executives regard it with pride. They think standard finger-print systems are dated and unsuited to an approach based on identification rather than criminal detection. These files and photo systems have simplified the problems of reemployment and fraud prevention to a point that would have been unthinkable twenty years ago.[35] Computers, in other words, make possible a degree of control and regulation that no amount of coercion could achieve. And, most important of all, the control is combined with the flexibility that is the characteristic of modern global capitalism. Over wide areas of southern Africa, traditional field recruiting, so essential to operations for a century or more, has become increasingly redundant (see Chapter 6).

Management refers to computerized migrancy as "stabilization." Compared with the previous situation of totally irregular periods of work and returns home, as well as the arbitrariness of which mine would provide the next job, it undoubtedly is "stabilization" of a kind. But the normal use of the term would imply that the worker has settled, usually with his family, in a family home near to the place of work, living at home, and commuting every day to work. In this sense of the term, the migratory labor force on the mines cannot be described as stabilized. A more satisfactory description, in fact, would be "pseudo-stabilization." The employer gets some of the benefits of a stabilized work force in which workers can be trained for a specific job and career path in a particular mine, their productivity can be maximized through training, and their reliability and discipline can be ensured through the guaranteed return to the same job, after a short and defined absence. By contrast, the employee loses the freedom he had enjoyed in the bad old days of migrancy without gaining the security, status, and improvement in living conditions implied by the normal use of the term "stabilized." This is one reason, among others, why the mining houses built so little housing for black workers in the early 1980s (see Chapter 7).

The new pattern of migrancy arises not only from policy initiatives and computerization but more importantly from circumstances that constrain workers' options. Workers stay with the mines because they have little choice in the matter. High unemployment across southern Africa (worsened by forced resettlement in South Africa proper) has made the mine job a prized possession. Large crowds of unemployed workers congregate outside mine recruiting offices throughout southern Africa in the hope of securing an elusive mine contract. In addition, the modern black miner is more an industrial, proletarianized worker. He has a much smaller stake in the increasingly depressed rural areas and is better educated than his predecessor. He is both more bound to mine employment and more likely to be dissatisfied with it. When the NUM began to organize in the mines after 1982, it recruited a work force already experiencing these new circumstances.

As long as the mines continue to draw labor from outside the country, that portion of the work force is likely to remain fully migrant, though under the constraints of computerized migrancy. But it is no longer certain that the old pattern of migrancy will endure within. Inside South Africa, migrants close enough to home are increasingly engaged in a form of monthly or biweekly commuting to the mines. In Lesotho, migrants working in the neighboring Orange Free State gold fields are now known as "weekenders." This practice is becoming more common as many mines now prefer to draw their labor from sources close at hand. The state's new urban labor policies will further hasten this process, as migrant miners avail themselves of the opportunity to move their families to townships and squatter camps closer to the mines. Rights of urban residence are now supposedly conditional upon access to secure employment and housing. These changes mean, at the very least, that the state has belatedly recognized the inevitability of black urbanization. This development has led to the concession of long leases and home-purchase arrangements in the townships.

It is by no means clear that the new strategy will succeed any better than the old. Already the state is struggling to find the resources for township development on the scale required. Large new squatter camps and settlements are springing up around major urban centers. Existing townships are growing dramatically. In any event, the collapse of old-style influx control has opened up the way for new forms of labor mobilization and control in the mines.

The pressures to transform the migrant labor system have been building for over a decade. These have come from two directions. As the skill levels of the black work force rise, so the case for continuing to treat black labor as undifferentiated units weakens. Second, stabilization has increasingly come to be seen as an industrial relations strategy by management. Once the NUM was permitted access to (some) mines, the compounds proved to be an ideal organizing environment (see Chapter 8). A fierce battle for control of the compounds ensued, culminating in the 1987 strike. Before the 1980s, stabilization was largely seen by management as a logical requirement of mine mechanization. In the 1980s, the delivery of family housing to skilled and semiskilled black miners was seen as a way of depopulating the compounds, dividing the work force, and damping militancy.

This housing model, first articulated in the 1970s, was based on a two-tier labor force, part-migrant, part-stabilized. The stabilized labor would be a permanently employed, skilled, homeowning, group of "permanent" miners with secure union rights. Unless mechanization produces large-scale redundancy, the industry will continue to source its unskilled labor from a rotating, vulnerable reserve of rural and urban labor held in place by the large pool of unemployed. More and more of these workers are likely to become commuters, leading to a further distinction between long-distance migrants and short-distance commuters. Large-scale stabilized labor in the existing gold mines is unlikely for most mineworkers in this century but the process has begun. The NUM has already called on the mines to dismantle the migrant labor system and commissioned its own research on ways to provide alternative accommodation for members. The extent, pace, and precise direction of change will be fiercely contested between labor and management over the next several years.

2

The Foundations of
Northern Expansion, 1920–1948

Throughout most of its history, the gold mining industry's recruiting system expanded into ever more distant regions. The Chamber of Mines always had to deploy its recruiters on the furthest edge of South Africa's labor frontiers. This situation developed not only because of cost considerations—the need to get labor where it was least expensive—but also because mine work is difficult: hard, dangerous, often unhealthy, and poorly paid. Unless without choices, most workers avoided it. Industry recruiters did better, therefore, in the least-developed areas where wages were low and employment opportunities poor. In these distant regions, the mining companies could outbid local employers and keep their South African competitors at bay.

Apart from their monopoly of recruiting for South Africa in Mozambique, only the mining companies had invested heavily in the elaborate recruiting networks that long-distance labor mobilization required. Expanding an existing system cost much less than building one from scratch. Moreover, wherever possible, as for instance in Mozambique and later Nyasaland (Malawi), the industry negotiated agreements that gave it exclusive rights to recruit for South Africa in order to cut out other low-wage employers, principally the farmers.

Northern Expansion

After 1920, the Chamber of Mines worked vigorously to enlarge its labor supplies and expand its influence. Its special objective was to penetrate the tropical labor pools of northern Bechuanaland (Botswana), Northern Rhodesia (Zambia), Nyasaland, and Southern Rhodesia (Zimbabwe). Earlier, the Louis Botha government had banned employment of workers from these areas in gold mines because of the disastrous rates of mortality, principally from pneumonia, experienced by them before

1913.[1] The ban did not entirely cut off the flow, but it severely restricted it. Workers still made their own way south, crossing into South Africa via Southern Rhodesia, Mozambique, and Bechuanaland. Some of them were able to pass themselves off as local residents and to secure mine recruitment at Native Recruiting Corporation camps in the northern Transvaal and southern Bechuanaland. Most of them found employment with farmers and in coal mines and other industries. Resumption of formal recruiting by the mines in the tropical areas after 1932 worked to entrench the whole labor supply system more firmly. The doubling of the gold price with devaluation at the end of 1932, and major new gold discoveries, meant that a program of large-scale expansion was in prospect. Industry analysts doubted that sufficient labor would be available locally. Access to the north gave mine migrant labor an assured future. Such access rendered unnecessary any effort to bring fresh thinking to bear on the problem of the long-term labor supply or to consider real alternatives to migrancy. This had been, in any case, less necessary because of the widespread view in the industry and the government throughout most of the 1920s that the life of the industry was coming to a close. The events of the early 1930s completely transformed the prospects for the future.

The mining companies' Mozambique recruiter, the Witwatersrand Native Labour Association (WNLA), became the instrument of renewed expansion; by the 1940s, its influence extended across southern Africa (Figure 2.1). The industry already had access to southern Mozambique and the monopoly of the recruiting for South Africa there. A long-standing intergovernmental agreement, the Mozambique Convention, confirmed this. It was renegotiated in 1928. One of the terms of the new agreement was a reduction in the number of Mozambique workers who could be recruited annually by WNLA from the pre-1928 average of about 100,000 to 80,000 per year. This goal was to be achieved in stages over several years. By the mid-1930s, however, as the depression deepened, the Portuguese became more interested in ensuring a high minimum flow to the mines and secured agreement from the South Africans on a 60,000 annual minimum. Once the South African government lifted the ban on the employment of tropicals, WNLA was able to open up northern Mozambique as well. With the whole northern tier of the subcontinent now potentially available to mine recruiters (once the governments there agreed), major consequences followed, both for the development of government labor policies and for South Africa's relations with its neighbors.

In the subcontinental political economy, the Chamber's recruiting arm became a major actor in its own right. Its representatives, particularly William Gemmill, conducted quasi-diplomatic negotiations with regional governments on a regular basis. Gemmill became Chamber general manager in 1923. In that capacity, he had responsibility for running the

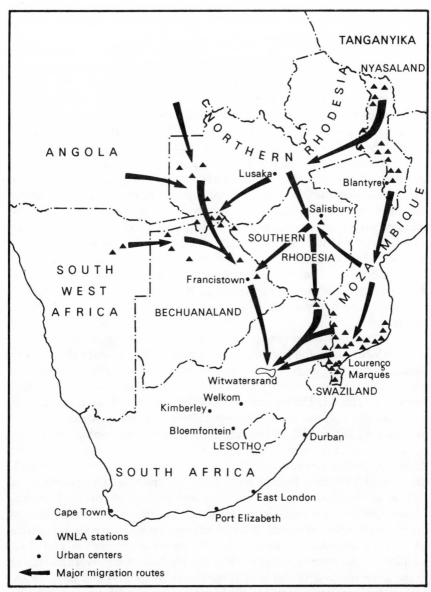

Figure 2.1 Major migration routes to South African gold mines, 1940–1970. *Source:* Adapted from Francis Wilson, *Labour in the South African Gold Mines, 1911–1969* (Cambridge, Cambridge University Press, 1972), p. ix.

recruiting system. Well connected in business circles and in high levels of the state bureaucracy, he was shrewd, able, and tough. The northern governments found him a formidable antagonist. Their various projects for closer union in Central Africa stemmed partly from the need to challenge and to contain the gold mining companies' labor demands.[2]

In some ways, Gemmill's instrument in the north, WNLA, became the successor to Cecil Rhodes' British South Africa (BSA) Company, a new instrument of southern economic power beyond the Limpopo River. The BSA company had counted on gold and rich grazing lands to attract investors into these regions. By contrast, the Johannesburg mining industry coveted the human potential of the area. Rhodes and his agents had relied on heavy-handed political manipulation and military force to pursue their objectives. More subtly, WNLA's master strategist, Gemmill, exploited the rivalries among the northern governments on migrant labor and deftly maneuvered to control the labor supply. The result was to extend the competition for labor between mines and farms which had long prevailed within South Africa.[3] In the target areas, the gold mines, with covert backing from the South African government, took on local employers and allied politicians. The main challenge to the South Africans came from the government of Southern Rhodesia. It struggled to retain control of the supply and to divert southward-moving labor flows to its own mines and farms.

These years saw the emergence of an intense struggle for low-wage migrant labor along the previously untapped northern tier of the subcontinent. When the mining industry asserted its power throughout the region, local labor markets were disrupted and interstate relations fundamentally altered. The requirements of the South African mines shaped the regional labor and immigration policies of the South African government during this period. In London, the Johannesburg mining houses put pressure also on the Colonial and Dominions offices for support of their access to Central African labor. They worked to the same end through the United Kingdom High Commission in Pretoria. The portrayal of WNLA as the champion of free labor was pushed at the International Labour Office (ILO) in Geneva. Although the imperial governments of the period worried about the adverse effects of migration to South Africa on regional colonial economies, for the workers themselves and their families official interventions worked mainly to support WNLA's access to the labor markets of the British territories in Central and East Africa, against the protests of settler politicians in the two Rhodesias and Nyasaland.

Before accepting recruiting arrangements, however, London insisted on health safeguards and imposed quotas designed to limit migration and minimize social disruption among the target populations. While privately critical of the gold mines, publicly British officials rarely challenged the idea of the mines as a progressive employer in the region. Mining representatives made sure that the imperial government received constant reminders of its direct stake in these matters. The South African economy was a major market for British goods; the gold mines sustained that economy. The South African devaluation at the end of 1932 substantially raised the gold price and stimulated unprecedented mining expansion. It ended the depression in the local economy. Thus South Africa became an even more important market for stagnant British industry. Finally, since South Africa remained part of the sterling currency area, its gold propped up the British pound.

By 1932, the Chamber of Mines had secured the permission of the South African government to recruit north of 22° south latitude, initially on a small-scale, experimental basis (the line runs across the subcontinent just beyond South Africa's northern border and bisects Mozambique, Botswana, and Namibia). Gemmill immediately opened negotiations with the Southern Rhodesians and later with the Northern Rhodesian and Nyasaland authorities. Since the Southern Rhodesian mines and farms paid even lower wages than the Rand mines, their owners feared a WNLA challenge to their de facto recruiting monopoly further north.[4] The negotiations were tough. The lure of higher wages in South Africa and the determination of thousands of northern workers to get to them forced the neighbors to negotiate. Their labor was going south anyway and they lacked the bureaucratic and police capability to control their borders. Negotiating with the South Africans offered the hope of getting some control over the migration and possibly putting some enforceable limits on it. In a series of agreements between 1932 and 1939, William Gemmill secured access for WNLA to Northern Rhodesia and Nyasaland, first on a limited, experimental basis and then more permanently.[5]

Although the number of workers flowing to the mines from the tropical regions was small up to 1939 (less than 10 percent of the total supply; see Figure 2.2), WNLA and the Chamber saw tropical workers as an investment for the future.[6] The industry's recruiting experts judged that their expanding needs required new sources outside South Africa and Mozambique. Analysts feared that the gold mines were increasingly uncompetitive in South Africa's own labor markets. They knew that the potential of the southern parts of Mozambique had been largely tapped. The tropical northern areas were the only remaining unexploited labor source. Hence in the late 1930s and the 1940s WNLA developed transport networks (road and air), rest camps, and medical facilities to gain access to the labor there.[7]

Northern Bechuanaland was the key to Gemmill's strategy in the trans-Limpopo. This area was important for itself as a potential source of new

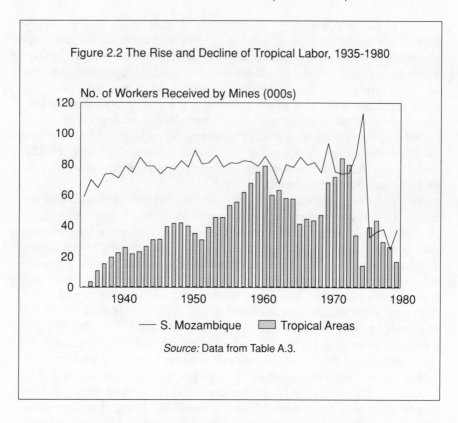

Figure 2.2 The Rise and Decline of Tropical Labor, 1935-1980

—— S. Mozambique   ▨ Tropical Areas

Source: Data from Table A.3.

recruits (novices), though the area was thinly populated. It was more important as the mining industry's recruiting highway into the north and northwest. By establishing bases there, WNLA could tap the labor of the entire region. Though Rhodesia and other governments were hostile to South African recruiting, it was enough for WNLA to put its camps on their borders. Voting with their feet in response to the lure of higher gold mine wages, workers from areas in which WNLA was restricted or denied access simply crossed the Bechuanaland borders to WNLA camps on their own.

In the era of subcontinental labor mobilization, Bechuanaland retained every bit of the strategic significance it had enjoyed in the days of Rhodes. In the 1880s, the imperial government established a protectorate in this huge, semidesert wilderness, acting from a variety of strategic motives. Cape Colony merchants and politicians, including Rhodes, saw this very much in terms of securing their commercial access to the African interior. In those days, the principal enemy of Cape expansion had been Kruger's Transvaal government. The acquisition of Bechuanaland opened the way for Cape commercial and railway expansion to outflank Kruger on the west. By the 1930s, WNLA had inherited the mantle of South African expansion, and it came to need access to the territory as much as Rhodes and his associates had. The rivals too had changed, of course. Now, WNLA confronted the formidable Godfrey Huggins (later Lord Malvern), from 1932 the premier of Southern Rhodesia. Ironically, the legatee of the defensive, protectionist policies of the great Ndebele leader, Lobengula, and the legendary Afrikaner, Paul Kruger, Huggins now became, in his turn, the leading political opponent of southern imperialism and the advocate of Central African economic autonomy. The Rhodesian government said repeatedly that it would do everything possible to thwart WNLA's plans. To counter Huggins, WNLA had few options. Communications were difficult through Mozambique. This left Bechuanaland.

Huggins came, reluctantly, to the negotiating table between 1936 and 1939. He knew that WNLA was already establishing itself on his borders. Using Bechuanaland, the association, with or without the cooperation of the other governments, could tap the labor supplies of the entire region. From its new depot at Francistown, it built roads north to Kazungula on the Zambezi River, west to Ghanzi, and on to Grootfontein in South West Africa (Namibia) (Figure 2.3). WNLA's roads extended across the central Kalahari Desert where only tracks had existed before. It was WNLA and not the colonial government that opened the modern road from Francistown via Maun to Mohembo on the Okavango River. Eventually, WNLA constructed over 1,200 kilometers of roads in northern Bechuanaland alone. It had in addition established motor barge transport on the Zambezi and through the Okavango. The association also built roads and camps in northern Nyasaland and Barotseland. After World War II, WNLA moved into air transport, establishing a scheduled service with over thirty flights per week from Francistown alone by 1955.[8]

The Chamber of Mines underwrote the expansion of colonial medical services in Bechuanaland and the other High Commission Territories with modest grants-in-aid. The money, derived largely from the unclaimed deferred-pay fund of the workers themselves, supported the training of paramedical staff and funded mobile clinics. This service was provided partly to improve the chronically poor health of the target population. Many of the males had to meet the medical standard established by WNLA for mine recruits and loss of labor through medical rejection was wasteful. High rejection rates also affected the willingness of all blacks to come forward from long distances (thousands of them made their own way every year to WNLA's far-flung recruiting camps) when there was a high risk of being turned back on health grounds. Through its modest grants-in-aid, the Chamber sought to cultivate the goodwill of the impoverished Bechuanaland administration at Mafeking.[9]

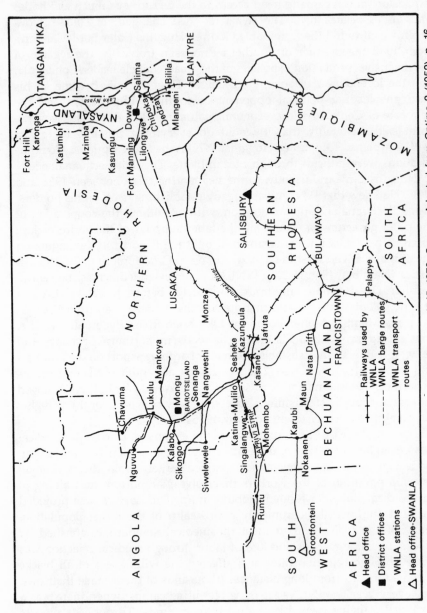

Figure 2.3 WNLA recruiting operations in tropical areas, 1945–1970. Source: Adapted from Optima 2 (1952), p. 16.

The medical problems that arose with the proposed recruitment of mineworkers from these areas were not new. In the earlier "experiment" with tropical labor, high death rates from pneumonia eventually compelled the mining companies to transform their hospitals from badly supervised death traps to modern facilities with improved supervision. The companies also introduced slightly more thorough medical examinations at recruitment and as needed during the worker's contract. At the time of Union in 1910, the industry joined with the state in establishing the South African Institute of Medical Research. It specialized in the study of diseases to which miners were especially susceptible. An extensive debate among public health experts, mine medical officers, and Chamber executives took place during the 1920s on the appropriate forms of preventive and curative medicine for black miners. In this context, the medical community addressed the tropical health question.

Migrancy and the Economics of Miners' Health

Despite major improvements in medical facilities in the mines, black miners remained at serious risk.[10] While the banning of tropical recruitment in 1913 led to sharp falls in the occurrence of pneumonia, tuberculosis and other lung ailments continued to exact a heavy toll. Few of the black miners served long or continuously enough to display acute symptoms of miners' phthisis or silicosis, the chronic lung disease caused by prolonged exposure to the rock dust from drilling and blasting, which was the principal health risk of the white workers. The dust problem was gradually controlled but not eliminated by the mandatory use of water sprays on the pneumatic drills, extensively employed to prepare the rock at the stope face for blasting. The health precautions and compensation for victims mandated by the state under successive Phthisis Acts gave blacks little benefit. For them, tuberculosis, complicated by or confused with incipient silicosis, was a major killer.

The Chamber of Mines recognized only slowly the gravity of the health problems that were endemic among its target population. As late as 1943, Gemmill informed the Lansdown Commission on black miners' wages that there was no serious health problem affecting miners:

Another parrot cry in regard to the Native Territories is the allegation that the health conditions of the native population in the Reserves are exceedingly unsatisfactory. . . . It seems that here again the unfortunate conditions prevailing in Urban Locations and in some small Native Reserves . . . have been confused with the general position in the Native Reserves and a mistaken and highly dangerous idea of the conditions in the Reserves has been propagated. . . . The increase in the population of the Transkei and also Basutoland is over 2 per cent per annum, one of the highest rates of increase in the world. Such a rate would not be possible if malnutrition were rife and general health conditions bad.[11]

This was his usual brazen performance. Data readily available in the Chamber library contradicted Gemmill's argument.

Using the 1924 Tuberculosis Survey by Dr. Peter Allan, reports of the Native Affairs Commission, the findings of the Native Economic Commission of 1932, and other sources, the Lansdown Commission easily demonstrated that Gemmill's assessment of conditions in the territories was false: "The Commission is satisfied that the allegation as to the unsatisfactory state of health of the rural natives and the existence of malnutrition in the Reserves generally is no 'parrot cry', but, on the contrary, that the conditions give cause for grave concern."[12] Reporting in 1943, the Miners' Phthisis Acts Commission echoed this judgment. It expressed alarm about the incidence, treatment, and compensation of lung diseases in black miners. It urged the creation of a nationwide system of health care for Africans suffering from phthisis, tuberculosis, and other lung diseases. During 1943 and 1944, the National Health Services Commission underlined the urgent need of a universal health-care system, particularly for blacks.[13] There was growing unanimity among the medical experts on the deplorable state of health conditions in the reserves. This was not a conclusion that Gemmill could accept.

From the beginning, Gemmill and his associates knew that British officials in the tropical areas would demand health safeguards for tropical migrants at least as effective as the industry's existing standard for other workers. In an effort to satisfy the Colonial Office and officials in the target colonies, the Chamber of Mines ordered new studies. Reflecting an awareness of the disastrous results of high tropical mortality in the early years of the century, the mines conducted their new round of experiments carefully.[14] No tropical labor ended up in mines with compound rooms housing more than twenty workers or bad health records. Each worker began in the mine with twelve shifts on the surface and another fourteen days of acclimatization in light underground work. At the end of each shift, these workers received examinations for abrasions, since earlier experience had shown that disastrous infections could erupt in minor, untreated wounds. Compound staff inspected the rooms each morning and sent for treatment any workers apparently ill. As an additional precaution, they weighed the workers on pay days. Miners who sustained weight loss over successive pay periods went to hospitals for observation.

Tropical workers faced an extra risk from pneumonia; this had been the experience of the first round of "experiments" with these workers. Thousands died from the lung infection. In the early years, lack of proper hospital facilities and medical care had contributed to most of the pneumonia deaths. By the 1930s, the mines had developed much better methods of coping with pneumonia. Nearly twenty years of medical research, jointly sponsored by the Chamber of Mines and the government, led to the development of the Lister anti-pneumococcal vaccine. Though its efficacy was challenged, especially with the careful studies of Dr. A. J. Orenstein, its routine administration to tropical workers on recruitment showed industry concern about the pneumonia problem.[15] The frequent monitoring of the recruits in the compounds and their transfer to hospital at the first sign of trouble were important. They reflected an awareness that pneumonia caught and treated early was likely to be much less serious than if neglected. Only later, during and after the war, with the development of sulfa drugs and penicillin, did the treatment of pneumonia patients become straightforward.

The failure to introduce routine X-ray chest examinations of workers not suspected of lung disease showed that containing costs remained paramount to mining companies even on a politically sensitive issue. The X-ray screening was important if the industry was to deal effectively with tuberculosis. During the intense debate on tropical labor in 1935, C. F. Rey, the resident commissioner of Bechuanaland, wrote to Gemmill.[16] Following the recommendations of his principal medical officer, Dr. H. W. Dyke, Rey argued that the mines should provide an X-ray examination for all returning mineworkers. Their idea was to catch tuberculosis early, when treatment and isolation were most likely to prevent the spread of the disease. Rey pointed out that the mine medical departments had the facilities and the staff to do this readily. His scattered medical officers lacked needed equipment and had to depend on the unreliable physical examination.

In response, Gemmill referred to the minimum standard of the Phthisis Act which included no such requirement. The incidence of tuberculosis among black miners generally had been falling sharply since the 1920s and this must have contributed to the reluctance to sanction additional, expensive measures. He added that an X-ray exam for all returning mineworkers would be "very expensive" and "wholly unnecessary." He agreed to forward particulars on those Tswana workers found with tuberculosis (those with acute and obvious symptoms) but not to examine every Tswana worker before repatriation. Neither side recognized that comprehensive X-ray screening would do nothing to address the underlying causes of the scourge. These causes lay in the deteriorating economic and social conditions throughout the black rural areas and in migrancy itself, a primary means of infection and reinfection. However, the exchange with Rey did reveal the limits of the Chamber of Mines' willingness to address the health problems of its workers.

Gemmill and his colleagues argued that TB was not a mining disease and, therefore, not the responsibility of their medical system. Yet every contemporary study showed that tuberculosis was a major menace to the mining companies' target population and that mine work was a principal source of infection and reinfection.[17] Industry spokesmen often denied this connection; when they did admit that TB was a serious problem they refused to accept a conclusion that found the mining industry mainly responsible. Industry medical experts took the view that blacks were predisposed to TB, more by racial and physiological than by environmental conditions.[18] If TB was endemic in rural society, how could this be the companies' responsibility, they seemed to say. Dr. Orenstein pointed out that the death rate in the mines from acute tuberculosis had fallen dramatically over the previous twenty years.[19] If partly this decline was due to better methods of early detection, then the industry itself could take credit for that. Yet TB patients after diagnosis remained in the hospital only until "fit to travel." Officials justified early repatriation on the grounds of the restorative effects of country living. Their reasoning might have been correct but for the malnutrition, bad health conditions, and high incidence of the disease which were endemic there. In any case, owing to early repatriation, industry mortality rates did not reflect the real toll from the disease. Sent back as soon as "fit to travel," workers died from TB at home rather than in the mines. Industry medical statistics did not, of course, record these deaths.

Mine officials took the view that if death rates in the countryside from TB remained high then surely that was a general health problem, not the industry's responsibility. Without question, routine X-ray examinations would have reduced the incidence of tubercular infections of mineworkers and checked its spread. Equally, the mines, with or without mandatory X-ray examinations, were by themselves incapable of solving a problem rooted in black poverty, chronically low wages, and malnutrition. In any case, the X-ray screening would have dramatically increased costs, both for the examinations themselves and even more for the treatment which would have been necessary.[20] To say that this step was expensive was correct; to argue that it was "wholly unnecessary" contradicted known facts. Although its medical facilities and health precautions far exceeded what governments and other employers provided, the gold industry failed to take all the health precautions available to it. It found a variety of sociological, racial, economic, and medical reasons to justify this inaction. Later, after World War II, the mining industry did introduce a comprehensive program to provide X-ray examinations for all black miners, belated recognition of the gravity of the tuberculosis scourge, and of the role of migrancy in it.

Despite the precautions taken by the Chamber of Mines, tropical recruits fell ill and died in larger numbers than other workers. Gemmill and Dr. Orenstein argued that this was "normal" and predictable in worker populations that were without previous exposure to crowded urban environments. As larger numbers came to the mines, the Chamber predicted, a "herd immunity" would develop. A generation earlier, industry officials had offered the same reasoning when pneumonia was the major killer. Over time, the death rate would fall dramatically, they insisted on both occasions.[21] While correct, this was a Darwinian approach to industrial health policy, which proposed to sacrifice the weak and to focus on the lower morbidity rates of the survivors. It allowed medical officials to justify rates of illness and death that continued to be higher than for other workers in the mines.

The Northern Rhodesian administration wrote to London explaining the inadequacy of the medical facilities for migrants on its roads. Africans had to walk for hundreds of miles before they could get any medical attention from a European practitioner. Against comparisons of this type, the Rand looked presentable. Such arguments provided the justification both in southern Africa and in London for British officials to authorize limited expansion of the recruiting quotas allowed to WNLA.[22]

WNLA's Empire

Even before the Northern Rhodesian government had decided to authorize recruitment on a permanent basis, WNLA established its depot at Kazungula to tap the labor districts of Barotseland. Eventually northern Bechuanaland became a central corridor for WNLA operations extending into adjacent parts of Northern Rhodesia, Angola, and South West Africa. WNLA's many depots, fleets of passenger lorries, and network of airports gave the agency a presence in the region which, at least initially, dominated that of governments. New villages grew up along its routes; its motor lorries provided the only transport and mail service in many areas.[23]

This network cost large sums but failed in the short run to provide the increased labor, which mining executives wanted eventually to draw from "their" hinterland. In 1939, WNLA still had only about 20,000 tropical workers on its books (see Appendix, Table A.3). Partly this slow penetration of the northern areas was the product of political calculation. Preferring to secure the cooperation of the northern governments, Gemmill and the Chamber advanced slowly. They agreed to initially small experimental recruiting targets. They provided elaborate, time-consuming studies to give assurances on the health issues. Like the colonial governments, the British Colonial Office, and the South African government, the Chamber of Mines knew of the interest of the International Labour

Office in recruited labor in Africa. With London and Geneva watching developments closely, it was expedient for Gemmill and his colleagues to work for agreement with the northern governments. Conflict would bring bad publicity and that did not serve the interest of any of the employers. Thus, keeping these political calculations in mind, they moderated their demands and tolerated the interminable negotiations with Huggins and his Rhodesian associates. There were limits, however. Often, blunt threats extracted further concessions from the northern governments.[24]

By 1939, WNLA had its northern strategy in place and was accepted by the governments there. It established a regional headquarters in Salisbury and concluded a formal agreement with the three Central African governments. This agreement gave the association the right to establish its depots, camps, and transport systems throughout Barotseland and northern Nyasaland. In return, Gemmill undertook that the mines would not engage northern voluntary labor within South Africa itself.[25] This was an important concession. The northern governments knew that the mines were the magnet for most of their clandestine migrants. They had introduced regulations to monitor and control emigration of workers from their territories. One motive was to ensure that taxes had been paid prior to departure. Throughout southern Africa, however, no government was able to control its borders or restrict or even accurately monitor transborder population movements, in or out. From the Zambezi River south to the Limpopo, the wild untracked wilderness along Mozambique's western border provided perfect cover for southward-moving migrants. Thousands never returned, becoming the "lost ones." The 1939 agreement promised to check that unregulated flow of labor, which neither police border patrols nor pass laws and other controls had been able to contain or prevent. Under the agreement some of this labor could now be diverted into WNLA channels with repatriation guaranteed. What force had failed to achieve, the northern governments sought now to secure by agreement with WNLA.

During World War II, WNLA found other means to help the hardpressed Rhodesian employers, as labor shortages mounted. Because of the poor physical condition and indifferent health of the recruiters' target populations, medical rejection rates at the Bechuanaland camps remained high. These rejects hurt recruiting levels because they showed that migrants who traveled long distances on foot with much hardship could not count on securing employment. Southern Angolans who crossed the Caprivi Strip to join at one of WNLA's northern Bechuanaland camps suffered particularly. The industry knew that news of high rejection rates would get back to Angola and the supply would dry up. To counter this setback, the Chamber of Mines developed a farm labor scheme to provide employment for large numbers of these rejects while recovering part of its recruiting costs and earning itself some goodwill with Rhodesian farmers. Rejects who were fit enough for farm work could take employment on "approved" Mashonaland farms at low pay. Initially, the labor involved came principally from Angola.

WNLA made its arrangement with the Southern Rhodesian National Farmers' Union. Farmer members with certificates of approval from their local native commissioners were eligible to receive this labor. The association sent thousands of Angolans to Rhodesia over the next several years. It tried but failed to persuade the Bechuanaland authorities to handle their "TNB" (Tropical Northern Bechuana) mine rejects in the same way. By 1947, wages had increased slightly for experienced workers but remained low. The contract period was lengthened to 395 days with an optional extension for an additional 210 days.

The effect of this change was to create in the north conditions that had evolved informally in South Africa overall during the previous half century. Because the gold mines paid premium rates, they got the pick of the long-distance migrants. Increasingly, farmers had to be content with the mine's medical rejects, the aged, juveniles, and women. Moreover, the scheme kept the rejects under WNLA supervision while on the Rhodesian farms. The objective was to ensure proper treatment and feeding, and evidently it was successful. After a period on the Rhodesian farms, many of the medical rejects became fit enough to pass the mines' medical examinations and to go to the Rand. This is additional evidence that the major effort by the industry to deal comprehensively with the medical problems associated with long-distance migration had finally paid off. Eventually WNLA extended the scheme to Nyasaland and Northern Rhodesia as well.[26] In this way, Rhodesian farms could become, despite themselves, staging points for the Rand mines' labor supply.

These dealings between Gemmill and the northern colonies had serious implications for WNLA's South African competitors, especially the mines and farms of the northern Transvaal. Many of the clandestine immigrants, although bound for the gold mines, ended up working for farmers when they crossed the Limpopo. Either they never got to the gold mines at all or they did so only after an interval of low-wage employment on some border farm or mine. During the 1930s, the South African government had established depots and police patrols to catch these laborers and force them either to accept local employment in the border area or to return home. Although ineffective in stopping the inward flow, these measures forced many immigrants to seek shelter in uncongenial, low-wage employment on local farms or mines.[27] Private recruiters prowled in these regions touting for labor in the service of individual estates and various farming collectives. Clandestine migrants now had no prospect of employment in gold mines by the terms of Gemmill's 1939 deal with the supplying governments. To get to the mines, they had to use the WNLA system. They could no longer count on mining employment even if they successfully evaded the cordon thrown up by predatory farmers and labor touts in the border areas. WNLA had managed to divert at the source part of the migration which formerly had provided northern Transvaal and Zululand farmers with much of their labor.

Although the pay-off in additional labor was slow to appear, WNLA had committed itself by the mid-1930s to an expensive extension of its recruiting network into the north as reflected in the increase of tropical labor (Figure 2.2).[28] The emergence of this system brought major social and economic changes and had a decisive impact on the economic future of the whole subcontinent. Equally with railway development, WNLA's commanding presence throughout the region bound the periphery to the mining heartland. Labor flows to the higher wages and opportunities of the South African economy predated the mining industry's tropical recruiting policy. However, that system ensured that the resulting regional subordination would endure. Yet there were limits to South African hegemony, despite the economic weakness of its neighbors. The experience of the supplying colonies, led by Southern Rhodesia, showed that they were no happier with their dependence on South Africa than were the successor governments, organized in the Southern African Development Co-ordination Conference (SADCC). It also shows how political arrangements could at least partially offset economic weakness.

Rhodesia's Huggins did not prevent WNLA's expansion into the north, but he did influence its shape and timing and successfully restricted its scope for many years. The target British territories to the north were uneasy allies with sharply different economic interests and objectives. Yet they did share an interest in controlling, restricting, and profiting from the penetration of the South Africans. As a result, Huggins's efforts to unite them against their domineering southern neighbor met with some success. Gemmill and his colleagues in the Chamber of Mines had to conciliate, not merely confront, the Rhodesians.

WNLA in the Northern Territories

Competition for labor in the northern tier of the subcontinent intensified rapidly in the 1940s. In March 1940, the Inter-territorial Council, representing the three British Central African governments, renewed its approaches to Pretoria with a request for a meeting on joint control of migration. Although supporting the principle, the Smuts government had its hands full in 1940, and the proposed conference never took place. Furthermore, mounting labor shortages on farms probably restrained South African action on the clandestine immigration problem during the war.

Farmers' complaints had been growing since the mid-1930s. They reached flood proportions in 1942–1944. Individual farmers and their associations wanted more control of their workers. They also demanded effective action against squatters, which farmers had been calling for for over fifty years, access for their recruiters to the tropical areas, more protection from the mine recruiters, the right to employ child labor without the permission of the parents, and other measures. Official replies were often unsympathetic and stressed that labor shortages on farms were related to conditions on farms and that the black worker had the right to sell his labor in the best market.[29] To act against the illegal immigrants who were flooding in would have led to even harsher complaints. It was prudent, especially on the eve of the 1943 election, given the resurgence of D. F. Malan's National party, to put off the northern governments. After the war, in 1947, the three northern territories again took the initiative with a new request to the South Africans for joint action on clandestine migration. Mounting labor shortage in the supplying areas was the main concern, but the territorial governments also worried about the criminal activity associated with the migration. Brigands and labor touts in the pay mainly of South African farm employers continued to exploit the southward-moving traffic, as they had done for three-quarters of a century. During 1947, South Africa came reluctantly to the bargaining table but two conferences produced no agreement. Meanwhile, in April 1948, the three Central African territories developed a new agreement to regulate the flow of labor among themselves. The lead came, as always, from Southern Rhodesia which wanted to enhance its control of the flow of labor south. Like earlier control schemes, the new plan failed completely. The South African high commissioner suggested that because of the transportation provided under the scheme to the southern parts of Southern Rhodesia, the flow to South Africa may have increased.[30]

Toward the end of 1948, the Southern Rhodesian authorities approached the new rulers in Pretoria to discuss labor control. The Malan government declined, stating that it was in the midst of negotiations on the distribution of the labor resources of the country.[31] Ideological preoccupations and political interest both suggested that the Malan cabinet would be unsympathetic to the concerns of the northern neighbors. The National party wanted above all to reverse permanent black urbanization. Foreign workers were almost all prohibited immigrants and unable to qualify even for limited urban rights under the Section 10 of the 1945 Native Laws Amendment Act. Even more docile and rightless than South Africa's own black workers, the immigrants posed no threat to the government's restrictive policies. Second, the farmers wanted much more of this labor not less, and they had been crucial to the National party's 1948 victory.

In October 1950, the South African delegation traveled to Salisbury for the talks.[32] The South African high commissioner, T. H. Eustace, led the delegation. It included the director of Native Labour, the under-secretary of Native Affairs, F. Rodseth, the commissioner of Immigration, and various subordinates. Because of his knowledge of the issues involved, Rodseth became the effective spokesman and chief negotiator for the South Africans. The Chamber of Mines and the South African Agricultural Union sent observers. The union officials agreed to consider steps to identify and trace workers but not to impede the inflow.[33] This labor remained too important to northern Transvaal mines and farms to contemplate restricting it.

Given the hostility of South African mine owners and farmers, there was little chance of South Africa accepting the 1948 agreement on migration that the Central African colonies had already signed. The supplying states had practically nothing to offer their southern neighbor. The labor was going south anyway; at a conservative estimate some 200,000 northern workers were continuously in South Africa. Nyasaland and Northern Rhodesia governments could do little to stop it, and anyway needed the flow of repatriated earnings. As the Union's main competitor, Southern Rhodesia was in an even weaker position; its farms, mines, and industries paid less and offered inferior conditions of service. South Africa's capacity to dictate the terms to its British neighbors emerged in a 1951 exchange of correspondence between the secretary of External Affairs and the South African high commissioner in Salisbury. The secretary pointed out that the Union would prefer to see larger recruiting quotas from the northern territories but recognized that the governments would not agree. Nyasaland and Northern Rhodesia should not expect South Africa to turn back needed workers who had walked hundreds of miles to get there. He instructed High Commissioner Eustace to ask the Rhodesians to set up depots where Union employers could receive voluntary workers who wanted to work in South Africa. Since workers from Nyasaland and Northern Rhodesia viewed Southern Rhodesia as a corridor to the higher Union wages, the negative reaction of Southern Rhodesia was predictable. In any case, the Malan government demanded that Salisbury undertake not to discourage such workers. In other words, the Malan government agreed to turn illegal into legal immigrants but only on the condition that Rhodesia not impede the flow.[34]

Northern Hegemony

While rival recruiters slugged it out on the ground, Gemmill carried the propaganda battle for the mines into the diplomatic arena, including the ILO in Geneva. He continued to battle with the Southern Rhodesian rivals who represented employers as hungry for labor as his principals.

He also had to worry about the northern supplying governments in Nyasaland and Northern Rhodesia, which had a growing concern with the disruptive social effects of large-scale absences of most of the young males. Local employers there also used these arguments against WNLA, disingenuously, to serve their own interest in maintaining the size of the captive local labor pool. In the struggle to control the regional flow of labor, both the South Africans and their northern neighbors appealed beyond the region for support, and both grounded their arguments on high principle. Nyasaland and Northern Rhodesia had argued since the 1930s for emigration restriction because of the disruption of family life that followed from the absence of so many males. Southern Rhodesia claimed that its workers were unrecruited, voluntary laborers who were free to come and go, whereas the WNLA indentured its workers and bound them to contracts enforceable with criminal penalties.

Stung by these criticisms, WNLA began to produce propaganda of its own. Gemmill and others asserted that WNLA labor was not recruited labor either. The association merely provided facilities for voluntary workers who were determined to get to the higher wages of the Rand. WNLA presented itself as the champion of free labor in southern Africa (for WNLA, worker freedom stopped at the South African border). It attacked neighboring governments for the restrictions that compelled the would-be miner to work at very low rates of pay in his own country when much more favorable employment was open to him elsewhere "under International Labour Organization conditions."[35] Gemmill failed to note that the Union was not a signatory to the ILO convention on migrant labor and did not adhere to its terms. He also used the spurious advocacy of a free labor market effectively with the Dominions Office against the northern governments' efforts to get British approval for their restrictive emigration measures.

A WNLA statement to the ILO, following the failed negotiations with the northern governments in 1950, put the case succinctly for the mining industry.[36] Although the association was itself an employers' cartel designed to restrain wages and strengthen labor controls, it employed the language of labor rights. Second, the memorandum distinguished between its own organized, humanely conducted migration in which deferred pay and the eventual return of the workers were assured and the hardships imposed by the much larger, uncontrolled migration. Few of the second group ever returned, but WNLA's workers almost always did. South African law and WNLA's agreements with the northern governments required repatriation. The uncontrolled migration disrupted the social life of the supplying states, while WNLA's operations helped to sustain it. The recruited workers came back in better health than when they left, bringing with them substantial sums in deferred pay and cash to support their extended families. Although a few never returned, death rates were low—five per 1,000 per annum from disease and two from accidents.[37]

The association contrasted its own benevolence with the restrictive practices of the northern governments. WNLA found itself routinely harassed in these regions, prevented from establishing its depots and transport systems, and restricted to limited quotas. The governments of the supplying territories policed their borders to keep would be migrants at home and coerced the chiefs and local elites for the same purpose. Though ineffective, these measures did drive the workers into clandestine channels and increased the hardship involved in the migration. WNLA argued that such measures contravened the Declaration on Human Rights, which the United Nations had recently adopted, particularly Article 13, affirming the right to leave one's country, and Article 23, concerning the entitlement to choose one's employment. The document concluded with a stirring peroration: "The Witwatersrand Native Labour Association submits that the African is entitled and should be permitted freely and openly to sell his labor in the best market available to him, even if it is outside his own country, provided the conditions of engagement and employment are satisfactory."[38] In this way, WNLA posed as the champion of freedom in colonial southern Africa.

These exaggerated claims had the ring of Gemmill about them, and he presented much the same case at an ILO conference in June 1951.[39] Apart from overstating the benefits that derived from migrancy to the gold mines, the statement obscured the real purpose of the mine labor system. It was organized specifically to constrain labor freedom, to prevent competition between the mining groups themselves to the disadvantage of workers, and to keep wages down. In discussing the target areas, Gemmill, of course, emphasized free labor markets. WNLA paid more than its local rivals in these regions and so in the absence of government restrictions could corner as much of the supply as it wanted. At home, however, it ensured that quite a different set of rules applied. The Articles of Association of WNLA, which defined its methods of operation, were written to rule out wages as a mechanism for allocating available labor. Moreover, the association had always been at the forefront of a wide range of other restrictive practices, including support of criminal penalties for the enforcement of labor contracts and the refusal to recognize African trade unions. The gold mines had long been one of South Africa's least progressive industrial employers. To accept Gemmill's arguments, and he was accorded a sympathetic hearing at the ILO, required a breathtaking suspension of critical faculties.

However, compared with most southern African employers, the gold mines, after much prodding by the South African government, had taken important steps to secure workers' welfare. They did look after workers' health better than other employers, creating a uniquely elaborate medical system that far exceeded what any other major employer, including the government itself, provided for its workers. In the 1930s, after several disastrous decades of carnage through the rampant incidence of preventable disease and accidents, the mine medical services began to benefit from a shift in emphasis to sanitation, nutrition, and disease prevention, as opposed to cure, that had begun twenty years earlier; some of the earliest research on diseases afflicting the black community was funded by the industry through the South African Institute of Medical Research. The gold industry paid more than its northern competitors and provided, despite the sterile, artificial, and restrictive life of the "bachelor" compounds, vastly superior basic living conditions. By the 1940s, most workers were returning from the mines in much better physical condition than when they left their homes. Since WNLA required the repatriation of its workers and provided for deferred pay, some benefit from the migration did result to the home districts, and there was less disruption of family life than with the clandestine migration. Nevertheless, the WNLA presentation before the ILO gave only one side of the story.

The generation of self-serving propaganda at the ILO was not the only weapon available to the association. Through the Union minister of Finance, N. C. Havenga, the Chamber of Mines badgered the United Kingdom to support its northern recruiting effort. In the early 1950s, Chamber president, S. R. Fleischer, whose son Tony would later become Chamber general manager at another pivotal time for the industry, explained to the secretary of external affairs that the industry currently employed 287,000 black miners who produced 11.5 million ounces of gold. He estimated the current shortage at 78,000 workers. If they could be found, it would mean another one million ounces per year. With the opening of the Free State and West Wits mines, the total requirement would grow to 414,000 black workers by 1956. Writing in 1952 to R. A. Butler, then Churchill's chancellor of the exchequer, Havenga used Fleischer's brief. The most effective action his government had available to help with the sterling crisis was to increase the gold supply. The industry's efforts had suffered from persistent labor shortage, resulting, he complained, from the restrictive practices of the Central African governments. He asked Butler to use his influence, particularly with Nyasaland. The chancellor in reply was sympathetic but noncommittal and merely urged the continuation of direct talks. Butler's diffidence with the South Africans was feigned. Immediately, he asked officials at the Central African Council to take "as sympathetic an attitude as possible" to the Union's labor needs. Within two months, Gemmill reported an improvement. To intensify the pressure, the high commissioner in London called at the Colonial

Office to reiterate the objections to Nyasaland restrictions on WNLA recruiting there.[40]

WNLA had objected to Nyasaland policies for some time. The association resented the favored treatment given to the Southern Rhodesians at its expense. In 1952, the competition became more serious when a labor-starved Southern Rhodesia threatened restrictions on coal exports to its northern neighbors unless they agreed to increase the emigration of labor.[41] Interventions by Butler and Colonial Office officials headed that off. In addition, WNLA objected to its exclusion from the southern districts of Nyasaland and to other restrictive measures. It feared, above all, efforts to divert the growing flow of workers from northern Mozambique and Tanganyika, an increasingly important element in the labor supply (Appendix, Tables A.3 and A.4). Finally, WNLA opposed the reduction in its quota from a high of 12,500 workers in 1947–1948 (up from 8,000) down to only 7,000 in 1952.[42]

By 1953, Gemmill had concluded that his campaign was having significant effects. In an interview with the Union high commissioner, he noted that relations with the Nyasaland governor, Sir Geoffrey Colby, were now much improved. Havenga's intervention with Butler had helped, and Gemmill believed that Colby would ease the restrictive 7,000-worker quota. Nevertheless, as the high commissioner warned in his report on the meeting with Gemmill, problems remained.[43] When the Central African Federation came into being, he suggested, the northern governments would lay stronger claims to their own labor. High Commissioner Eustace would have known that concern about growing South African influence across the Limpopo, particularly the inflow of Afrikaner settlers, had been a major consideration in London's decision to back closer union in Central Africa. The Southern Rhodesians had been pushing this argument to build support for federation in the United Kingdom.

Officials in Salisbury probably worried much more about Union economic power, the pull of its labor markets, and the inflow of Rand capital to the Copperbelt than they did about Afrikaner settlers. Perceiving this, Eustace was giving notice that restrictive economic and labor policies could follow the establishment of the federation. On the labor front, however, events did not bear out Eustace's prediction. Recruiting figures for the tropical areas continued to increase steadily through the 1950s and early 1960s, despite the loss of access to Tanzanian and Zambian labor at independence in 1961 and 1964.

3

South African Recruiting:
Crisis and Recovery, 1946–1965

The appointment in 1940 of William Gemmill as labor czar in the north with headquarters in Salisbury underlined the importance attached to tropical labor by the mining industry. Yet progress in the development of these new sources was slow and did not really take off until the mid-1950s. The serious problem in the 1940s and early 1950s had to do with the South African part of the supply. During World War II, South African workers began to leave the mines in large numbers and the trend accelerated after the 1946 strike (Figure 3.1). Because the tropical numbers remained small, a policy of substitution of foreign tropical labor for local South African labor was not workable. The industry was forced to address its domestic recruiting apparatus.

The Chamber of Mines commissioned an overhaul of the Native Recruiting Corporation and began to reconsider its relationship with the hundreds of trader-recruiters in the countryside whom it had neglected for a generation. More important, the Chamber began to examine the structure of the rural social order which underpinned the flow of migrants to the mines. Industry testimony to the Fagan and Tomlinson commissions in the late 1940s and early 1950s provided a revealing glimpse of how alarmed its analysts had become about agricultural decline and proliferating rural deprivation in the black peasant communities which had always supplied much of the mine labor. Whereas an earlier generation of mine controllers had wanted the state to use its taxes and other devices to undermine rural self-sufficiency, create rural poverty, and force peasants into the labor market, the Chamber had by the 1950s concluded that without large-scale government investment, the black rural economies would collapse, putting the mines' labor system further at risk. This evidence, which has been in the public record since these commissions reported, challenges the so-called "labor-reserve" theory that has dominated thinking on this issue since the early 1970s.[1]

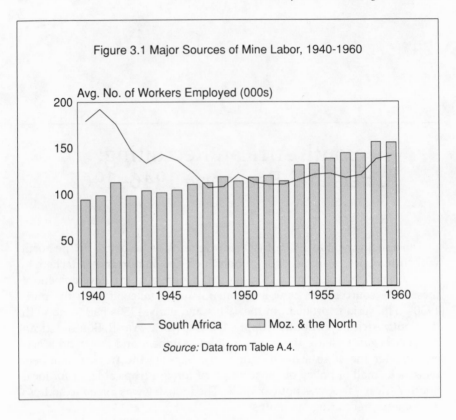

Figure 3.1 Major Sources of Mine Labor, 1940-1960

The 1946 Strike and
the Tropical Labor Strategy

Coming at the beginning of one of the industry's most profitable periods after 1932, the emerging tropical labor strategy did much to determine the mines' general labor policies for the next thirty years. Despite the disappointing numbers initially, the heavy investment that tropical recruiting required discouraged serious consideration of alternative ways of organizing the labor force. With vistas of inexpensive, docile tropical labor opening before it, the Chamber of Mines could afford a tough line on the black wage issues, which became acute during the war. Static wages and high inflation combined with deteriorating conditions in the countryside to promote discontent in the mines, which became chronic in the last years of the war.

Yet the intransigent position on wage increases and other concessions that the industry took during the war was a significant gamble. No one could be sure that enough labor from the northern territories would be available to replace dissatisfied South African miners, who were increasingly seeking other employment. Wages in manufacturing industries rapidly outstripped those in mining after the war. As a result, the leakage of labor from the mines steadily worsened.[2] Because the tropical recruits were unavailable in sufficient numbers at first, the mines had no choice but to improve their competitive position within the South African recruiting zones. Yet they were slow to see the need for improvement.

The Chamber opposed major concessions, especially wage adjustments, to black workers at the time of the Lansdown Commission in 1943. The industry was vulnerable to the rising cost of supplies. Because the stable gold price meant that the mines had to absorb their cost increases, a profitability crisis followed. It threatened returns on investment and jeopardized their ability to raise the capital required for expansion on the Far West Rand and in the Orange Free State. As in the past, the Chamber of Mines arranged that the burden of adverse economic circumstance would fall on the poorest, most vulnerable component of the labor force. Holding the line on blacks' wages was the most important strategy to achieve this goal. It went with a variety of coercive measures inflicted on black miners designed to enhance labor productivity.[3]

The Lansdown Commission looked carefully at wage levels in relation to cost of living increases and the deterioration of agriculture in the main recruitment centers. It endorsed the conclusions of many knowledgeable observers that the living standards and health of Africans had declined disastrously throughout the countryside. Although a small wage increase finally went ahead following publication of the Lansdown Report, the state paid most of the cost through an adjustment in tax rates. The increase fell well short even of the Commission's modest proposals, which included also a cost of living allowance and a contribution toward the cost of boots (which workers had to buy themselves). The governments of the High Commission Territories, Nyasaland, and Northern Rhodesia submitted briefs to the commission, calling for a better deal for their workers in the mines. The mining companies rejected these submissions and remained unresponsive in dealing both with workers and with neighboring governments.

The hard line of the Chamber determined its response to the new African Mine Workers' Union (AMWU), set up in 1941. Wartime conditions, including inflation and low wages in most industries, had produced a rapid expansion of the black trade union movement, which was growing significantly before the war.[4] Emergency regulations were enacted in 1941 and 1942 to prevent work stoppages from disrupting production, but these measures could not easily be justified after the war. The draconian War Measure 145 (1942) banned strikes. It mandated stiff penalties for violators, including imprisonment for up to three years and heavy fines.

It provided for compulsory arbitration using a single arbitrator chosen from among officials in the Department of Labour.

Even before hostilities ended, some members of the Department of Labour had recommended legislation to give limited recognition to approved black unions. The minister, Walter Madeley, said as early as 1942 that he was considering such a step. Officials proposed to exchange black union recognition for control. They wanted to bring the black unions separately under a special version of the industrial conciliation laws. Another objective was to insulate black workers from the influence of radical whites, including Communist party members. The party had been influential in the growth of nonwhite unions from the late 1930s. Accordingly, the draft bill in 1946–1947 restricted membership in "native unions" to black workers and exworkers. The intention of the draft legislation was to co-opt and control the union movement and to move it into nonradical channels. While administrators in the labor department considered legislation, other elements in the government turned increasingly to repression. In this, the Chamber of Mines abetted them.

Throughout the discussions over the black union issue, the Chamber remained fiercely opposed to any form of recognition. The African Mine Workers' Union, skillfully led, had grown rapidly during the war, although it was in decline by the time of the 1946 strike. Under the terms of Proclamation 1425, police began to break up union meetings from 1944. The employers rejected any form of negotiation with the union before the strike.[5] Beginning in 1944, they prosecuted union organizers found on mine property for trespass. Nevertheless, the union continued to organize mineworkers and operated clandestinely in the compounds. Membership grew even as repression intensified. Dissatisfaction with low wages fed discontent, as did a cut in food rations in 1945, following a South Africa–wide drought and crop failure. Many of the protests before and during the strike on the East Rand involved conservative, nonunion members. They rebelled at the erosion of their wages through wartime inflation, just when the onset of crippling drought caused much hardship to their families. Elsewhere, the union played an important part in organizing and focusing worker militancy.[6]

During the year before the strike, the government responded to sporadic demonstrations with even harsher measures, including a ban on gatherings on mine property. When many workers finally left their jobs on a dozen mines, beginning 12 August 1946, the owners called in the police, who used force against them.[7] Perhaps 70,000 black miners came out altogether, of whom the police arrested about 1,000. There were over 1,200 injuries and nine deaths. Without the official repression in the prestrike period, which undoubtedly crippled the AMWU, the strike would have been a much more serious challenge to the industry. Nevertheless, the strike revealed a resurgence of worker militancy not seen since the 1920 strike.

Was the strike responsible for the sharp reduction thereafter in the number of South African workers accepting employment in gold mines?[8] It has recently been argued that "at a deep structural level . . . the 1946 Strike may be seen as a final spasmodic effort by 'militant' South African labor to force the Chamber to raise wages. The failure of the strike simply hastened their exodus from the industry."[9] The author also noted that the departure of South Africans from mining began years before. This was the result of the wartime growth of secondary industries with better wages, working conditions, and greater opportunities for advancement. Dissatisfied mineworkers now had a much wider range of employment choices.

An examination of the recruiting data seems at one level to support the conclusion that the strike was a factor in the sharp fall in the number of South African miners accepting contracts. Recruiting from South African sources did drop substantially after the strike. The reduction included a fall off in the number of "voluntary" (or nonrecruited) workers. As the most experienced miners, the voluntary workers could be expected to respond to adverse political circumstances such as the strike by refusing employment. However, the fall off in numbers in the voluntary category was within the normal year-to-year variation experienced since 1940 (Figure 3.2). Employment levels among this group were volatile and fluctuated wildly both before and after the strike. One reason the nonrecruited workers made their own way to the Rand was the prospect of securing nonmining employment. They chose the mines as a last resort. In the final stages of the war and after it, fewer of them were driven to this. Moreover, the fall off in the number of arrivals to the mines in 1946 represented a decline from the unusually high intake the year before, when serious drought racked the countryside. Mine employment levels always surged in these circumstances; so it was in 1945. From this standpoint, the reduced number of voluntary workers arriving in 1946 simply represented a return to the levels of 1943 and 1944. Unfortunately, the employment data themselves do not permit a firm judgment on the role of the strike in the later fall-off in the number of voluntary workers arriving in the mines.

The more significant figures are of the reduced number of recruits accepting contracts in the period 1947–1949. The recruits were represented disproportionately by workers on their first contracts (novices). They were among the least politicized members of the mine labor force. However, a significant number of them participated in the strike. This segment of the mine labor force was responding to the hardship produced by a combination of severe drought in the countryside and the erosion of real wages

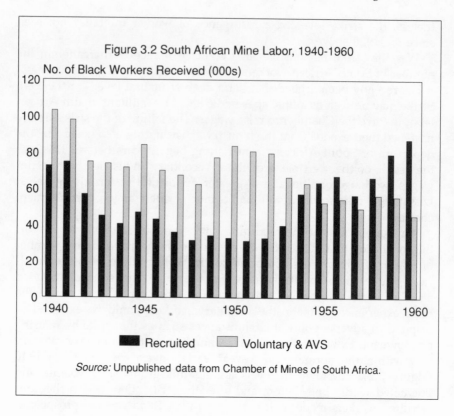

Figure 3.2 South African Mine Labor, 1940-1960

No. of Black Workers Received (000s)

■ Recruited   ▢ Voluntary & AVS

Source: Unpublished data from Chamber of Mines of South Africa.

through inflation. Although the resulting poverty was well known from the report of the Lansdown Commission and other sources, the Chamber of Mines took a hard line against higher wages. Support for the strike on the East Rand, where the African Mine Workers' Union had least success, has been attributed to "a deep sense of moral outrage on the part of workers about . . . the loss of buying power of their wages and drought in the countryside."[10] In its intransigence, the mining industry had broken its unwritten bargain with the workers. It had disrupted the "moral economy" and aroused the anger and hostility of large numbers of the least proletarianized miners.

Yet moral outrage eventually yielded to economic realities. South African workers' rejection of the mines in the 1940s was temporary. Less than a decade later, numbers were up again to the point at which the industry resorted to quotas to control the flow from within the country (Figure 3.2).[11] This fact suggests that a complete explanation of the workers' behavior needs to go beyond the impact of the strike. Industry neglect of the recruiting system, which became more pronounced during the war, was an important element in the erosion of the South African labor supply. When the NRC successfully argued for higher wages, shorter contracts, and improvements in the fees paid to recruiters, labor statistics responded immediately. By the mid-1950s, South African workers were returning to the mines again in something like the numbers experienced in the early years of the war.

The leaders of the Chamber of Mines might have reacted differently to the strike if had they not been confident of the eventual success of tropical labor. This confidence also made them less concerned about the competition for labor from other industries. Finally, it meant that the mines could continue to tolerate the rigid mine Color Bar despite the expense and inefficiency that it increasingly involved. By 1951, Gemmill envisaged 150,000 workers as a kind of minimum target for the tropical areas.[12] The industry might have moderated its intransigence concerning the demands of the South African workers but for the prospect that tropical recruiting would rescue the system.

The Postwar Domestic Labor Crisis

None of the industry's hopes for recruiting tropical labor meant, however, that the recruiters would abandon their South African sources of supply. Beginning in 1947, the industry undertook a detailed examination of the causes of the reduction and possible remedies. Two important meetings of NRC district superintendents in 1947 and 1949 focused mainly on internal difficulties affecting the recruiting system itself. By the early 1950s, however, senior mining executives were again calling on government to rescue them from their labor difficulties. Concern about the labor supply continued intermittently for roughly a decade until the Chamber's recruiters temporarily restored "labor surplus" by 1959. Even then the proportion of its total labor supply that the mines drew from South African territory remained far below prewar levels.

Despite the expected continued expansion in the supply of tropical labor, the mines could not ignore the decline of local sources because their labor requirements were growing so rapidly. As a result, analysts identified several problems, some internal to the mining industry and its recruiting strategies and some related to external economic circumstances. Significantly, however, the entire discussion over the period took place within the assumptions that underpinned the migrant labor system. The mine labor organizations never seriously considered adopting the alternative strategy of partial labor stabilization that Ernest Oppenheimer proposed for the Free State mines in the early 1950s. Instead they worked to "improve" the system that they had laboriously developed and defended over the previous fifty years.

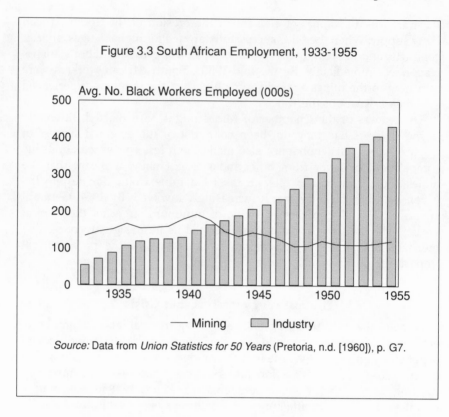

Figure 3.3 South African Employment, 1933-1955

Avg. No. Black Workers Employed (000s)

— Mining   ▨ Industry

Source: Data from *Union Statistics for 50 Years* (Pretoria, n.d. [1960]), p. G7.

This move was predictable. Those involved in the discussions had grown up with the recruiting system. They owed their livelihoods to it, and most of them knew nothing else. Moreover, they were in close touch with officials in the Native Affairs Department and the Native Labour Bureau and were well aware of the determination of the National party government after 1948 to entrench the migrant system. H. F. Verwoerd, while minister of Native Affairs, and W. M. Eiselen, the influential secretary of the department, developed harsher measures to arrest the influx of blacks into the cities as permanent residents and to make the black reserves the repository of the resulting "surplus labor." This worked to entrench the mines' long-established methods of mobilizing and using their black labor.

Concerning the causes of the reduction in the number of South African mine recruits in the late 1940s, the experts cited various reasons. Competition for labor had intensified dramatically with the expansion of secondary industries during the war. The industrial labor force grew from 55,638 in 1933 to 433,056 in 1955 (Figure 3.3).[13] Because these employers paid "extravagant wages," the mines' standard rates for underground work were no longer adequate. Manufacturing wages did increase sharply after the war and moved from rough parity to double average mine wages by 1951.

Belatedly in 1949, the Native Recruiting Corporation recommended the implementation of the increase advocated by the 1943 Lansdown Commission, which the industry had earlier successfully resisted. In 1943, the proposed increase had been modest enough; by 1949 continued inflation had substantially eroded its value. Citing increased competition, the chairman of the NRC justified his conversion to wage increases by referring to the increase in the gold price. The increased price meant that several marginal mines would continue production and further expand labor requirements. He now regarded raising wages as essential.[14] As in the past, adherence to the "target-worker" justification for holding the line on wages was speedily discarded whenever supply problems loomed. Equally, the chronic "crisis" of the low-grade producers could be forgotten as readily as, in different circumstances, it was invoked.[15]

The second major problem concerned recruiting operations themselves. The mine labor organizations had become bureaucratic and complacent. This problem was the burden of the self-criticism at the conference of district superintendents of the NRC in 1947.[16] The chairman, G. O. Lovett, stressed the importance of the superintendents keeping in touch with "recruits, headmen, chiefs and native women folk." This should be their main function, he emphasized, and "routine" office work should not take precedence. The personal touch had been the secret of the recruiting successes of the legendary H. M. Taberer, general superintendent of the corporation from 1912 to 1929 and the principal architect of the labor system, and of his successor, H. C. Wellbeloved.

The NRC had lost sight of this function since the retirements of Taberer and Wellbeloved. Lovett urged senior head office staff to resume the regular tours and meetings with "natives" on which Taberer had always insisted. The NRC had to defend its policies in open debate at these meetings. Discussion at the conference showed that much skeptical resistance to industry propaganda was present in the target population. When hecklers intervened, their criticisms should be addressed directly; it was a mistake to try to ignore hecklers, Lovett and others insisted. To counter such hostility, the recruiters dusted off a device widely used in the competitive era forty years earlier, namely, the employment of "native propagandists," mostly retired mineworkers, to tour the principal target areas. The 1949 conference noted that these agents were often not well informed of the latest developments and should come to Johannesburg for briefing tours around the newest mines before returning to the countryside. The managers decided to recruit more of these propagandists from the corporation's senior clerical staff.[17]

Of course, recruiting staff did not content themselves with defensive measures to answer their critics. Another idea they proposed was to launch a vigorous campaign of propaganda and advertising. More posters on bus routes would help, as would the distribution of sweets, tobacco, and other small gifts to potential recruits and their families, especially the women. Wrapping paper emblazoned with the NRC logo could be distributed to the trader-recruiters and this would keep the organization's name before the country population.

In some Bechuanaland districts, NRC agents had distributed carrier bags with the logo and name of the local office to black women. If anything the conference paid more attention to persuading native women than the recruits themselves. This strategy underlined the fact that the decision to accept mine employment continued to be, as from the beginning, a household decision taken for the young worker by his elders and by the experienced miner in consultation with his wife.

Touring film shows had been an important recruiting device since the 1920s. Several superintendents favored expanding this activity. The corporation had switched to the use of 16-mm film because the equipment was easier to use and could be set up and run by amateurs. They agreed to establish eight new film units for use throughout South Africa, Basutoland, Bechuanaland, and Swaziland. American cowboy films such as those regularly screened in the compounds would not be suitable for recruiting, the superintendents concluded. Instead, they recommended more use of cartoons. In addition, the corporation had commissioned a new film, *From Kraal to Reef*, portraying the life of the mineworker in idyllic terms that went "on the circuit." Also in the area of entertainment, one superintendent suggested that radios be set up in the district offices. Bored recruits waiting there could listen to the "Bantu programs" of the South African Broadcasting Corporation and the musical programs of the other services.[18]

Two years later at the 1949 conference, the superintendents still stressed the propaganda campaign. They now wanted to concentrate on school children. There were 260,000 black children in the Cape schools alone. Previously, the publications *Life in the Mine Compound* and *Mining Survey* had gone out to the schools. Superintendents considered but then rejected the use of more direct methods of recruiting in the schools. They feared that this might upset the school authorities. Worse, it might lead to requests for financial aid "unconnected with the mining industry." Recruiting school dropouts was one thing; but helping them to get an education risked funding their preparation for other, more desirable jobs.[19] Thus the superintendents agreed to continue with the indirect approach to the schools.

Both conferences addressed the important issue of the minimum contract period. In 1923–1924, the mines had lengthened the contract for recruits from the South African and High Commission Territories by a half to nine months. They knew that a nine-month minimum contract (actually 270 shifts, requiring substantially longer than nine calendar months to complete) for recruits would regularize the labor force and make it more efficient. Although still firmly committed to the longer contract, the superintendents reviewed the case for a six-month minimum. While both conferences rejected the shorter contract, the discussion did reveal the seriousness with which senior staff viewed the fall-off in recruiting levels. What told in the end was the recognition that lengthening the contract from six to nine months had enlarged the average size of the labor force even though initially the number of recruits had fallen off. By 1953, however, continuing disappointment in the numbers of South Africans recruited led to a decision to offer the six-month contract to recruits once again.[20]

The most important theme in this decade of anxious reappraisal concerned the corporation's relations with the trader-recruiters. Worry about the questionable loyalty of the country recruiters to the NRC had been growing for some time. Since the early years of the century, their importance had declined dramatically. Critical to the expansion of the labor pool in the decade after 1902, they became a liability as the Chamber of Mines imposed centralized recruiting after 1912. The state, too, wanted to reduce the number of trader-recruiters since competition among them had caused fraud, deception, and other abuses. With nonrecruited labor a central element of the supply by the second decade of the century, senior recruiting staff viewed the trader-recruiters as an expensive and unnecessary burden. Their numbers fell sharply.

New circumstances in the 1930s also undermined the position of the labor agents. With the spread of the depression in other sectors of the economy and the rapid expansion of the mining industry, which set in after devaluation in 1932, recruiting levels in the mines soared. This expansion enabled the NRC to impose quotas on its remaining agents, a step that curtailed their incomes and aggravated their disaffection. Increased medical rejection rates also cost the recruiters capitation fees. As a direct consequence of these measures, the agents switched to other employers in the farming and industrial sectors.[21] Large-scale farming, in particular, turned increasingly to organized recruiting. During World War II, the mines reduced their labor complements (to release whites for the army), and an additional contraction in the number of mine recruiters took place.

While labor flows remained adequate, the mining industry could afford to ignore the hostility of its former allies, the trader-recruiters. By the late 1940s, however, as recruiting levels plummeted, the NRC began a fundamental reappraisal of its policies toward them. In 1948, for the first time since 1925, the proportion of recruited South African labor (i.e., compared with voluntary labor and those hired locally) fell below 30 percent. Both the 1947 and the 1949 district superintendents' conferences had stressed the importance of the trader-recruiters and called for measures to win back their loyalty. The mines began to pay a small fee for each Assisted Voluntary Scheme worker sent forward by a recruiter and later raised the recruiting fees for each contracted worker. In the early 1950s, the NRC appointed a senior official, G. O. Lovett, to be its liaison officer with the trader-recruiters.

Reviewing the recruiting operation in 1953, Lovett rediscovered an old truth about the recruiting business: "The fact should never be ignored that traders exert a powerful influence on the Natives in their own districts, particularly when they reach the stage of wanting to seek work, and they should always be recognized as a necessary and integral part of the industry's recruiting machinery. Any act or policy likely to endanger relations with them should be avoided."[22] He stressed that earlier policies had caused the industry to lose the loyalty of the recruiters, who had begun to recruit in competition with the NRC for Cape farmers and other industries. His job and that of the district superintendents was to win back their support.

To achieve this objective, NRC executives began to spend large sums of money. The figures of recruited labor show that the renewed support of the recruiters began to pay off almost immediately. South African sources now provided more labor, and recruited workers constituted a much higher proportion of the total than in the late 1940s. The number of AVS workers continued to fall, maintaining the pattern of the 1940s, but the trend for recruited workers was completely reversed. Owing to expansion elsewhere in the system, the proportion of the total coming from the South African territories did not return to wartime levels. However, the South African recruiters did manage to increase the South African supply at a rate that kept pace with the growth elsewhere (Figure 3.2).

In the 1940s and 1950s, therefore, circumstances combined briefly to put the trader-recruiters back in control to an extent not seen in the industry since before 1914. Conditions of labor shortage always threw power and resources toward the labor supply districts on the periphery of the subcontinental mining economy. As a result, enhanced benefits and profits now began to flow to the private trader-recruiters operating under contract to the mines. By 1949, the corporation agreed to pay some of them a bonus for every AVS worker they sent forward. When the NRC reintroduced the six-month (180 shift) contract in 1953, it also raised its fees for recruiters. The forty-shilling fee formerly applied to the 270-shift contract became payable for the new six-month contract. For a nine-month contract, the fee became sixty shillings. Also, the new fee for AVS workers became available to all NRC recruiters and the amount doubled.[23]

Renewed emphasis on the importance of the trader-recruiters coincided with special efforts to win the loyalty of chiefs and local notables. In Swaziland, the NRC superintendent successfully organized a series of meetings during 1948, two of which King Sobhuza II himself attended. The Swazi royal family had been early converts to the cause. Now Sobhuza agreed to support the NRC against mounting local competition for labor. In return, he extracted the important concession, which he had long sought, of posting a representative at the NRC headquarters in Johannesburg. This gave the king much better access to and control over the young Swazi workers and meant better tax revenues for the Swazi Crown and the means to ensure the workers' return at the end of the contract period. Formerly, Sobhuza had posted his representatives at the individual East Rand mines where the Swazi congregated or in the township of Sophiatown. The backing of the NRC made the work of the new representatives more effective.[24]

The failure of these changes and adjustments in operating procedures to provide sufficient South African workers, when total needs were expanding rapidly as new mines came into production, led the Chamber of Mines to look for causes and remedies outside the recruiting system itself. A memorandum to government complained that the mines could never afford to compete with the "extravagant wages" paid by secondary industry.[25] Average wages for blacks in manufacturing had more than doubled between 1937 and 1950, while mine wages had hardly increased at all. Cash wages on the mines for positions requiring a degree of skill were much lower than for comparable jobs in manufacturing. As a result, the industry had been unable to hold its labor force. Most mineworkers who formerly returned seven or eight times to the mines now served far fewer contracts before moving to higher paid jobs in manufacturing.

The memorandum explained that the state's Color Bar and influx-control policies removed any possibility of labor stabilization and the higher wages that a better-trained, more-permanent labor force would permit. It suggested that the longer contract was one of the few means available to improve efficiency. It pointed to the recent modest increase in the minimum underground rate and the new service increment bonuses. Unfortunately, the effect of both of these measures had been more than offset by the higher wages in manufacturing. Longer contracts availed little when the average worker returned many fewer times.

In brief, the Chamber also called for government-mandated controls on the use of labor in manufacturing. The mines wanted labor allocation based on importance to the national economy, a criterion that they had always used against all other employers. With these curbs in place, more labor would go to the mining industry, "a vital national resource." Wage levels in the mining industry would then be set "not by reasons forced on it by necessity for competing for Native labour, but by the natural laws flowing from greater productivity per native worker."[26] The thinking of Chamber officials easily encompassed the idea of "natural laws" in the area of worker productivity. Yet, in their minds, notions of natural law had no role in the supply and demand for labor where the laws of the state, not those of the market, were taken to be fundamental. Whereas Gemmill had argued before the ILO that the mines provided additional job opportunities to Africans throughout the subcontinent, his colleagues saw nothing contradictory in asking the South African government to restrict the local labor market (and therefore job opportunities for Africans) in their interest.

A measure of the seriousness with which the mining companies viewed the situation was that their examination of the reasons for the fall-off in South African recruiting levels extended to the social order which sustained recruiting in the countryside. In evidence to the Tomlinson Commission on "The Socio-Economic Development of the Bantu Areas," the Gold Producers' Committee of the Chamber of Mines expressed concern at the deterioration of the reserve economies and tied it to the decline in its labor supply.[27] Tomlinson had been appointed to make recommendations on the implementation of the government's plans for social engineering in the so-called reserves in order to entrench further the migrant labor system, to intensify influx-control barriers to permanent black urbanization, and to resettle as many Africans as possible from the so-called white to the black areas. It was the most important government commission of the era, at least in the eyes of the authorities. Thus the mining industry's evidence before it constituted a major political statement.

It has been suggested that after World War II the mines welcomed the sharp fall of rural subsistence and intensified poverty in the reserves and may actually have been responsible for them.[28] According to this analysis, the mines needed the black rural areas sufficiently impoverished to force the adult males into the work force on a regular basis, yet still capable of providing a partial income and offsetting the low mine wage. Accordingly, the sharp fall in recruiting levels in the late 1940s should have prompted the mining industry, if it was behaving according to this theory, to call for more government-imposed deprivation in the countryside. The reality, in terms of what was actually happening in the countryside and in terms of policy, was very different.

By the 1940s, reserve agriculture was in terminal collapse. The mining industry's recruiters knew this, and their reports had begun to influence thinking in the Chamber of Mines. The evidence for this is in the important testimony to the Tomlinson Commission. The conclusion that the industry drew on the relationship between rural poverty and falling recruiting levels was the reverse of what later scholars have argued its interests required. Mining employment appealed only to the "tribalized native," the Chamber noted. For this class of worker, the mine wage had been an adequate supplement to reserve earnings. When the subsistence economy failed, as was then the case, the workers turned to other more remunerative employment. The Chamber representatives had by the early 1950s also developed quite a different analysis of what they wanted from government on this issue. While mining spokesmen had earlier been strong advocates of land alienation, higher taxes, and other measures to force peasants into their labor system, by the 1950s they rejected the notion that rural poverty served their interests. It was agricultural prosperity through government investment in the black rural areas that they advocated, seeing this, paradoxically, as a means of promoting mine labor supplies.

James Gemmill, who had earlier succeeded his father as senior Chamber advisor on labor matters, and several colleagues spent a morning with the Tomlinson Commission toward the end of May 1952.[29] They urged the development of settled peasant communities and villages with a high degree of self-sufficiency and called for the expansion of the existing "betterment areas," advocating large-scale government investment in the reserve economies. They argued that this policy would not lead to a diminution of the labor supply. It was the young, unmarried black worker who came to the mines and the number of tours rarely exceeded ten (their own figures showed to the contrary that nearly half of the miners were married men). Rural workers would continue to come, the Chamber believed, even if government capital investment successfully restored peasant agriculture in the reserves. There was no particular political need for Chamber representatives to take this line. Yet they returned to it several times in their evidence, calling for what a commissioner, summarizing their testimony, described as "[the development] of the native reserves to their fullest agricultural potential."[30]

Behind this suggestion lay, first, an awareness that if the reserves continued to decline, forcing more and more Africans into the white areas, the industry would lose its labor permanently. Once settled in the cities, African men came to the mines only when totally bereft of alternatives. Even the mine controllers knew this. Chamber spokesmen also apparently believed, second, that there would be a structural labor surplus in these restored peasant communities. They thought that heads of families would see the advantage of increasing farm income by sending younger sons to the mines during the slack times in the agricultural cycle. Just such a division of family labor had been common earlier in the century, when supplementary income from mining had helped to offset the decline of income from the land. At that stage, mining employment was often a way of preserving the economy of the rural household, not, as some historians have argued since, the primary means of its destruction.

In this testimony, the Chamber's representatives suggested that the complementarity of a conservative and stable peasantry and high rates of mine recruiting could be reestablished. Recruiting analysts also recognized that a restored peasant agriculture would tend to keep heads of families out of the migrant system but believed that the mines would continue to attract the younger workers from conservative households. Despite the success of tropical recruiting, James Gemmill stressed the importance of restoring the number of South African workers to prewar levels, which would require an additional 100,000 miners over the 1952 figure of about 160,000. A reconstituted peasant economy would have required, however, much state aid to rehabilitate the impoverished reserves.

Once the commission had completed its work, the National party soon revealed that it had no intention of funding even the inadequate but still expensive program of reserve development eventually proposed by Tomlinson. Few in the mining industry could have imagined how far the government through its minister of Native Affairs and later prime minister, H. F. Verwoerd, was prepared to go to enforce the influx-control laws. This fact coupled with population increase and further agricultural deterioration in the bantustans maintained, even enlarged, rural labor supplies. Later in the 1960s and 1970s, massive clearances of surplus black labor from white farms added hundreds of thousands of new families to the pool of labor available in the bantustans and the rural slums on their margins (see Chapter 5). These measures, not the rural-development program cogently advocated by mining representatives before Tomlinson, were what delivered the labor and helped to restore industry recruiting levels to something like expected levels.

In 1956, James Gemmill reviewed the measures that the industry had taken since 1947 to offset the decline in the number of South African recruits (see Figure 3.2). It was an optimistic report. South African recruiting had finally begun to respond to the changes introduced over the previous decade. The trend in South Africa itself had been consistently up since 1953.[31] Gemmill thought this trend would continue. He expected recruiting levels in Basutoland to increase, based on rates of natural population growth. Also, the policy of the National party to restrict the flow of Sotho workers into the urban areas left many of them with no option but mine work. Concerning Mozambique, he noted that the Convention limited the mines to an average of 100,000 workers. The Portuguese had recently agreed, however, that Portuguese East African blacks resident in South Africa could be contracted, and this source was slowly increasing. He reported that there were currently 5,000 of these workers in the Free State mines. Additional recruits from Mozambique would only become available if there was a substantial fall in world farm prices. This situation would throw the Mozambique estate producers into crisis and release more labor for the mines.

The trend in the tropical areas was also up encouragingly. Gemmill expected to achieve the Nyasaland target of 14,000 in 1956 and said the industry could plan to have it increased. He was hopeful also about Tanganyika, an especially valuable source, since the workers served 469-shift contracts. In both territories, however, the industry was vulnerable to political interference. He had heard that the Tanganyikan authorities were considering steps to reduce the flow of labor in the future (at independence in 1961, the Nyerere government ended recruitment for the mines). The average number employed should, he explained, reach 350,000 by 1958 and 355,000 by 1960. In the event, Gemmill greatly underestimated the improvement in the supply. The total strength reached nearly 400,000 by April 1961, giving the mines 106 percent of their underground complements. By this point, the proportion of South African recruits (though not the absolute numbers) had fallen dramatically. The buoyant figures had enabled the NRC to cancel the six-month contract for recruited workers. Longer minimum contracts were also under consideration for AVS workers and locals.

After outlining the efforts to make mine work more attractive to South African blacks, Gemmill noted that the industry still required additional numbers from South Africa and the High Commission Territories. This was despite the increase in the numbers of tropical miners. Although the tropical areas with their high rates of population increase and undeveloped economies offered the "best long-term prospect" for improving the labor supply, he worried about the recruiters' vulnerability to unpredictable political factors there. In any case, the increase obtained from the north could only be gradual. Thus, he stressed that the mine-labor organizations must continue to work on their South African sources. In this connection, he believed that the government's rigorous enforcement of influx control would make more "reserve natives" available for the mines.

However, the new labor bureaus, which the National party regime introduced in 1952, had emerged as competitors for labor in the black rural areas.[32] Gemmill warned that the bureaus would have the full backing of the Native Affairs Department (Bantu Administration) and that the bureaus would be able to use the chiefs and headmen, who were government functionaries, for propaganda purposes in a way not available to the private recruiters. Gemmill believed that the mining companies' labor supply problems were not the result of defects in the recruiting system itself. There had been administrative difficulties within the mine-labor organizations, but these were solvable.

In any case, the key to long-term stability of the supply was to get more of the workers to accept the longer contract. The 180-shift contract had been important in reviving the interest of the trader-recruiters in the mining industry (presumably because it was easier to recruit on short contract and the higher turnover meant more recruiting fees) but, he suggested, the increased turnover complicated management of the labor supply and impeded efficiency. Also, the competitors were continuing to bid aggressively for labor. The Natal sugar estates had recently increased its recruiting fee from forty to sixty shillings for the 180-shift contract. If the NRC matched this, it would cost the corporation 45,000 South African pounds (£) per year. He stressed that it was "vital" that the NRC have the resources to deal competitively with the recruiters. Finally, Gemmill noted that the mine-labor organizations were having trouble recruiting and holding new senior staff. Formerly, they had been able to recruit the sons of missionaries and country traders, people with a "profound sympathy" for the "natives." Increasingly, these employees were lured away by rival recruiting companies. He recommended an upward revision in the salaries of the senior officers.

By the mid-1950s, the extraordinary rate of labor inflow enabled the NRC to reduce the quotas of workers from the South African areas by 20 percent across the board. Despite the emphasis earlier given to the South African sources of supply, when conditions of labor surplus reemerged, the industry adopted policies favoring labor from Mozambique and the northern territories (Appendix, Table A.2). These workers served longer contracts and meant a more stable and efficient work force. When challenged by the government, however, the industry, worried about rising unemployment levels in the black rural areas, denied that it had changed its policies. Senior Chamber executives meeting with the minister of Finance, Dr. Nicolaas Diederichs, assured the minister that the mines remained committed to their South African workers. There were limits, however. If the mines had to pay competitive wages with manufacturing, many of the marginal producers would close. Responding to the minister's concern about the estimated one million "foreign natives" in the country (most of them not, of course, in mining employment), the Chamber's men stressed that they had to have a "large supply" of extra-South African workers. The long service contracts of the tropical miners made them especially valuable, and the Mozambique miners were the most cost-effective of the industry's workers.[33]

Government concern remained, however, and led to the appointment of the interdepartmental Froneman Committee on foreign labor in the early 1960s. Its recommendations came out firmly against the continued use of northern labor in South Africa and argued for a strict timetable to replace foreign labor within five years. This suggestion went too far for the Verwoerd government, which did not publish the report officially. Its recommendations struck not only at the mines but also heavily at agriculture, especially the border farmers who relied on low-wage foreign migrants. Furthermore, any cutoff in the flow of foreign workers would have led to a bitter battle between mines and farms. The mines would immediately have demanded removal of the restrictions on recruiting in the country's white farming areas which had been in place since 1911. Later, the authorities had to make this concession when, after 1974, the mining industry temporarily lost much of its foreign labor. Preferring to skirt around such potentially explosive issues, the authorities quietly shelved Froneman's recommendations.[34]

With the threat of government action against the mines reduced, foreign labor continued to grow as a proportion of the total through the 1960s and early 1970s (see Figure 5.1). In 1960, South African recruits still constituted 41 percent of the total received that year. A decade later, the proportion had fallen to 28 percent. However, the average contract period of these workers had increased significantly. In 1960, the mines had to hire 174,287 South African workers to maintain an average of 141,806 in the mines. By 1970, workers received from South African sources had fallen to 98,917. Because the average number employed from these sources was 105,169, the typical contract period now exceeded one year. A major increase, the longer average contract length undoubtedly reflected the further deterioration of economic conditions in the bantustans. During this period, the proportion of northern workers on the mines increased from 38 to 45 percent. Because these workers served much longer contracts than the South African or High Commission Territories miners, the mines needed fewer of them to maintain their labor complements.[35] Thus, although the geographical composition of the labor force was changing dramatically in the 1960s, when foreign sourcing emerged as the central element in the supply, the work force was becoming more stable, as average contract periods increased.

With stability came greater productivity and efficiency. In 1960 with an average black work force of 375,614, the industry processed 66,988,000 tons of ore, about 178 tons per black miner. A decade later, the total tonnage of ore treated had increased to 79,965,000, while the average number of black miners employed had remained stable at 370,312.[36] By

1970, therefore, the industry was processing 216 tons of ore per worker annually, an improvement of slightly over 23 percent. Working profits had increased from slightly above 3 rands (R) per metric ton of ore treated in 1960 to R4.5 in 1966, an advance of 49 percent. Because the gold price remained stable in this period, until the introduction of the two-tier pricing system in March 1968 (which had little effect on profits initially), the increased working profits can be attributed partly to containment of costs and to the enhanced productivity realized from technological changes and efficiency gains from the more stable black labor force. The productivity gains achieved in this decade were the most marked since the 1930s when mechanical scrapers replaced much of the lashing (shoveling) formerly required to clear the stopes (mine working faces).

Worker efficiency also benefited from technological innovation and from changes in the work process and the racial division of labor. The introduction of a new blasting technique called sequential firing (to focus the effect of the explosives and to raise the tonnage of ore extracted per blast) made possible concentrated stoping.[37] This improvement was largely responsible for the productivity gains. By 1970, the labor force could be maintained with 25 percent fewer recruits annually, owing to the longer average stay in the mines, which meant that significant savings in recruitment and training costs also emerged during the decade. Finally, the successful negotiation of some modest productivity concessions from white workers permitted more efficient use of the black labor force (see Chapter 4). Thus important improvements in productivity accompanied the shift toward greater reliance on external sources of labor (see Table 3.1).

Only the upheavals following the Portuguese withdrawal from Mozambique and Angola in 1974–1975 and the withdrawal of Malawian labor at the same time forced the mine labor organizations to rediscover the centrality of their internal labor supply (see Chapter 5). In 1976, for the first time since 1942, South African sources provided over half of the industry's migrant labor. Between 1942 and 1975, the local supply rarely exceeded 42 percent of the total and often less, as low as 27 percent in the early 1970s.

The supply crisis that overtook South African recruiting in the late 1940s, before large-scale tropical labor supplies had become available, briefly produced benefits for both the workers and the recruiters. It also forced the industry to look critically at the social and economic structures that underpinned its recruiting system in the rural areas. That little in the form of permanent benefits for the countryside resulted from this was due partly to the surge in the tropical labor supply in the late 1950s and 1960s, which made reliance on South African sources less necessary, and partly to the refusal of the government to implement the recommendations of its own Tomlinson Commission concerning agricultural rehabilitation

Table 3.1 Employment, Production, and Working Profits,
South African Gold Mines, 1960-1970

	Workers Received			Average No. Employed		Tons Treated (000s)	Working Profits (Rands/ m.ton)
	S. Africa	%	All Areas	S. Africa	All Areas		
1960	174,287	41	426,133	141,806	375,614	66,988	3.03
1961	170,151	40	426,951	146,605	388,345	68,547	3.48
1962	162,721	42	390,617	150,804	383,494	71,995	3.82
1963	149,446	42	353,764	150,049	373,958	74,087	4.04
1964	132,050	39	342,248	144,684	374,455	75,351	4.34
1965	128,311	37	350,382	136,551	369,161	75,396	4.47
1966	126,221	37	339,837	128,810	363,232	74,964	4.51
1967	124,062	38	325,467	126,862	353,198	74,038	4.24
1968	130,029	38	341,365	129,122	361,632	73,751	4.16
1969	116,373	36	321,176	122,319	354,814	76,280	4.29
1970	98,917	28	357,972	105,169	370,312	79,965	3.90

Source: Adapted from Chamber of Mines of South Africa, *Statistical Tables, 1980* (Johannesburg, 1980); Chamber of Mines of South Africa, *Annual Reports* (Johannesburg, 1960-1970).

in the reserves. Toward the end of the war, falling South African and High Commission Territories' recruiting levels had reproduced some of the recruiting conditions that had prevailed in the early years of the century. Once again the rising demand for labor moved the power equation away from the mining center toward the supply periphery. As a result, both the black miners and the recruiters secured benefits that they otherwise could not have expected. Blacks' wages, though still poor, increased measurably, and the recruiters secured much higher fees and other concessions. Shorter contracts, which South African recruits had always favored, became available (although only briefly) for the first time since the early 1920s. Another indicator of the change in the balance between center and periphery was the Chamber's call in its evidence to the Tomlinson Commission for government investment in the black rural areas.

The industry's recruiters expected that because of the nature of household production in the reserves, the industry would benefit from the establishment of reasonably prosperous, settled peasant communities. Impoverished rural areas fed one-way migration to the towns; such workers did not choose the mines. The mining industry wanted to see social and economic conditions developed that would sustain the conservative, rural communities that had always supplied most of its South

African labor. It believed that its interests would be served, not undermined, by rural prosperity. However, the black rural areas were set in a pattern of irreversible decline, which the state's increasingly callous relocation policies did much to intensify. When Pretoria rejected its proposals for agricultural development, the industry discovered that its tropical labor policies combined with the state's harsh enforcement of influx control at home would maintain the supply of workers without the requirement of any significant change in the system.

The Opening of the OFS Mines
and the Stabilization Experiment

The response to persistent black labor shortages in the decade after 1945 underlined the gold industry's commitment to the migrant labor system. The essential conservatism of the Chamber of Mines was intensified by the nature of its leadership in these years. The older mining houses whose properties were in the mainly declining fields of the Central Rand continued to be influential in the Chamber as they had since the 1890s. This was particularly the case of the long-dominant producer, Rand Mines Limited, and its London parent, the Central Mining and Investment Corporation.[38] Individual companies belonging to this group, particularly Crown Mines and the East Rand Proprietary Mines (ERPM), both mining vast reserves of low-grade ore and very sensitive to cost increases, had experienced recurrent problems of profitability. Like many companies, both had invested heavily in the migrant system by building giant compounds. For these mines and others like them, replacing the compounds with family housing units in large new residential townships made no economic sense.[39] Even had they been able to find the money, both of these centrally located mines lacked the space necessary to house their workers' families. Equally, mechanization to reduce the need for unskilled black labor was not an option for most of these properties. The older, still dominant mining houses were, therefore, those least likely to contemplate radical alternatives to migrancy when supply problems loomed.

It was no accident, then, that it was a newer firm, Anglo American, when it assumed a dominant position in the industry with the opening of the Free State gold fields at the end of the 1940s, that proposed a potentially important change of system for the new mines. Ernest Oppenheimer suggested that at least a small part of the regular black work force on the Free State mines could become permanent.[40] His better-equipped and lower-cost mines could face a departure from established policies with much less financial risk than the older companies. Furthermore, the new mines would build this family housing from the start. By contrast, the older mines could make the change only by first meeting the expense of scrapping their compounds just at the time when the mines were ending their productive lives. Like the older groups that now found their leadership superseded, Anglo American had declining Central Rand mines, which could not have afforded such a costly shift in labor strategy. However, the older holdings contributed less to Anglo American's profits than those of the long-established mines that dominated the holdings of declining groups, such as Central Mining or Johannesburg Consolidated Investment.

In the testimony to the Tomlinson Commission during 1952, James Gemmill and his colleagues gave a detailed assessment of the prospects for stabilized labor on the Free State mines. They started with an explanation of the effect of the Color Bar: "But given the existence of the legislative color bar on the gold mines, it means that to have labour permanently employed, instead of it coming for periods as they do [now], there is not the advantage of employing them [permanently] after they have acquired skill." As a result the industry could not contemplate stabilization of the unskilled pick and shovel men (the so-called "lashing boys"). Even within the constraints imposed by government and the white unions, the mines could do more to establish a settled labor force. According to James Gemmill, the industry thought that eventually as many as about 12 percent of the black work force could be stabilized. The continued commitment to migrancy was apparent in his thinking, however, and he referred to this percentage as "an extreme target figure."[41] In addition to the expense of the Color Bar, he stressed the prohibitive costs involved in building family housing for the whole work force. Running costs would also be much higher than for the compounds.

A study prepared by the Chamber for Tomlinson put the cost of a single family unit at £803 compared with the capital cost of £192 to house a single "bachelor" migrant in a compound. The estimate for the family dwelling came from the cost of a standard township, three-room house, but (unlike most township houses) equipped with running water, water-born sewage system, and electricity. For a new mine with a complement of 6,000 workers, providing family housing for the whole labor force would add £5.4 million to the development costs compared with only £1.2 million capital cost of compound accommodation. Thus stabilizing the entire work force would add about 36 percent to the capital cost of developing a new gold mine.[42] Despite these daunting figures, the mines showed greater interest in stabilization than ever before. This interest was the result of the dramatic fall-off in the supply of South African migrants. The simultaneous development of a whole new mining area on an unprecedented scale in the Free State provided the opportunity.

The practical results of Oppenheimer's proposal and the Chamber of Mines studies turned out to be small. On six of the new Free State mines,

Anglo American launched modest experiments, involving the construction of small villages of 150 houses adjacent to each compound. The company intended to investigate the prospects of larger-scale stabilization by offering permanent family accommodation to some semiskilled black workers, who were previously ineligible.[43] If the changing economics of gold mining, and the prospect of further domestic labor shortages, explains this sudden interest in stabilized labor, the new flexibility was soon overtaken by the determination of the National party government. Its leading ideologues, W. M. Eiselen and H. F. Verwoerd, had pledged to restrict the growth of urban black populations and to maintain the mine Color Bar.[44] Even so, over the next thirty years none of the mining companies even approached the 3 percent in family housing that the Verwoerd policy permitted. Flush with new supplies of long-serving migrant labor from outside the country, the mining companies lived comfortably within Verwoerd's policy.

Ten years earlier, if the mining industry had requested it, the authorities might have accepted limited stabilization of mine labor. During the war, the Smuts government showed some recognition of the inevitability of black urbanization. It had begun to relax the Color Bar and increase opportunities for black workers to obtain job skills. Smuts campaigned on the recommendations of the Commission on Native Laws, the Fagan Report (1948), which had called for recognition of blacks in the cities as a permanent feature of South African life.[45] With the Malan victory in 1948 and the subsequent formalization of the apartheid system, however, the halting, tentative pragmatism of the earlier period ended summarily. It ruled out any proposals to move away from migrancy, however modest. In responding to the mining industry, the government was never totally inflexible, particularly where its ideological imperatives imposed heavy costs. It demonstrated this on the issue of restricting the inflow of foreign workers. However, given that decreasing the permanent presence of black families in the white areas was a top priority for the party and that the mining industry was itself divided on the issue of stabilization (the costs and benefits remained murky and uncertain), Oppenheimer's proposal never took root. Only the more severe pressures of the 1970s, operating simultaneously on the industry and the government, combined to produce the first signs of the transformation of a system that had endured, little changed, since the 1920s.

4

White Labor and
the Color Bar, 1945–1987

In August 1987, the South African Parliament finally approved legislation abolishing the Mines and Works Amendment Act of 1926. Although not in force for another year, the new law did signal the end, after nearly a century, of the statutory requirement confining a wide range of skilled and semiskilled mining jobs to whites. This chapter examines the origins and development of the Color Bar in mining. It analyses the reasons for its persistence there long after the formal legislative and administrative protection of whites had ended in secondary industries.

A basic issue in the racial division of labor in the gold mines concerns the relation of the Color Bar, which protected white access to the best mine jobs, to the expansion and entrenchment of the migrant labor system. Most writers have seen the issue as a relationship of cause and effect. If the Color Bar came logically first, then labor migrancy was a consequence, forced on the industry as an offset to the higher labor costs imposed by the Color Bar. This argument meant that the origins of the system could logically be traced to racism among white workers and in the wider political arena. Conversely, if the real key to this peculiar labor system was low-wage black labor, then the Color Bar was the consequence, a defensive reaction by white workers who could not compete against low-wage blacks. This idea led to the conclusion that capitalist profit rather than white worker racism was the main determinant of the labor system.[1]

The connection between white and black labor policy in the mines had become an important political question even before the Anglo-Boer War. During the whole period up to 1924, the issue was at the center of an intense political debate on the future of white South Africa. There was an essential continuity between the political and trade union struggles in the early industrial period and the battles of the 1960s and 1970s over the future direction of labor policy on the gold mines. Management worried mainly about long-term profitability and maximizing the profits

79

from the industry. For the white labor leaders, job protection against the threat of low-wage black labor emerged as the major concern. Some of them argued more broadly to develop the idea that the Color Bar was essential to the maintenance of "white civilization" itself.

In the ranks of the industry, some mine controllers, as products of their society, sympathized with this idea. They agreed in effect to subsidize expensive white labor, fearing the social and political costs of not doing so. Experience showed that a full-scale assault on white workers' privileges could be dangerous politically. White workers, unlike blacks, were voters. However, when costs rose to threaten profits, even the more politically attuned owners usually quickly concluded that the industry needed much less white labor.[2] Primordial race prejudice affected the standpoint of white worker and capitalist alike. Nevertheless, motivations on both sides stemmed more from perceived economic interest than from traditional race prejudice or the more systematic, contemporary ideological racism.

The Mines and the Color Bar, 1902–1939

Recent radical scholarship has entrenched the view that the mine managers themselves supported the Color Bar. These writers acknowledged that, on occasion, the mines have attempted to shift the line in the direction of moving blacks into some of the more skilled jobs. Despite this, their argument went, the mines favored the Color Bar because it divided white from black labor. It inhibited the emergence of common purpose and helped to preserve the economies of the migrant labor system.[3] Furthermore, it served mining interests because it justified the pass laws and other controls on blacks. White racialism provided a convenient rationale for the regimentation of the black work force. The racial despotism that the Color Bar entrenched suited the owners, according to these writers, as a control device. As a group, the white miners were often lazy, violent, and unpredictable. In the front line of mine supervision, however, they drove the black miners relentlessly in pursuit of the productivity demands of the owners. Since the real savings came from low-wage, unskilled "native" labor, the Color Bar was anyway a small price for management to pay for the system.

Much evidence reveals that the mining companies have learned to live with the Color Bar and to off-load most of its costs onto their black workers. Yet their efforts to modify its application were important. As early as 1906–1907, the legislative and customary protection of white jobs on the mines came under scrutiny by the Chamber of Mines. One reason for this was a severe profitability crisis following the Anglo-Boer War. White labor was expensive, and the mines could have realized significant savings by shifting the bar decisively and opening the semiskilled jobs to blacks. Another event turning the companies against their white workers was the strike of 1907, which underlined the increasing radicalism and volatility of the white miners. The owners broke the strike and production hardly declined. They did this by replacing the strikers with out-of-work Afrikaners whom they recruited as supervisors at low wages. Recent refugees from the impoverished countryside, most of these white recruits had no mining experience at all. Underground operations could not have continued as they did during the strike without the skill of large numbers of black workers. Working under the supervision of mine officials, they now began to do many of the tasks formerly undertaken by the immigrant white miners.

It was this strike that brought to the attention of management the growing capacity of the black workers. This realization led to the first major debate in the Chamber on the possible reduction in the number of white miners.[4] Had the owners proceeded to reduce the number of white miners, the act would have had long-term implications for the migrant labor system. Large numbers of semiskilled black workers would have meant much greater wage differentials within the black work force than had existed up to that point. To make the most efficient use of the upper strata of black labor, the mining companies would have needed to stabilize it, which would have required permanent family housing for growing numbers of black miners. Because the state had yet to introduce influx-control restrictions on black urbanization, the whole pattern of urbanization on the Rand would have assumed a different course. In these years, the owners had several times considered labor stabilization and a few mine managers had introduced it.[5] Even partial moves in this direction, if introduced more widely in 1907, would have meant a different historical development of the labor system.

The Chamber of Mines did not expect labor peace, but it needed the assurance of state support, which it had by 1908. The struggle with white labor continued much more intensively in the decade after 1913. Once again declining profitability led to a concerted Chamber of Mines attack on the Color Bar in the area of semiskilled work. Once again the miners' union responded with radical industrial action, leading to the warfare of the 1922 strike. Once again the state, both under Jan Smuts from 1922–1924 and under J.B.M. Hertzog after that, intervened to impose a settlement. The government-mandated solution recognized the economic realities, as the industry defined them. It permitted the mining companies to make major productivity gains at the expense of the white miners.

However, the state and the industry decided that a legal Color Bar would remain to limit severely the access of blacks to the higher job categories. Even under the Pact government, however, white labor received a sharp lesson on the limits of its power. In the aftermath of the 1922 strike, over 2,000 white jobs were retrenched and the crucial ratio of white to black in the mines shifted decisively toward the latter. The pre-1922 ratio appeared again only in the late 1930s. By this time increases in the gold price had brought renewed prosperity to the industry and lessened pressure to retrench more whites.[6] Whites' wages also fell dramatically, nearly 20 percent in real terms, as a direct result of the crushing of the Rand Revolt.[7]

Despite these setbacks for whites, the objective was to co-opt rather than to destroy the white miners. In 1926, with the Mines and Works Amendment Act, the Color Bar had been firmly redrawn in the industry. The act probably still protected more white jobs than the industry wanted. However, the owners quickly learned to live with it. They had made major savings in the cost of white labor; the new industrial conciliation legislation gave them the assurance of labor peace; the role of the Color Bar in sustaining an authoritarian system of control had not been weakened. Although sometimes divided, the state, the mines, and the white workers could readily agree that the blacks would pay for the Color Bar in forgone wages and lost opportunities.[8]

The Mine Workers' Union and
the Defense of White Privilege, 1945–1987

After the Second World War, conditions affecting labor in the mines began to put more pressure on the Color Bar than had been the case since the struggles of the early 1920s. Increasing demand for skilled labor in other economic sectors produced a growing shortage of white labor, while the expansion of the gold industry put heavier demands on the recruiting system to continue to enlarge the black labor supply and maintain costs at the same low level. The rapid growth of secondary industry during the war opened thousands of better-paid, more-congenial jobs. Because the gold mines were always an employer of last resort, their ability to recruit South African black labor declined drastically. Intensified competition came also from farmers and other low-wage employers who were beginning to recruit more aggressively, which threatened to bid up the black miners' wage bill. Steady postwar inflation made the Color Bar more of a problem for the managers because it prevented needed economies in the use of labor. Over time, more of the gold-bearing ore fell outside the pay limit and was unprofitable without an increase in the price of gold or decreased costs. Ernest Oppenheimer's proposal in the early 1950s to operate the new Free State gold fields with a higher proportion of stabilized black labor reflected this situation. To work, Oppenheimer's proposal required an important erosion of the Color Bar

Table 4.1 White and Black Mine Labor, 1940-1953

| | Average Employed | | | | |
| | White | | Black | | Ratio |
	No.	%	No.	%	Black:White
1940	42,852	11.0	347,766	89.0	8.11
1941	41,424	10.2[a]	363,908	90.8	8.78
1942	40,555	10.2[a]	355,086	90.8	8.76
1943	38,508	11.3	301,869	88.7	7.83
1944	37,166	11.3	292,993	88.7	7.88
1945	36,328	10.7[a]	302,337	90.3	8.32
1946	39,642	11.7	298,891	88.3	7.54
1947	38,829	11.8	288,957	88.2	7.44
1948	39,019	12.6	271,399	87.4	6.96
1949	39,527	12.1	286,076	87.9	7.24
1950	43,109	12.5	294,425	87.5	6.83
1951	44,291	13.4	286,688	86.6	6.47
1952	45,105	13.6	286,329	86.4	6.35
1953	46,355	14.3	278,327	85.7	6.00

[a]Percentages do not add up to 100 because of rounding errors.
Source: Adapted from Chamber of Mines of South Africa, *Annual Reports* (Johannesburg, 1940-1954).

and a corresponding shift in the ratio of black to white labor at those mines.[9]

In the 1950s successive National party governments under Malan, Strijdom, and Verwoerd extended the mining Color Bar and entrenched it in the 1956 revision of the Mines and Works Amendment Act. As the politicians protected more white mine jobs, the ratio of black to white labor narrowed (Table 4.1). The white wage bill grew at a much faster pace than the black, widening the already yawning wage gap between the races (Figure 4.1). To some extent, the mining companies could offset this gap with the higher profits of the richer Free State mines. They also made significant extra returns on the sale of uranium as a by-product of gold mining.[10] But stability in the gold price and declining gold yields in the older mines meant that the industry was bound to address its labor costs. In this connection, the Color Bar offered a most tempting target.

Ten years after Ernest Oppenheimer developed his modest stabilization proposals, the mining industry began to press for changes in the pattern of work to improve productivity and make better use of black labor. The 1960s were a strained decade for the industry when costs pressed heavily

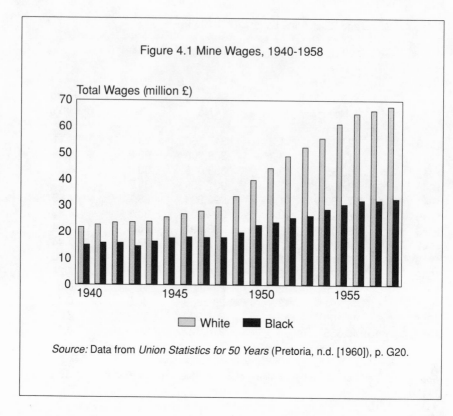

Figure 4.1 Mine Wages, 1940-1958

Total Wages (million £)

☐ White   ■ Black

Source: Data from Union Statistics for 50 Years (Pretoria, n.d. [1960]), p. G20.

on profits, and the mining companies had to economize wherever they could. From early on, the Chamber always argued that the white workers' interests would be best served by labor policies permitting maximum expansion and lowest costs. Some white jobs would disappear. This decline would be more than offset by the new posts which would go to whites as the industry developed and by jobs created elsewhere in the economy through gold-induced expansion. Remembering the jobs (and lives) lost in the battles of the 1910s and 1920s, the Mine Workers' Union (MWU) and its allies in the Council of Mining Unions always rejected these arguments. They jealously resisted efforts to erode their legislatively entrenched racial privileges. Since the mid-1960s, MWU leaders have tried to minimize the concessions extracted from them in productivity bargaining. Nevertheless, over the course of twenty years of tortured negotiations, the companies did extract productivity concessions in return for improvements in wages and working conditions for the white miners.

At first, the MWU was briefly more cooperative, but the membership quickly rejected this strategy, which led to the emergence of a new hard-

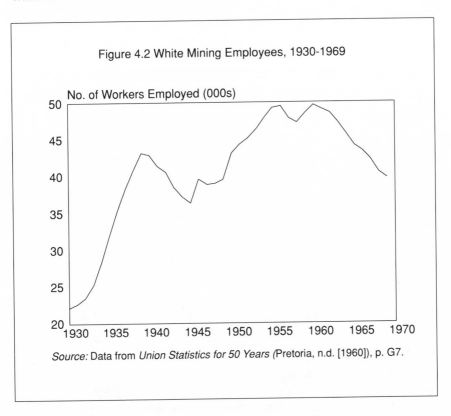

Figure 4.2 White Mining Employees, 1930-1969

No. of Workers Employed (000s)

Source: Data from *Union Statistics for 50 Years* (Pretoria, n.d. [1960]), p. G7.

line executive in 1966–1967. The union then embarked on a determined defense of its position which continued into the 1980s. By the early 1980s, this industry remained as the one industrial sector where whites continued to enjoy formal, legislative protection of their most vulnerable jobs. It may be true that the recent history of organized labor in the mines reveals its "relative impotence"[11] but in defending the Color Bar, the white miners fought a skillful rear-guard action. The owners made important productivity gains in this period, but they paid for these. The improvements that they did achieve fell short of their minimum agenda.

As always on this sensitive issue, the smallest effort to make more productive use of low-wage black labor could produce a sharp reaction. By the 1960s, costs and mounting shortages of white labor were once more pressing heavily on some of the marginal mines (Figure 4.2 and Table 4.2). In 1964–1965, the Chamber of Mines embarked on an experiment in twelve mines to make better use of selected black "boss boys" by giving them additional responsibility in return for slightly more money. This act may have been merely the first step in a planned thoroughgoing

Table 4.2 White and Black Mineworkers' Wages, 1945-1960

	Average Wages for Whites Per Capita (S.A.£)	Average Wages for Blacks Per Capita (S.A.£)	Ratio of Wages White:Black
1945	646	47	13.7
1946	657	45	14.6
1947	675	45	15.0
1948	621	46	13.5
1949	763	49	15.6
1950	846	53	16.0
1951	919	56	16.4
1952	1,003	58	17.3
1953	1,044	61	17.1
1954	925	63	14.7
1955	971	66	14.7
1956	1,023	66	15.5
1957	1,057	67	15.8
1958	1,106	69	16.0
1959	1,151	69	16.7
1960	1,136	70	16.3

Source: Data from Union Statistics for Fifty Years (Pretoria, n.d [1960]), p. G20.

restructuring of the Color Bar. However, the immediate proposal affected it only marginally. The "boss boys" would do a small amount of "scheduled work," work formally reserved for the white miners under the schedules of the Mines and Works Amendment Act.

Practice in the industry had been moving in this direction for some time. Since the early years of the century, many experienced black miners had the ability to undertake much of the work reserved in law and custom to the white miner. Often, because of skill shortages and productivity demands, white miners required blacks to do part of their work for them. The African worker received neither pay nor recognition for this, and the white ganger (or supervisor) risked prosecution. The experiment negotiated between the Chamber and the MWU tried to formalize and extend what had been going on clandestinely. The "boss boys" would get pay increases of about £6 per month. Some MWU members would also receive larger pay increases and improved pension and leave arrangements. Numbers of them became salaried staff paid monthly. Monthly pay had been for some time a major goal of the union.[12] The experiment resulted from the cooperation of the MWU executive which had made the arrangement as part of a package of concessions on both sides. The union began discussion of monthly pay in 1963, which gave the companies the opening to demand productivity concessions in return. The Chamber accepted an MWU demand to protect the jobs of all existing whites. The government mining engineer initially agreed to grant the necessary exemptions.

Initially, the position of the MWU executive and its general secretary, Eddie Grundlingh, seemed unassailable, but was actually weak. By the 1960s, the union leadership had grown bureaucratic and complacent. Claiming to be well connected politically, the executive enjoyed a cozy relationship also with the Gold Producers' Committee of the Chamber of Mines. Dissatisfaction among the rank and file had been growing for some time. Unconvinced that miners' interests were secure in the proposed "experiment," a rebel "action group" denounced the agreement and began to campaign against it. By early 1965, violence and wildcat strikes erupted, as the opponents of the experiment intensified their opposition. Grundlingh defiantly defended the deal that his executive had made and stated that he would extend it to include the colliers (coal miners). The action group responded with more strikes, and the MWU executive called out the colliery workers to show their support for the extension of the experiment. At the local level, in several mining districts, anti-experimentalists tried to take control of MWU offices.[13]

Because of the political sensitivity of miners' privileges, there was an immediate reaction in Parliament; and the government had to set up an inquiry, the Viljoen Commission, to investigate.[14] The rebels campaigned on the unedifying but politically potent slogan: "The kaffirs are pushing out White workers in all industries." Their spokesman was not a mining man at all but a far right Nationalist attorney with an L.L.D. from Leyden, "Ras" Beyers. According to one source, Beyers' motivation was less the Color Bar itself and more his hatred of Grundlingh, "the English," the "Anglo-Jewish" mine owners, and even the Afrikaner secret society, the *Broederbond*. The last he attacked both as "too liberal" and for harboring Grundlingh.[15] Beyers had evidently come to these views as a result of his membership during the war in the Afrikaner extremist group, the *Ossewa Brandwag* (OB). His activities were probably an attempt to revive the struggle for control of Afrikaner trade unionism which the OB had fought (and lost) with the *Broederbond* during the 1940s.[16]

When the rebels threatened to put up National party candidates at the next election, a dispute over a small-scale productivity experiment became by mid-1966 a major national issue. Even before Viljoen reported, Prime Minister Verwoerd and his Labour minister, Sam Haak, had begun to distance themselves from the affair. Finally, the authorities ordered the whole "experiment" cancelled. Productivity bargaining continued between the Chamber and the white miners' unions during 1965–1966, but the action group made it clear that they would never yield more than token concessions. Nevertheless, the Chamber persevered with its bargaining, offering a monthly pay system, which was high on the rebels' own bargaining agenda, in return for agreement on the productivity issues. Though the union executive was increasingly in disarray and at odds with an important element of the membership, it was not yet clear that the more moderate Grundlingh faction would have to go.

With union elections pending in mid-1966, the Chamber of Mines suggested a compromise. The white miners would still exercise direct supervision during safety inspections as required by regulations under the act. Whites would continue to inspect the stope face, but the black team leaders could take the workers into parts of the stope where no blasting had been carried on. The proposed arrangement would save some time. The new MWU executive (Grundlingh was out by this point) rejected the proposal and renewed the demand for monthly pay and various changes aimed at increasing white manning levels. The Chamber refused to yield on the monthly pay issue unless the union agreed to offsetting productivity improvements. In December, the Chamber submitted a revised offer of monthly pay in return for agreement to reorganize work arrangements.

The Chamber advanced the usual arguments to justify its stand. It pointed to the plight of the low-grade mines that already faced drastically shortened lives—by as much as one-third—and would have had their position made impossible by the union's proposals. This suggested that the Chamber expected another cave-in by the government. Predicting the imminent collapse of gold mining was always an effective way to frighten government. At the end of the year, the Chamber had, however, to make the damaging admission that its revised proposals would eventually lead to a reduction in the number of white positions in the mines (it had promised to protect the jobs of all existing white employees). The MWU took the admission as evidence that all along the mine owners had been intending to replace them with blacks and became even more intransigent. Mining industry pressure on the legislative Color Bar had by mid-1966 produced a result that was the reverse of the intended one. Not only was Grundlingh displaced and the hostility of the MWU aroused, but also the MWU's traditional nonpolitical policies were under attack from the radical right within the union.

The defeat of Grundlingh in the 1966 union elections was extraordinary. A member of the National party, he had joined the union in 1955. He was also prominent in the local politics of Westonaria and Carletonville. In addition, by the early 1960s he was a businessman of some standing in the area.[17] The ouster of such an important establishment figure suggested that the MWU was moving in a much more militant direction. Grundlingh gave way to Fred Short as general secretary, and Maurice

Meiring came in as president. The victors found no place on the executive for Beyers, who continued to act as informal advisor. Their oath of office left no doubt about their standpoint on the issues that had doomed Grundlingh: to keep "Kaffirs, Moors and Indians" out of white man's work "so help me God and strong my sword arm." The real victor, however, was Arrie Paulus who soon replaced Short, while Cor de Jager became president. A founding member of the action group, Paulus had avoided prominent involvement in the original dispute but supported a hard line on the Color Bar.

During the struggles within the MWU, a radical group had emerged that challenged not only the mining companies but also the National party government. "Ras" Beyers had links to the group that broke away under Albert Hertzog to form the *Herstigte Nasionale Partie* in 1969. The tactic of the radical right, frequent and repeated use of the wildcat strike, threatened the mediation and conciliation machinery that the state had used since the 1920s to co-opt the white unions and to discipline their wage and other demands. Government sensitivity appeared in its efforts to dissociate itself from the productivity experiment despite its earlier acceptance by the state mining engineer and officials within the Department of Labour. Recovering from the failures of 1964–1966, the Chamber of Mines continued to press for changes in the organization of underground work. However, the Chamber now knew that it could count on receiving no political support if the MWU took the issue, as it often did, into the public arena.[18]

Once in office, Paulus and his associates did not have everything their own way. The bitter contest for control left the union deeply divided. Partly the issues were personal, involved with competing loyalties to the Grundlingh and Paulus factions, but partly, too, they were over tactics. Many MWU members apparently objected to the overtly political stance taken in the 1964–1966 period and the challenge to the National party government that Beyers and others were posing. The early policies of Paulus suggested that the rank and file supported a defense of the Color Bar, but was divided on the attack on the government. Perceiving this, Paulus shrewdly moved the MWU's agenda back in the direction of more narrowly defined trade-union issues. Productivity bargaining continued with the Chamber of Mines. Paulus sought large salary increases, the five-day week, and improved benefits for his members, while resisting any erosion of the white miners' prerogatives under the Mines and Works Act.[19] Although the government repeatedly stressed in private its sympathy with industry objectives, it always drew back when publicly challenged by the MWU on the Color Bar issue.

In 1967, the Chamber secured minor productivity improvements in return for pay concessions and guaranteed retraining of any white miners displaced as a result. The white unions had successfully demanded terms, including an immediate wage increase, so that part of the productivity increase achieved went to their members.[20] However, two years later, the Labour minister canceled a scheme (begun in 1966–1967) to train blacks as ventilation recorders and samplers, jobs that whites had abandoned. The National party M.P. for Carletonville, an important mining center, demanded job determinations for the positions.[21]

Disputes continued throughout the late 1960s and early 1970s. The next flare-up occurred in 1968–1970 on the government's own ideological terrain and concerned mining operations in the nearby "homelands." The issue was simply whether the Color Bar would apply also to those mines such as Rustenburg Platinum or Impala Platinum that lay wholly or partly in the bantustans. If the government's policy of "unlimited opportunity for the Bantu in the Bantu areas" had any meaning, there was no room for the Color Bar there. Paulus and the MWU fought against any breach in the Color Bar even in the few homeland mines. The government could not obscure the issue, since the safety argument for excluding Africans from the "white" jobs had disappeared decades before. Prime Minister John Vorster therefore faced the embarrassing choice of repudiating the racial protection of whites in the country's most important industry or publicly giving the lie to its promises of bantustan advancement. Elements of the Afrikaans press attacked the MWU and denounced its hostility to the National party, but the government itself refused to confront the union.

When the issue arose initially in 1968, the government caved in to the union and promised protection of white jobs at Rustenburg Platinum. This move had some slight justification in that the mine was only partly in Bophuthatswana. Later, when mines entirely within the homelands became involved, the authorities offered a settlement:

> The compromise he now offers seeks to reassure the White mine workers that never will a Homeland African: Replace a White mineworker; Have authority over a White mineworker; Do the same work in the same mine, except in separate shifts or separate sections of the mine. In addition, exemptions from the Colour Bar section of the Mines and Works Act will be granted only on application by individual mines, and not to the industry generally. And the government affirms that in the White areas the Colour Bar will last as long as there is a Nationalist government.[22]

Persistent MWU resistance forced the authorities to embarrassing public delays in their promises to open these jobs to blacks in the homelands. Two years after the issue first arose, homeland mines were still operating with a Color Bar, and there had been no progress at all in dismantling it.

At the Rosslyn Mine the Department of Labour tightened up the Color Bar, opening itself to ridicule in the press.

By the early 1970s the Chamber of Mines believed that the main barriers to the elimination of the archaic racial restrictions lay with the mining unions rather than with the government or with generalized racial prejudice. In private, the owners had found the government increasingly accommodating, though still ideologically sensitive to open pronouncements against the Color Bar. A former senior Chamber official made this point at a conference in 1971. R. S. Cooke, a past president of the Chamber of Mines, registered a strong plea for relaxation of job reservation in the mining industry. He gave as his reasons the shortage of white mineworkers, estimated to reach 4,000 by 1973; the potential release of white miners to alleviate the general shortage of skilled labor in the Republic; and the reduction of mine working costs. Cooke laid the blame for the industry's antiquated labor system squarely at the door of the mining unions: "Basically it is the opposition put up by the trade unions which is the restricting factor. The government has been very reasonable with the mining industry in these matters." No doubt simple prudence and the hope of favors to come also inclined Cooke toward generosity in his public assessments of the standpoint of government.[23] In 1973, Vorster acted in much the way Cooke had predicted and announced that nonwhites, including Africans, could do skilled work. He added the important proviso, however, that the white unions must agree.[24] Growing shortages of skilled workers in manufacturing explained the change, but the requirement of union agreement revealed that the issue remained sensitive.

While quick to resort to extremist rhetoric in defense of its privileges, the MWU under Paulus did finally agree to the introduction of some of the work practices proposed but aborted in the 1964–1965 experiments in return for wage increases. By the terms of this 1973 agreement, selected black team leaders would undertake some of the safety inspections, mark certain noncritical holes for drilling, and charge-up for blasting on condition that they work under the direct supervision of a white miner.[25] While of some help in improving productivity, these changes fell well short of the industry's objectives.

The slow progress on the Color Bar issue forced the mining companies to search for other ways of increasing efficiency and lowering costs. The need to contain costs seemed particularly urgent in the early 1970s before the gold-price increases after 1973 took off some of the pressure. Tighter management and the system of production bonuses yielded productivity gains, estimated at 15 percent between 1973 and 1975. While the rising price of gold eased one set of pressures impelling the owners to act against the entrenched position of white labor, mounting concern about black labor availability pressed on them from another direction.

As the supply of foreign labor dried up and the political risks involving use of foreign labor became more apparent, the Chamber of Mines rediscovered domestic sources largely forgotten since the 1950s (see Chapter 6). Local labor was bound to be more costly because the mines were now competing directly with secondary industry. Furthermore, there was every prospect that South African miners would demand better jobs underground. Thus, the new circumstances of the 1970s continued to push the mining industry toward radical proposals to restructure the racial division of labor. As always, the MWU's response aimed to achieve maximum gains on wages and conditions while giving as little as possible on the Color Bar. Since many MWU members were not highly qualified miners, the blasting certificate was their only real protection against ouster. They knew that the companies could replace them with equally competent but much lower paid black team leaders.

Not all the mining unions proved to be as recalcitrant as the MWU. In 1973, the Chamber made a settlement with the winding drivers, who left the Council of Mining Unions followed shortly thereafter by the artisans' union and the reduction workers. By isolating the MWU in the council, the Chamber hoped to weaken its resistance to productivity bargaining and to work around its obstructionism.[26] Other cost-cutting measures continued simultaneously, including the long-standing mechanization program, designed to reduce labor needs, both white and black. By 1975 or even 1986, however, little in the way of productivity improvement could be attributed to mechanization.

The biggest barrier to greater efficiency was the blasting certificate, its confinement to whites, and the way the MWU used it to frustrate the advance of blacks. To circumvent this obstacle, the industry developed two strategies, one for the long term and one an interim measure. Both strategies reflected the expectation that the continuing political efforts to secure the withdrawal or at least the modification of the Color Bar itself would yield little result. For the future, the industry began the development of a boring machine that could cut the gold-bearing ore from the stopes without the need for blasting.[27] In the short term, the mining companies worked to reduce the involvement of the white miners in the stope, in effect to make the white miner more concerned with production in his section, while shifting the supervision of stoping operations to the black team leaders. In particular, the companies wanted to get rid of the requirement that a white miner do the preshift inspection. This change would have meant that the black miners could begin work an hour or two earlier, before the whites came underground.

In 1975–1976, the Chamber again went to work on the MWU. Once again, it tried to get productivity concessions in return for accepting the union's long-standing demand for a five-day week. The issue was the protection of 18,000 white mining positions. Under the Chamber's proposals some of these would inevitably go, although not the jobs of the incumbents.

Complicated negotiations lasting over eighteen months followed. Twice the MWU formally declared a dispute, in 1975 and 1976, before finally accepting a compromise.[28] Following the declaration of the first dispute and the intervention of the minister of Mines, the government appointed a commission to sort out the competing claims of the MWU and the Chamber. Before the commission had properly begun, the parties managed to agree in principle on how the industry might move toward a five-day week. However, the MWU tried to minimize or avoid completely further productivity concessions. Another year passed before the mines secured agreement. A reason for delay was the industry's demand to extend a five-day week to the artisan unions. The Chamber wanted from them the same kinds of production concessions that it had negotiated from the miners themselves. Early in 1976, the union declared its second dispute, and the matter went to a conciliation board which failed to get an agreement. In midyear, the MWU took a strike vote on the five-day week issue, and a majority voted in favor. The state again intervened and called the parties to a series of meetings that succeeded in averting a strike. In the end, the industry agreed that the scheme could go ahead without the artisan unions. The MWU for its part accepted something less than the full five-day week. The productivity concessions, though significant, still fell short of what the industry wanted.

In March 1977, the Franszen Commission, which the government had appointed to investigate the issues involved, submitted an interim report.[29] The commission opposed the five-day week if any loss of production would result. Meanwhile, events overtook the work of the commission when the Chamber of Mines proceeded to put in place the compromise eleven-shift fortnight which it had negotiated with the MWU the previous year. In return, the union accepted an extension of the productivity changes which it had permitted in 1973. This enabled the companies to use the team leaders more productively. By easing the requirement of direct white supervision of safety-related activities, they reduced delays, particularly at the beginning of the shift before work could start. Under the scheme, the white miners would have the option of alternative Saturdays off, but work would continue on a six-day basis.

There was never any thought of a five-day week for blacks. According to the Franszen Commission, the black miners themselves opposed this, because it would lengthen the contract periods they had to spend on the mines. They complained also that they were already working twelve-hour days and objected to the even longer day resulting from the five-day week. With typical civic-mindedness, local white politicians who lived near the mines complained that a shortened work week would lead to their shopping districts being invaded on Saturday mornings by off-duty black miners. Finally, the Chamber of Mines said that it could not support a five-day week for blacks (although it later conceded this point to promote the move to commuter migrancy). In a revealing admission, the Chamber stated that recreational facilities in the compounds were inadequate if the miners were to have an additional day off on the weekends. Executives claimed that rioting might result from the blacks' inability to occupy themselves on their Saturday holiday.

Because these negotiations yielded less than the industry wanted, the industry tried to find other ways to minimize the effects of the Color Bar on operations. These efforts included the development of concentrated mining techniques and other changes that eliminated the need to place the drill holes with precision to maximize the tonnage of broken rock in each blast. Location of the holes for drilling had always been a task requiring both knowledge and experience. The Mines and Works Act reserved this task for the white ganger and produced an operational bottleneck, which slowed production of the whole team. Under the new system, the white miner had only to mark the first hole, and black assistants placed the others according to a standard pattern, using a template. The companies introduced other changes designed to enlarge production units and make them operate more efficiently. Improvements in the production bonuses for white miners gave them a direct interest in maximum efficiency, which, according to most of the blacks who worked with them, came at considerable cost to workers' safety.[30]

Production changes of this sort could help make an inefficient, cumbersome system work more productively. Yet the need was still, from the companies' point of view, to negotiate an end to the racial division of labor. Despairing at the highly effective guerrilla tactics of the MWU over the previous decade, by late 1977 Anglo American Corporation had developed an elaborate plan to appeal to the union membership over the heads of the executive. The idea was to take productivity bargaining to the grass roots. Dealing with the individual miners on each mine, the company would try to get agreement on more efficient work practices. Such tactics had been a highly successful means of promoting black advancement against union opposition in other industries, notably the iron and steel sector. In this way, Anglo executives apparently hoped to avoid the chronic politicizing of the issues experienced earlier.

The announced goal, to integrate the black and white work forces and do away with job reservation, was not new—Anglo had been calling for integration for years. The new dimension came in the attempt to undercut the MWU leadership by appealing directly to the membership. More daringly, the strategy envisaged a wide-ranging training program for blacks with the apparent intention that companies should be able to maintain production in case of a white miners' strike. This was no far-fetched proposal; during the white miners' wildcat strike in 1979, the blacks, working under mine officials, did run the mines, and underground operations continued throughout. Unfortunately for Anglo, the plan was leaked to the press and immediately denounced by Arrie Paulus as a nefarious plot to break his union. Anglo executives responded that the proposal intended no threat to whites. They began by acknowledging that continued white presence in the mines was essential. Undoubtedly, the leak of this document did considerable damage and further entrenched the position of the MWU chief.

Suspicion of Anglo American's intentions continued for years. In 1981, a row occured when the MWU got wind of new training schemes for team leaders at Anglo American group mines. The union believed Anglo was training its team leaders for protected jobs, which it thought the government was about to open to blacks. There was even a report that the company had trained one of these team leaders as a mine captain, the second-ranking management position underground. On this occasion the MWU took the same hard line that it had always taken, threatening a general strike if there was any such breach of the Color Bar. Anglo denied both the mine captain story and that it was training team leaders for white jobs. Anglo did not deny it was providing additional training for team leaders, however, and concluded, rather lamely, that the company also trained whites.

These moves by Anglo American underscored the dramatic changes taking place in the pattern of race relations in South African industry. An even more important development was the government's appointment in 1977 of commissions to investigate and report on the two central features of the labor system: influx control and the Color Bar. P. J. Riekert chaired the commission on influx control, while Professor N. E. Wiehahn was in charge of the commission on industrial legislation and trade unions. When Wiehahn began his work, the legal structure of job reservation remained largely intact. White workers were sheltered under an umbrella of protective laws. These both secured their access to industrial concili-ation machinery and protected them from black competition.

Although the structure remained in place on paper, there had been a large-scale erosion of the Color Bar, particularly in manufacturing. Es-calating manpower shortages had created openings for the advancement of whites, leaving the places vacated for blacks. On occasions, the positions which thus became available were formally reclassified. At other times there would simply be an informal agreement between the employer and his white workers to open a specified number of reserved jobs to blacks in return for wage or other concessions. As early as 1973, the Vorster government had officially opened skilled work to blacks, provided the white unions involved agreed.

Two consequences flowed from this development. Despite lack of formal recognition and initial, active discouragement by state and industry, black trade unions began to emerge, especially in the wake of the 1973 Durban strikes. Second, white labor became divided both on the issue of black unions and on the Color Bar. In a range of manufacturing industries, the white unions ceased to be much of a concern. In the extractive industries, nowhere more than on the gold mines, white unions mounted a ferocious defense of their privileges and the legislative protection that guaranteed them. The campaign began even before the Wiehahn Commission released its first report. When management at the O'Kiep copper mine in the northern Cape decided to employ three mixed-race artisans, the MWU members at the mine struck work. Before long nearly 7,000 union members on seventy gold and coal mines were out. Paulus intended to bring off a major general strike as a preemptive blow against what the MWU feared in the Wiehahn reports. Government assurances that any changes recommended by Wiehahn would require negotiation with the union were not believed.

On this occasion the MWU leader overplayed his hand. The government did not intervene; despite various threats against those who did not strike, the MWU rank and file did not unite behind Paulus. Other mining unions did not support him and the companies were able to maintain production, using blacks, white strike breakers, and senior management in supervisory positions. Intended as a major blow against erosion of the Color Bar, the strike petered out. Over the following two years, the government released six reports from the Wiehahn Commission. To minimize damaging political consequences, the commission only published its last report on the mining industry after the 1981 election. In the final report, Wiehahn's major recommendations struck directly at the basic position of the MWU. He recommended official recognition of black trade unions and formal registration (if they met certain criteria) under the industrial conciliation legislation. This condition had applied to white unions since the 1920s. He also proposed to extend the same right to strike that the white unions enjoyed. Equally important, Wiehahn advised abandonment of job reservation and the whole edifice of the legislated industrial Color Bar.

Since Arrie Paulus had been fighting the mining industry on its modest proposals, his reaction to this recommendation of the Afrikaner professor was predictable. He condemned Wiehahn, denounced his proposals on black unions and the Color Bar, and attacked the government for the greatest betrayal of the white working class since the 1922 strike. Paulus and the MWU led the most conservative white unions, organized in the Afrikaner-dominated South African Confederation of Labour, in die-hard opposition to the proposed reforms. The MWU went to the lengths of changing their membership rules to admit as members whites who had left integrated unions. The MWU also drew closer to the Afrikaner opposition.[31] In areas outside the gold mines themselves, the Botha government tried to ignore Paulus. It moved by stages to accept Wiehahn's proposals, both those regarding black trade unions and those concerning the dismantling of job reservation. On the mines, the government had to be more cautious. It conceded partial recognition of the black miners' union but hesitated to take Paulus on directly.

In August 1987, after years of intermittent negotiation, Parliament abolished the legislative Color Bar. The government at last moved to honor its long-declared intention to phase out racial discrimination in mining. However, the white electorate's swing to the right in the May 1987 election and the strong opposition of the Conservative party, now elevated to the role of Official Opposition in Parliament, made the government's position more delicate.

Until the matter came to a vote, it remained doubtful that the authorities would summon the courage to act. In any case, the amending legislation gave ample scope for prevarication. The government could use its discretion to slow or even prevent the access of black miners to the more skilled jobs. The key section of the Mines and Works Amendment Act, Section 12(1)n, stated that the minister, before announcing regulations for issuing certificates of competency (including the key blasting certificate, for nearly a century the license of the white miner), should seek the advice of the owners and of the organizations whose members hold a majority of the certificates, that is, the white unions, including the Mine Workers' Union. He was to do this through the formation of advisory committees.[32]

These clauses of the bill, together with the prolonged reluctance of the government to push it through second reading (and then to proclaim it), suggested that progress toward the integration of skilled job categories in underground work in the mines would be slow. The Parliamentary Conservatives, Arrie Paulus now among them, worked to make the political cost of integration high. They fought the Mines and Works Amendment Bill at every stage of its passage through Parliament. The introduction of the bill required years of negotiation involving the Chamber, the white unions, and the Department of Mineral and Energy Affairs.

The Chamber of Mines had been negotiating separately with the white unions on the Color Bar since 1981. Wiehahn's recommendation to scrap the racial barriers in the mines focused on the need to provide security for the white miners. This recommendation was part of his general view that the phasing out of the Color Bar throughout the economy would require steps to reassure the threatened whites. Soon the industry did secure the agreement of the six white artisan unions to the appointment of black apprentices and to the integration of their training with that of the whites. In 1985, 140 black apprentices came onto the mines, slightly less than 10 percent of the 1,560 white apprentices employed that year. Otherwise, before 1985, progress in the mining industry toward accepting Wiehahn's ideas was slow. The MWU would only participate in the negotiations with the Chamber as an observer.

Finally, during 1985, the Department of Mineral and Energy Affairs began to press for serious negotiations and agreement by the end of the year. When that deadline passed without a settlement, the department published a draft which gave the MWU an important role in regulating entry into the scheduled jobs in a proposed Mine Labour Selection Board. Responding to this draft, the Chamber and nine of the white unions (excluding the MWU) proposed an alternative approach, more in keeping with Wiehahn's recommendations. They proposed scrapping the racial definition of scheduled persons in the 1926 act, ratification of the closed shop, agreed participation in an industrial council, and job security through an "Industrial Council Security of Employment Agreement." The security agreement required appointment of a Dismissals Appeals Board and other measures to reassure the white unions. These conciliatory proposals were a measure of the eagerness of the Chamber to get rid of the Color Bar. Once again the MWU, now joined by the much smaller Technical Officials Association, rejected the proposals, claiming that the proffered guarantees were valueless. Meanwhile, Chamber negotiators also began to back away. They warned the unions that did sign that the industry would not honor its undertakings if the government operated the revised act on a racial basis.

Throughout these prolonged discussions, there was virtually no involvement of blacks at any stage.[33] The Chamber hesitated to consult openly with the National Union of Mineworkers (NUM), fearing that to do so would make the prospect of agreement with the MWU even less likely. Although excluded from the negotiations, the NUM leadership emphasized its opposition to any form of racial discrimination in the mines. Moreover there was a high degree of militancy on this issue among the rank-and-file membership. The general secretary, Cyril Ramaphosa, told a Parliamentary Standing Committee in 1986 that to scrap the racial definition of scheduled persons under the act and simultaneously to provide job protection for whites was contradictory. He urged deletion of Section 12(1)n of the draft act, because its retention would open the way, through the exercise of ministerial discretion, for the resumption of discrimination. He argued against efforts to retain these clauses on safety or health grounds; existing regulations were perfectly adequate to protect the workers. Although Ramaphosa's views on these points coincided with the thinking of the Chamber of Mines, its representatives prudently refrained from associating themselves publicly with his ideas.[34] Although a color-blind Mines and Works Amendment Act has finally passed Parliament, the tortured history of these negotiations, extending over nearly a decade, suggests that progress toward achieving racial integration in the skilled jobs in the mines will be slow.

Racial Privilege and Worker Safety

With the official abandonment of the final elements of the legislative Color Bar in 1987–1988, the emphasis of the National Union of Mineworkers shifted toward demanding improved training for team leaders and other black supervisors. Its objective was to make health and safety a shared responsibility between management, the state, and the workers themselves. To emphasize its independent standing on the safety issues, the union has also underwritten its own studies on the causes of dangerous working conditions.

In a paper written for the NUM before the formal abandonment of the Color Bar in underground work, Jean Leger, a Witwatersrand University researcher, discussed the safety aspects of the management system underground. Management, he concluded, "has separated the control functions of direction and evaluation from discipline. The racial divisions in the underground work force have facilitated this division and have been exploited [by management to this end]."[35] Increasingly, he pointed out, the white miner had become the main engine to intensify work pressure underground, because his earnings depend on maximum production. The actual supervision of operations in the stopes is no longer the function of the white ganger but now of the black team leader (the former "boss boy"). According to Leger, the mining industry has used the racial division of labor to maximize production at the expense of worker safety. Leger's point seemed to be that these organizational changes threatened the long-established safety programs of the Chamber of Mines and the individual companies.

On the available evidence it is beyond dispute that the mines, always dangerous places to work despite great emphasis by management and workers on safety, remained hazardous. This situation was partly because of the intensification of production associated with the racially based management system. The white ganger, who had the responsibility by regulation under the Mines and Works Act for ensuring that the work places were made safe, did not spend much time in the stope. It was in his direct financial interest to minimize or eliminate the periods when production halted for safety reasons. The supervisor who really knew whether conditions were safe or not was the black team leader. He always worked with his men at or near the stope face but lacked the authority to order the workers out when he perceived a safety hazard. Also, he received much less training than the white ganger. Who was responsible?

To attribute the safety problem exclusively to the managers is possibly to slight the reasons they acted as they did. For decades the companies could not get agreement from the white workers for the introduction of a more efficient system, leaving them with little alternative but to work within the restrictions imposed by the Color Bar. It was their effort to wring maximum productivity out of an inherently inefficient racial system that produced the problems noted by Leger. Management has long struggled to erode the restrictive practices in which the white ganger had responsibility both for discipline and maximizing output and for safety, while the team leader supervised production at the stope face. Repeated efforts by the Chamber of Mines to secure agreement from the miners' unions and the government to reorganize this system have always failed. These efforts went back to the early 1930s. For instance in evidence to the Native Economic Commission, a Chamber representative complained:

> If we had a free hand to re-organize our work, with all due regard to safety and health, there is not the slightest doubt that we could do with a materially smaller number of men, Europeans; and that in consequence of the re-organization, we would have to employ a larger number of leading hands and Natives of the boss-boy type. We would have to increase their number; and to that extent there would be an enlarged scope for the employment of natives at a higher rate of pay.[36]

The Chamber tried for decades to put more of the underground management function in the hands of black supervisors (while proposing to pay them more than before but much less than the whites were getting), which would effectively have eliminated the system of divided responsibility that now prevails. It was this system that caused the safety problems noted by Leger. Of course, senior management shared the responsibility. Because their efforts to reorganize the management system always fell short, they worked aggressively to offset the inefficiencies of the racial system imposed on them by custom, the political power of the white unions, and legislation. These efforts to make a bad system more productive by intensification of the work process, in turn, exacerbated the safety problem. To that extent the owners have put production and profits ahead of safety. They also connived at work practices that left more of the safety-related inspections to the black team leaders. The team leaders did not have the specific training given to the white gangers because of their statutory responsibility, which put the safety of everyone at risk underground. Yet the responsibility was not that of management alone. It was the MWU's relentless defense of the Color Bar that led the managers to act as they did.

5

The Sourcing of
Foreign Labor, 1973–1990

The boom in South Africa's manufacturing industries in the aftermath of the 1960 Sharpeville massacre ran parallel to a decade-long stagnation in its mining industry. With inflation and rising competition for black labor from secondary industries, the fixed price of gold meant that the mining companies' top priority was cost containment. Because labor from outside South Africa cost less and was more readily available, the industry's dependence on it grew in the late 1960s. By 1973, foreign migrants made up almost 80 percent of the black work force. In some mines, the figure was 90 percent (Table 5.1).

Three years of turbulence beginning in 1974 were sufficient to undo this predominance of foreign workers and to drive the mines back to domestic sources of labor (see Appendix, Table A.5). South African labor had been leaving the mines in ever-greater numbers; quite suddenly that trend was reversed. The number of foreign workers dropped from 336,000 at the end of 1973 to fewer than 200,000 by late 1976. Over the same period, the proportion of non–South African labor in the work force fell from 80 to 40 percent (Figure 5.1). The decline in northern labor accounted for much of the reduction. In late 1973, there were 227,000 Malawians and Mozambicans in the mines; six years later only 56,000. Conversely, labor from the "inner crescent" of foreign suppliers (Botswana, Lesotho, and Swaziland) increased over the same period from 108,000 to 120,000. Rhodesia (Zimbabwe), barely represented in the mines in the early 1970s, sent 29,000 workers there in 1976.

In the late 1970s, the labor supply pattern stabilized. The proportion of non–South African workers reached equilibrium at about 40 percent.[1] After a decade of stability, however, foreign labor in the gold mines is again said by some to be under threat of removal. Following repeated warnings, the South African government ordered the mines in late 1986 not to recruit Mozambicans and not to renew existing contracts. The

Table 5.1 Foreign Labor by Mine, 1972 and 1984 (percentages)

	December 1972			April 1984		
	Moz./Mal.	BLS	Total Foreign[a]	Moz./Mal.	BLS	Total Foreign[a]
Anglo American						
Western Deep	33.7	40.2	74.5	14.7	37.7	52.4
FS Saaiplaas	33.4	53.0	86.4	2.3	46.1	48.4
Vaal Reefs	33.8	40.3	74.5	6.2	39.6	45.8
Elandsrand	14.3	31.3	45.6			
Welkom	24.1	44.3	68.6	2.4	40.3	42.7
Pres Brand	28.5	45.5	74.0	1.7	37.9	39.6
Pres Steyn	30.2	42.8	73.2	2.2	37.3	39.5
Western Holdings	34.7	33.2	68.1	4.1	32.3	36.4
FS Geduld	21.3	51.3	75.6	2.1	26.5	28.6
Gencor						
Beisa	27.4	24.4	51.8			
Kinross	62.1	24.9	87.0	17.7	28.3	46.0
Bracken	43.6	35.7	82.8	8.3	34.1	42.4
Beatrix	18.1	23.8	41.9			
St Helena	53.0	30.4	83.4	14.2	26.0	40.2
Unisel	18.7	18.1	36.8			
Marievale	39.4	30.6	71.6	1.3	34.6	35.9
Stilfontein	70.3	14.4	87.0	17.3	17.7	35.0
Winkelhaak	59.8	18.1	79.8	19.0	15.6	34.6
Leslie	55.7	25.7	84.3	7.9	25.1	33.0
West Rand Cons	61.7	16.9	83.0	10.9	16.3	27.2
Grootvlei	32.3	21.7	61.5	6.8	18.1	24.9
Buffelsfontein	41.9	30.8	74.3	5.2	19.3	24.5

(continues)

government found, as it had sixty years before, that getting the mines to repatriate Mozambicans is no simple matter. In 1987, Malawians working in the mines were informed that they too would not be allowed to return to South Africa once they went home. The International Labour Organization (ILO) has argued, on tenuous statistical grounds, that, quite apart from dramatic political gestures, up to two-thirds of foreign workers will retire from the mines by 1992.[2]

The voluminous recent literature on foreign labor in the gold mining industry mostly relies on a notion of unilinear displacement ("internalization") of foreign by South African labor.[3] The theory of internalization assumes that the interests of the South African government and the

Table 5.1   *(continued)*

Goldfields						
Doornfontein	76.3	7.0	84.5	17.1	43.5	60.6
West Driefontein	68.6	11.5	82.1	17.1	42.8	59.9
Kloof	79.0	9.9	89.6	14.1	43.1	57.2
Libanon	74.3	6.4	85.3	12.7	43.4	56.1
East Driefontein	53.3	24.8	78.2	8.9	43.8	52.7
Venterspost	80.4	6.3	89.5	11.2	40.8	52.0
Deelkraal	2.3	49.1	51.4			
Rand Mines						
ERPM	84.8	3.9	90.5	64.7	9.8	74.5
Harmony	33.5	35.8	69.4	19.9	42.5	62.4
Blyvooruitzicht	58.7	15.2	77.7	25.2	20.9	46.1
Durban Deep	71.6	8.7	83.9	24.4	18.0	42.4
JCI						
Western Areas	77.2	13.8	92.7	31.2	22.2	53.4
Western A. (Elsburg)				28.5	15.0	43.5
Randfontein Estates				17.2	18.7	35.9
Anglo Vaal						
Hartbeesfontein	75.5	12.7	89.1	17.1	36.8	53.9
Loraine				20.8	18.1	38.9

ªIncludes all foreign sources.
Source: Unpublished data from Chamber of Mines of South Africa.

employers are congruent. It makes no distinction between the South African government and state, ignoring the role of the bureaucracy and the military. Finally, it assumes that the mining houses and their member companies speak with one voice on the issue.

This chapter explores the break-up of the mines' northern labor empire and the changing role of foreign labor in the two decades following 1970. It considers four related issues: why foreign labor is still employed in the mines, despite massive domestic unemployment; the sourcing strategies of the mining companies; the relationship between the mining industry and the South African state on the issue of foreign labor; and the relationship between the supplier states and the mining industry. The four

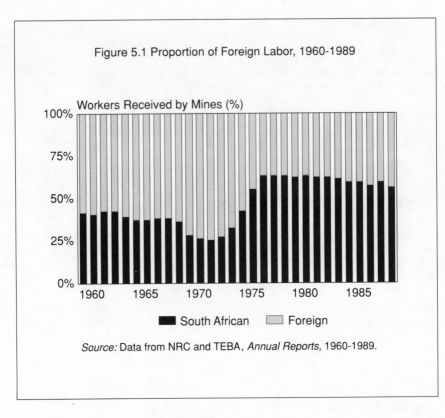

Figure 5.1 Proportion of Foreign Labor, 1960-1989

Source: Data from NRC and TEBA, *Annual Reports*, 1960-1989.

issues are used to test the notion, first, of industry-wide solidarity on sourcing policies and second, that the interests of industry and state are congruent. The concept of symbiosis, or mutual dependence of industry and state, is compared to that of congruence.[4]

The End of Empire

The last three decades reveal a history of often unpredictable political intervention in the migratory labor system. These periodic pressures, which have come both from within and outside South Africa, have helped reshape the system in significant ways. In the 1960s, newly independent Tanzania and Zambia gave notice of the impending break-up of the mining industry's northern labor empire. In 1961, Tanzania announced the recall of its 14,000 black miners, and by 1966, they were all home. Zambia's withdrawal came later but more suddenly; in 1965 there were some 6,000 Zambians in the mines; by 1968, none remained (Appendix, Table A.2). Despite the warning, the Chamber of Mines did not take steps to reduce dependence on the other important northern supply areas. The number of Malawians in the mines tripled between 1967 and 1973, for example.

A combination of factors in the early 1970s marked a decisive break in the mining companies' foreign labor policies. The freeing-up of the international gold price was pivotal. The price rose slowly, then explosively. Windfall profits explain why the mines could pay their migrant workers more, but not why they actually did so.[5] In the early 1970s, the Chamber of Mines faced a groundswell of international criticism which was brought to a head by the publication of Francis Wilson's influential book *Labour in the South African Gold Mines*. Wilson demonstrated that real wages in the mining industry had actually fallen over the previous eighty years.[6] The Chamber prepared a 53-page summary of the book, which it circulated throughout the industry.

The strikes in Durban in December 1972 and January 1973, while not affecting the mines directly, reverberated around South African industry, signalling a more militant mood among black workers.[7] Labor unrest in the mines, beginning at Carletonville in September 1973, soon followed. Alarmed too by the continuing hemorrhage of South African blacks from the mines, some mining houses reevaluated their wage policy. The continued rise in the gold price—64 percent (in rands) in 1973—made it possible to pay more. In 1973, Anglo American and Johannesburg Consolidated Investment (JCI) rejected the "maximum average clause," which had long constrained competition among the groups for labor by requiring adherence to Chamber-set wage levels.[8] After resistance from the other mining houses, the defectors accepted a compromise.

The next year, Anglo American again broke ranks. It wanted to raise the minimum underground wage to 200 cents a shift, while Goldfields would agree to no more than 150 cents. The Chamber negotiated a compromise of 160 cents.[9] The higher rates stemmed from efforts to close the widening differential between mine and factory wages. Anglo American and JCI also pushed for above-average wage increases in semiskilled and skilled job categories to attract more educated and skilled South African blacks.

Although the mine owners could increasingly afford a new sourcing strategy focused on the domestic labor market, it took the events of April 1974 for them to see this. That critical month focused as nothing else the debate about foreign versus local recruitment, low versus higher wages. First came an aircraft crash in Francistown, Botswana, which killed seventy-four Malawian miners. Pending the report of a Commission of Inquiry into the crash, the Life president of Malawi, Hastings Banda, suspended mine recruiting in Malawi. The commission blamed technical incompetence in Francistown for the crash. Banda nevertheless denounced the mines and ordered all 120,000 Malawians home.

For some years, the Chamber of Mines had worried about this possibility. However, the conventional wisdom held that the suppliers needed to send the labor more than the mines needed to receive it. In 1971, the Association of Mine Managers argued that Malawi was too dependent on the mines to follow Tanzania and Zambia. In early 1974, a report by an industry researcher reached much the same conclusion.[10] Banda himself had visited the mines in the early 1970s and been feted by management and Malawian workers. His sudden decision shocked the mining industry.[11] The Chamber of Mines and the South African government dispatched high-level delegations to Malawi to urge Banda to reconsider. Banda rejected all offers of conciliation.[12]

The number of Malawians officially registered in the mines plummeted from 120,000 to no more than a few hundred in less than eighteen months (Figure 5.2). The Chamber of Mines initially thought it was the victim of a ploy to force it to pay for the transport of all Malawian workers on Air Malawi planes. Fearful that its own monopoly would be replaced by Banda's, the Chamber offered to share the transport of workers with Air Malawi. In September 1975, the Malawi Congress party gave Banda the authority to suspend recruiting permanently; he then did so.[13] In meetings with a Chamber of Mines delegation, Banda was harshly critical of the mines' air service but still repudiated the plan to give more business to Air Malawi. Subsequent Chamber speculation focused on Banda's quixotic personality, because the Chamber's analysts could see little economic rationality in the withdrawal.

Later commentators emphasized an element of calculation, relating the decision either to Banda's need to avoid isolation as the Mozambique and Rhodesian regimes crumbled around him or to the labor requirements of the expanding agricultural plantation sector in Malawi.[14] Banda himself subscribed to the latter analysis on at least one public occasion. At the opening of Malawi's 20th Parliament in 1983 the Life president proclaimed that he had "killed" mine recruiting in Malawi. He continued that foreign mine labor recruiting organizations no longer recruited in Malawi because the majority of the people had responded to his appeal to stay and work in their own gardens or on plantations. Banda reminded his audience that the plantations operating under his own company, Press Holdings Limited, now employed between 25,000 and 30,000 people.[15]

Although some returning mineworkers went to work on the plantations, many refused to work at lower wages than their mine rates. A considerable number returned clandestinely to South Africa and Rhodesia. Some went to the mines, and the NRC made plans to establish a border reception point for workers crossing into South Africa.[16] In the late 1970s, as expansion in the Malawian plantation sector slackened and domestic unemployment grew, Banda softened his hard line on

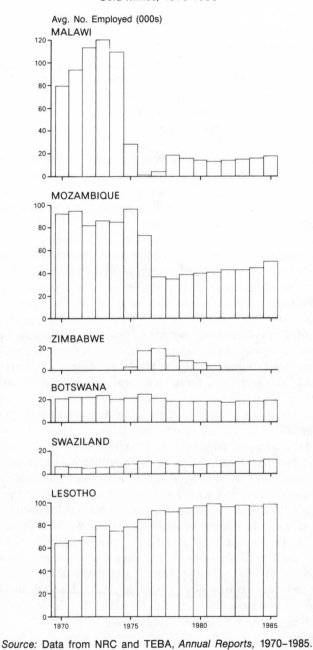

Figure 5.2   Foreign Migrants to South African
Gold Mines, 1970-1985

Avg. No. Employed (000s)

Source: Data from NRC and TEBA, *Annual Reports*, 1970–1985.

mine employment.[17] It was too late; the terms of the labor market had turned against the suppliers. Now in a much stronger position, the mines took back fewer than 20,000 Malawians, though they made certain concessions to Banda.

In an agreement signed by the Chamber of Mines' recruiting arm, TEBA (The Employment Bureau of Africa), and the Malawian government in 1977 (and ratified in 1983), TEBA agreed not to recruit labor and to allow the government to vet all prospective employees. Malawian miners had first to obtain the approval of the local Department of Labour. That department refused to provide letters to workers who had not first obtained clearance from their rural chiefs. The Chamber offered, and Banda agreed, to charter jet planes from Air Malawi to transport workers directly to Johannesburg (at their own expense).[18] From there, TEBA sent most of them to the poorer, lower-grade Witwatersrand mines, such as ERPM and Durban Deep, which were unpopular and chronically short of labor.

The second major upheaval for the mining industry in April 1974 was the overthrow of the regime of Marcello Caetano in Portugal. Later that year, in September, the new rulers in Lisbon negotiated a transfer of power to the Mozambique liberation movement, Frelimo. On 25 June 1975, the Portuguese left Mozambique for good. The loss of Mozambican mine labor at any stage in 1974 or 1975 would have completely crippled the South African gold mining industry. For a time this seemed probable. In an atmosphere of restrained panic, the Chamber's immediate goal was to hunt heads whatever their quality or source. Preferring South African labor, the recruiters mobilized locally. Contrary to the precepts of the "internalization" thesis, however, they also scrambled for labor throughout the region to replace the Malawians. Despite intense unease about Frelimo's takeover, the mines took labor wherever it was offered, including Mozambique, Angola, and Rhodesia.

For some decades, the mines had drawn significant labor from Portugal's other southern African colony, Angola. Between 1967 and 1973, the South Africans negotiated with the Portuguese to stabilize the Angolan supply at 5,000 per year. During this period, several thousand Angolans continued to reach the mines via well-established overland routes through Botswana. In 1974, after the news from Malawi, both the Chamber of Mines and the South African government made secret approaches to the Portuguese to lift the quota. In the aftermath of the Spinola coup, however, there was no one with whom to deal.[19] Instead, the Chamber established a recruiting office on the Namibia-Angola border to recruit Angolans who could pass themselves off as Namibians.

In contrast to earlier times, labor from Rhodesia proved easier to acquire. Following government-to-government negotiations in late 1974, the Rhodesians agreed to allow the controlled recruiting of up to 20,000 men per annum.[20] Though they finally had access to the Rhodesian labor market, the mines soon had cause to regret it. The recruits were more militant than most other foreign workers and were heavily involved in the industrial unrest that racked the industry beginning in the mid-1970s (see Chapter 8).[21] Unwilling to tolerate this, the mining companies began to send them back.

The Chamber of Mines also focused considerable attention on foreign sources closer to home. The mines considered Botswana, Lesotho, and Swaziland as low-risk areas. All three were deeply dependent on the South African economy and had good relations with Pretoria. Lesotho's proximity to the Orange Free State gold fields gave it an added attraction. Though Prime Minister Jonathan's attitude toward South Africa would later become more hard-line, the Chamber of Mines calculated that barring massive (and unlikely) international aid he could not afford to alienate Basotho mineworkers known to be sympathetic to the opposition Basutoland Congress party.[22] In Swaziland, King Sobhuza had always been a great friend of foreign capital and the mines. Botswana's President Khama was more critical but his economy was in no position to reabsorb repatriated migrants.[23]

The mining industry's new sourcing strategy combined crisis management with longer-term contingency planning. There is no evidence that mining officials ever wanted to displace all foreign labor or mount a systematic policy of withdrawal from the supplier states. Initially aiming for an equal split, they later settled for a 60:40 ratio of domestic to foreign labor. The industry learned two main lessons from the Malawian debacle: cultivate multiple domestic and foreign sources and avoid excessive reliance on foreign labor without phasing it out altogether. The general manager of TEBA noted that the industry's objective was "to encourage inter-dependence between the countries of southern Africa" while simultaneously "reverting as much as possible to the situation 40 years ago when nearly sixty per cent of mine labour was South African."[24]

By late 1975, however, many mines had become critically dependent on Mozambican labor, particularly given the large increase from there in the preceding year. This influx had two disadvantages for the mine owners: It made their mines more vulnerable to a Frelimo-inspired withdrawal and it increased their real losses through the operation of the gold premium.[25] The Chamber of Mines moved to renegotiate the gold premium but did not want to antagonize Frelimo since it desperately needed Mozambican labor. In early 1976, the Chamber became convinced that a Frelimo-ordered pullout was imminent and responded with a contingency plan to replace departing Mozambican workers with workers from all the remaining foreign suppliers, as well as South Africa itself.[26] The fear of withdrawal thus etched the principle of diversified sourcing more firmly into mine policy. The Chamber also developed plans to begin reducing the industry's Mozambican complement as soon as it could.[27] But events in Mozambique soon took matters out of its hands.

In 1976, Frelimo set up new administrative procedures which drastically cut the outflow of labor to South Africa by closing seventeen of WNLA's twenty-one offices in Mozambique. For three months the flow of labor from Mozambique was negligible. It later picked up, but numbers fell from 114,385 in January to 48,565 by the end of the year.[28] In the end, the Chamber of Mines got the reduction it wanted without the political fall-out.[29] A flood of applicants from across the subcontinent quickly replaced the Mozambicans. The Chamber made its new accord with Malawi and increased the flow of labor from Rhodesia, Botswana, Lesotho, and Swaziland (Appendix, Table A.2). The importance of a policy of diversification was later underscored by Lesotho's erratic posturing against the gold mines and by the withdrawal of Zimbabwean miners by the new Mugabe government.

Industry and State

The role of foreign labor had long been a topic of conversation between the mine controllers and the South African state. In the 1960s, the state tightened up on the use of foreign workers by other sectors and approached the Chamber of Mines several times to express its concern.[30] The Chamber replied that it was perfectly prepared to recruit South African blacks but that they would not work for the wages that the industry could afford. The state generally went along with this rationale for several reasons. It was reliant on industry data and could not readily support counter arguments with evidence. Apart from the mining companies, there were powerful interests in favor of foreign recruitment and even possibly extending it to other sectors of the economy. White farmers did not want more competition from mining companies at home. Finally, the state was internally divided on the issue. The bureaucrats dealing with South African blacks were opposed by the foreign-affairs functionaries. The former worried about domestic unemployment and tended to oppose foreign mine labor, while the latter wanted the leverage and diplomatic advantage gained from employing foreigners. These differences were important but not fundamental. Like the employers, both groups understood the need always to balance domestic security and foreign influence.

In 1970, Chamber of Mines representatives met with Piet Koornhof, then deputy minister of Bantu Administration, on the issue. The Chamber underlined the industry's preference for South African workers and its growing problems in keeping them. The deputy minister suggested that his labor bureaus could take over mine recruiting functions within South Africa, set up training centers, increase the prestige of mine work, and solve the problem of insufficient local recruits. The Chamber quickly rejected potential state intrusion into its labor market, though it did agree to accept any labor forwarded by the bureaus.[31] Mine recruiters regularly addressed large crowds at the bureaus. The workers usually refused to listen and subjected them to ridicule and abuse. In one case, a Bantu Affairs Commissioner told the Native Recruiting Corporation that he had a surplus of 700 men whom he could not place in employment. An NRC official went to the office and addressed the work-seekers; only two signed up.[32]

In 1975, the South African Agricultural Union, increasingly fearful of competition, repeated the call for state control over mine recruiting (see Chapter 6). In response, the Chamber reiterated its case, based on the observations of its recruiters, against state intervention. The Chamber argued quite accurately that the labor bureaus had forwarded negligible numbers of workers to the mines, that the bureaus would be unable to provide the multitude of services performed by NRC offices, and that in many bantustan areas tribal labor bureaus were either nonexistent or in disarray.

The logic of the symbiosis defining the relations between state and capital was seldom clearer than in the crisis of the mid-1970s. Both state groups backed the industry's recruiting efforts. The Department of Bantu Administration did all it could to promote the employment of more South Africans in the mines; the Department of Foreign Affairs met with Chamber representatives to see how they could help to increase labor flows from foreign sources, including Rhodesia, Mozambique, and Angola. Only in the late 1970s, when it become apparent that the mining companies had restored stability and that they intended to continue employing foreign labor, did the Department of Co-operation and Development (the former Bantu Affairs) renew its calls for expulsion.

Periodic demands to phase out foreign labor continued. In the early 1980s, official concern about black unemployment mounted and with it came more efforts to push the industry away from its established sourcing policy. The minister of Co-operation and Development recommended in mid-1983 that foreign labor should only be used underground, that training schemes should be directed at South African miners, that a principle of not employing a foreign worker when a South African was available should be adopted, and that the industry should reduce its foreign labor component to 20 percent.[33] Most vociferous were local officials working in Co-operation and Development and Nationalist M.P.s on the East Rand where mines such as ERPM in Boksburg still employed more foreign than local labor. The Chamber of Mines repeatedly deflected criticism by arguing that individual mines were responsible for their own sourcing decisions and that the industry's policies had cabinet approval. Only one mining house, Afrikaner-controlled Gencor, adjusted its policies.[34]

In mid-1984, another round of attempted state intervention became imminent. Ironically, the renewed pressure this time came not from the Department of Co-operation and Development promoting local recruiting, but from Foreign Affairs, which began to pressure the mines to take more foreign labor. The political context was the Nkomati Accord with Mozambique. In May, the Joint South Africa/Mozambique Economic Working Group, set up under the terms of the accord, met in Cape Town and discussed a list of Mozambican demands. These demands included a request that the mining industry take responsibility for flying Mozambican workers to and from the mines, that the proportion of compulsorily deferred pay be increased, and that the number of Mozambicans in the mines should be increased to 80,000 in the short term (and ultimately to 120,000).[35]

Initially, the Chamber of Mines resisted this new interference. Acutely aware of past attempts by the South African government, the bantustan administrations, and the foreign supplier states to influence foreign sourcing, the Chamber argued that the mining industry had the right to pursue its own foreign policy. It emphasized the industry's historical debt to its foreign workers and stressed the importance of maintaining diversification. The mines needed the freedom to choose from ethnic groups with particular skills and intended to continue to employ an "appropriate" number of foreign workers. In a "free enterprise system," furthermore, the employer had the right to choose his own employees.[36]

Later that year, however, pressure increased to help make the Nkomati Accord work by accommodating more Mozambican labor. The government wanted this done without increasing the total number of foreign workers in the mine work force, by reducing elsewhere. They suggested cutting back in Lesotho. Chamber of Mines officials met several times with the Mozambique government. The mines wanted specific concessions related primarily to the transport, health, and physical safety of workers and recruiting officers in exchange for increasing the intake of Mozambican laborers. The Mozambican minister of Labor offered TEBA free rein in Mozambique by agreeing to remove all locally imposed restrictions on the age and geographical origins of new recruits. These restrictions were lifted but Mozambique was less able to deliver on the other demands because of the deteriorating security situation in the country.[37] Nevertheless, the number of Mozambicans in the mines rose by about 12,000. There was no offsetting cutback in Lesotho. In the aftermath of the coup that overthrew Jonathan, the mines reaffirmed their commitment to Basotho labor by increasing their orders and building a new TEBA recruiting complex in Maseru, Lesotho's capital.

In late 1985, the Nkomati Accord fell apart, when it became clear that elements in the South African state had no intention of fulfilling the military provisions of the agreement. Furthermore, mounting international pressure on the South African economy, through disinvestment and the threat of sanctions, provoked South Africa's white politicians to retaliate. State President P. W. Botha went in search of a stick to brandish at the front-line states and found one on the gold mines. In August 1986, Botha threatened to expel all foreign workers should the United Nations invoke mandatory sanctions against South Africa. The figure quoted—1.5 million "foreign" workers—included those from the Transkei and other "independent" bantustans. In October 1986, in retaliation for a landmine blast on the Mozambique/South African border, attributed to the African National Congress (ANC), Botha summarily announced expulsion of Mozambique's 60,000 mineworkers on the termination of their contracts.[38]

The Chamber of Mines vigorously lobbied against this, with some success. By December, a compromise emerged, involving a partial reprieve for the Mozambicans. A ban on novices would remain, but workers in the upper skill categories, or with more than seven-years experience, could stay (an estimated 40–50 percent of the total). Mines with more than 20 percent of their work force in the lowest skill brackets would be given three years to phase the Mozambicans out. Applications could also be made for individuals "on compassionate grounds."

During the course of 1988, the state quietly withdrew its demands, and Mozambican labor stabilized at its pre-Nkomati levels. This is not to suggest that the state would be unable to enforce a policy of expulsion should it wish to do so: it clearly could. What it shows is the inescapably symbiotic nature of the relationship of state and industry. The state could not seriously harm the industry without harming itself: It can categorically order the repatriation of Mozambican miners; the following day the Chamber would pull together the historical precedents and the list of costs to the industry, to the government, and to the government's allies, such as the farmers. The day after, this material would be put before state bureaucrats and the age-old minuet resumed. Before long the bureaucrats will explain to the state president just how far he can go without treading on his own toes, and how he can appear to put the industry in its place without actually doing anything. The outcome of the dance is not predetermined, but neither partner intends to finish it alone. When and if Mozambican labor is finally phased out it will be because both state and industry want it to happen. There is no sign that such a consensus is imminent.

Sourcing and Symbiosis

For the last decade, the gold mining industry has operated with full complements and in market conditions of domestic surplus. In 1978, TEBA calculated that it could recruit an additional 500,000 workers if the mining companies needed them.[39] The figure would undoubtedly be much higher now. A unilateral withdrawal by foreign supplier states poses little threat. The mining companies could doubtless decide to dispense with foreign labor altogether. This might have been the lesson to take from the disruptions in the 1970s, but it was not. That foreign workers continue to find employment in the mines in such numbers is important to the workers, their home communities, and their governments.

The proportion of foreign workers in the mine labor force has remained relatively constant at around 40 percent since the late 1970s (Figure 5.1). With the obvious exception of Zimbabwe, the number of workers from the individual foreign suppliers also remained relatively steady in the 1980s, even increasing slightly in the late 1980s (Figure 5.2). In 1980 the TEBA general manager, Tony Fleischer, argued that the mining companies should make a systematic effort to reduce foreign labor to 30 percent by 1982, replacing them with South African, particularly Zulu, labor. His plan for a further centrally planned reduction of foreign labor was ignored by the mining industry. Company officials rejected Fleischer's argument for an industry-wide policy and offered reasons why they wanted to retain existing levels of foreign labor. Anglo American highlighted its preference for Basotho workers in its Orange Free State mines. Others pointed out that many key posts in the mines were occupied by foreigners. All argued that each mining group should be free to decide its own sourcing strategy.[40]

This exchange with Fleischer came at a time when the labor market had turned irrevocably in favor of the employers. With labor in abundance, workers could no longer choose their mine; the mine owners, on the other hand, could choose labor from where they wanted. The mining groups clearly relished their new powers and rejected the inflexibility of a centralized policy. For the first time, mine labor mixes became a relatively unambiguous reflection of management strategy. Sourcing strategy varied from group to group and mine to mine, though all listened carefully to the strategic arguments of Chamber officials and still relied on the Chamber, through TEBA, to deliver the labor they ordered. When the state tried directly to intervene, however, the groups rallied behind the Chamber banner to ward off any threat to their autonomy.

Only two of the six mining houses (Anglo American and its affiliate JCI) adhered at all closely to the Chamber's guideline of 40 percent foreign labor (Figure 5.3). Goldfields held its foreign labor component at 50 percent and another, AngloVaal, to 40 percent from 1980–1985 (Table 5.2).

Figure 5.3 Composition of Labor Force by Mining House, 1985

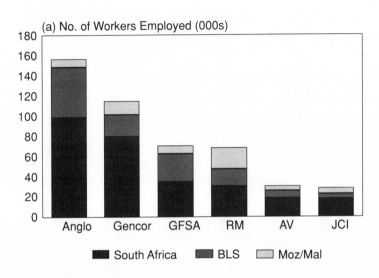

(a) No. of Workers Employed (000s)

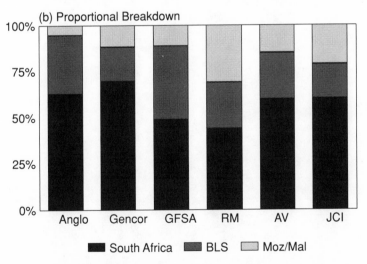

(b) Proportional Breakdown

Source: Unpublished Data from Chamber of Mines of South Africa.

Table 5.2 Proportion of Foreign Labor Employed by Mining Group, 1972-1985[a] (percentages)

	1972	1973	1974	1975	1976	1977	1980	1981	1982	1983	1984	1985
Anglo American	74.4	74.7	71.8	60.0	50.7	46.6	41.2	38.9	37.9	36.9	36.9	39.6
Gencor	79.6	81.9	77.3	66.7	54.0	47.3	34.8	35.0	35.0	32.0	29.9	27.6
Goldfields	85.0	85.9	81.2	74.4	64.0	55.5	51.4	49.0	49.0	49.0	48.8	49.1
Rand Mines	79.9	81.3	74.2	69.7	61.0	54.3	52.0	51.0	53.0	55.0	56.9	58.4
JCI	88.1	85.1	82.5	76.3	61.8	51.9	42.7	36.0	44.0	41.0	39.0	41.0
Anglo Vaal	83.4	82.5	73.8	71.4	58.4	51.2	39.4	37.0	39.0	40.0	43.0	40.0

[a]Figures for 1978-1979 not available.
Source: Unpublished data from Chamber of Mines of South Africa.

Rand Mines rose to nearly 60 percent foreign labor. At the other end of the spectrum was Gencor, the only one of the six mining groups that continued to shed foreign labor through the 1980s (from 47 percent in 1977 to 28 percent in 1985). Yet, while Gencor dispensed with several thousand Basotho workers in the mid-1980s, in 1985 it employed more Swazis, Mozambicans, and Malawians than it did in 1981.

Even within one group, no two mines maintained an identical labor composition. In 1984, the proportion of foreign labor in individual mines varied quite considerably from a low of 24.5 percent at Gencor's Buffels-fontein mine to a high of 74.5 percent at Rand Mines' ERPM (Table 5.1). In consultation with head office, individual mine managers—the "men on the spot"—tended to make the detailed decisions about labor mix. Management autonomy varied from group to group. On Goldfields mines, management followed head office directives more closely and labor composition tended to be more uniform. In Anglo American mines, local management had considerable control over sourcing leading to greater inter-mine variation. To determine the precise (and changing) mix of variables operating on every mine requires an investigation beyond the scope of this study.[41] For our purposes, it is sufficient to identify the common elements in sourcing strategy that explain the continued attraction of foreign labor to most mines.

One argument used by the Chamber of Mines itself is that the industry has a "historical debt" to the foreign suppliers. Another old argument is that certain ethnic groups are better fitted for particular jobs. As one official pointed out, "we say that the Welsh sing well and no-one bats an eyelid, but say that the Basotho are naturally good shaft sinkers and everyone accuses you of being a racist."[42] Whether these stereotypes are true or not, mine officials believe them, as do many workers. They do influence policy.[43] More recently, a new stereotype has emerged. Certain ethnic groups are supposed to be "less interested" in union activities than others. In a buyer's market for labor, the idea only had to be stated, and workers were seen to behave as if ethnicity actually did determine affinity to collective bargaining. Reflecting dependence on the receipts from migrancy, the governments of Malawi, Lesotho, and Mozambique have all felt the pressure to see that their workers act according to the stereotype. To various degrees, they all undertook privately to steer their workers away from the National Union of Mineworkers. For these and other reasons, the position of foreign workers in the mines has tended to be structurally weak. Their behavior reflected this weakness and helped to explain why the mines wanted to retain them. Since the 1987 strike, mines hardest hit by violence and mass dismissals have replaced hundreds of Transkeian workers with Mozambicans who are considered more "loyal" to management.[44]

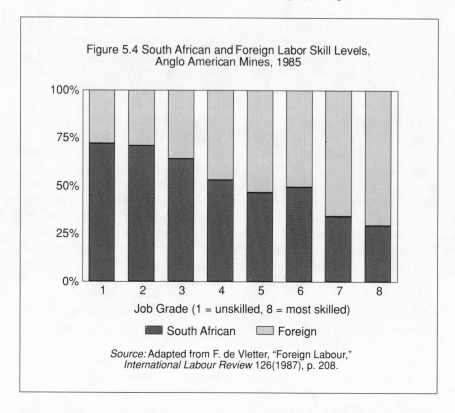

Figure 5.4 South African and Foreign Labor Skill Levels,
Anglo American Mines, 1985

Job Grade (1 = unskilled, 8 = most skilled)

■ South African   ☐ Foreign

Source: Adapted from F. de Vletter, "Foreign Labour,"
International Labour Review 126(1987), p. 208.

In sourcing policy, all mines subscribe to the principle of diversified sourcing. There is hardly a mine without some foreign labor, usually from several different sources. The geographical location of supplier areas also carries weight with management. Both Rand Mines and Anglo American have declared that their policy is to employ workers from the sources closest to the respective mines,[45] a clear endorsement of "commuter migrancy" (see Chapter 7). Workers living close to home can return there more often, supposedly alleviating some of the hardships of migratory labor. The best example of this policy is in the Orange Free State where many mines employ a disproportionate number of workers from neighboring Lesotho, QwaQwa, and Botshabelo. A constant stream of buses and taxis ply the roads on weekends taking Basotho workers home for short visits.

Foreign miners constitute the most experienced and the more skilled component of the work force. They are disproportionately represented in the better-paying, skilled categories (Figure 5.4).[46] Although they are not indispensable, the mines have an incentive to keep them and to avoid or

Table 5.3 Sources of Novice Workers, 1978-1985

Year	Total Novices	South African Novices	Foreign Novices	Foreign as %age of total
1978	68,960	56,924	12,036	17.5
1979	56,223	45,138	11,095	19.7
1980	67,149	57,271	9,878	14.7
1981	64,879	55,051	9,828	15.1
1982	65,364	54,088	11,276	17.3
1983	50,265	44,279	5,986	11.9
1984	53,239	43,914	9,325	17.5
1985	50,699	37,849	12,850	25.3

Source: Data from F. de Vletter, "Foreign Labour on the South African Gold Mines: New Insights on an Old Problem," International Labour Review 126 (1987), p. 213.

defer heavy new training costs. Whether these considerations will continue to operate is now less clear. Since the mid-1970s, Chamber strategists have argued that the mining industry's skilled black workers would eventually have to be South African since foreigners could not be settled in family housing. Now that progress is being made in that direction, the historical hold of foreign workers on skilled posts must inevitably loosen. As skilled and semiskilled foreign workers do retire, they will be replaced not by other foreign workers but by South Africans who are now heavily represented in the middle categories of the job hierarchy. The foreign labor suppliers will increasingly be relegated to supplying unskilled make-up labor.[47]

For most of the 1980s, the mining companies clearly preferred domestic sources for new or "novice" labor. Since 1980, over 80 percent of new workers have come from within South Africa (Table 5.3). Because so few novices are recruited at present (less than 10 percent of the total labor force, down from 35 percent in the mid-1970s) and because there is a large foreign reserve of unemployed workers with mining experience, the mine owners' preference for domestic novices has so far had little effect on the proportion of domestic compared with foreign labor. The foreign work force is aging, however, and there are signs that the number of novices from outside South Africa may begin to rise.

Foreign migrants tend to congregate on some of the oldest and most dangerous mines. They do not do this out of choice. Workers have clear ideas about which mines they prefer but few have the luxury of choosing where to go. Despite the benefits of labor abundance, these mines have still found it difficult to hold South African workers. Labor turnover has declined but is still unacceptably high for detailed manpower planning. Foreign workers—particularly those from Mozambique—tend to stay on and return. For them, a job at ERPM or Durban Deep is still better than nothing at all.

Workers' ability to affect directly the labor composition of a mine is limited. Nevertheless, by returning regularly and repeatedly to a mine they constrain management's ability to effect rapid change. Similarly management is acutely aware of the possibility of worker resistance to overt attempts to substitute workers from one area with those from another.[48] Beyond that, mine management is inundated with requests to sign on unemployed relatives languishing in the rural areas. Others are more creative. In 1983, management discovered a group of Mozambican miners on one West Rand mine with forged South African passports, obtained from a syndicate in Germiston that supplied South African papers to foreign workers for R100 apiece. A year later, the police caught several Angolans with forged documents from the Lebowa bantustan in the northern Transvaal.

Despite the relative safety of foreign jobs in the mines, one recent development that could fundamentally affect the future of foreign migrancy to South Africa is the spread of AIDS through the subcontinent. AIDS has already had a large impact in mines in Zaire and Zambia. Some spokesmen there have predicted that it will soon affect production levels. In 1986, the Chamber of Mines introduced HIV screening, a tacit admission of the vulnerability of its own labor system to the AIDS epidemic. The South African state has characterized AIDS as the new "black peril" and foreign miners as agents of the peril.[49] The Chamber of Mines put pressure on Malawi Life President Banda to allow testing of workers in Malawi, before they travel to South Africa. Banda refused. The Chamber refused to accept untested workers. Malawians going home on leave were blocked from returning to the mines. By the beginning the 1990s, the Malawian complement in the mines fell to under 1,000. Initially it was unclear whether this was mere maneuvering or marked a genuine break with the past. Historical precedent and the logic of symbiosis suggest that as long as both sides need each other an accommodation remains possible. But an issue as explosive as AIDS either could be used as a pretext, if the mining houses wanted one, or—more likely—could become important enough in its own right to force the mines to abandon what remains of their northern labor empire. This would not, of course, be the first time that the politics of disease have constrained the industry's ability to choose the source of its labor. For almost twenty years between 1913 and 1932, the Chamber was barred from recruiting labor from north of 22° south latitude after pneumonia decimated the black mine work force in the first decade of this century. The ban was lifted only on the condition that the most vulnerable workers were protected and after the application of intense political pressure spurred by the industry's expanding labor needs. Subsequently, the development of the Lister anti-pneumococcal vaccine, sulfa drugs, and penicillin neutralized the pneumonia threat. With more than enough labor from other sources, the Chamber of Mines is highly unlikely to lobby as intensely for access to Malawian labor in the 1990s. A medical breakthrough on the treatment and prevention of AIDS, akin to pneumonia treatment in the 1940s, will probably not have the same effects. What is more likely to happen, as it did between 1913 and 1932 (and between 1974 and 1977), is a clandestine movement of Malawians to South Africa where there will always be some mining companies happy to employ them.

The Supplier States: Toward a Labor OPEC?

Over the last twenty years, as regional and international pressure on South Africa escalated, the front-line states faced the policy dilemma of their own citizens migrating to South Africa. Their responses differed markedly despite ten years of effort to evolve a common policy. In April 1978, the United Nations' Economic Commission for Africa and the ILO cosponsored a conference in Lusaka on migratory labor to South Africa. Representatives of twelve black states and the major liberation movements including the African National Congress, the Patriotic Front of Zimbabwe, and the South West Africa People's Organization attended. Also present were researchers from the ILO, and several South African historians, who gave a series of papers highly critical of the migrant labor system. To the general consternation of those present, the ILO's Duncan Clarke argued that "internalization" meant that any leverage the supplier countries might have was fading fast.[50]

Two important decisions came out of the conference. First, the delegates adopted a "Charter of Rights for Migrant Workers in Southern Africa," aimed at improving the lot of foreign workers in South Africa. Second, they committed themselves to "a concerted and collective effort . . . at the national, subregional, regional and international levels to hold the labor-supplying states to withdraw and finally to abolish their supply of migratory labor to South Africa."[51] Planning began for what became the Southern African Labour Commission (SALC) with a brief to carry out the conference resolutions. Simultaneously, the ILO drew up plans for a suppliers' cartel to be called the Association of Home Countries of Migrants that would commit itself to the phased withdrawal of mine labor from South Africa.[52]

The proposal caused sufficient alarm in South Africa to attract a detailed rebuttal by the Chamber of Mines research organization. The critique was despatched to the governments of Lesotho, Mozambique, and Botswana, which were urged not to go along with the plan.[53] In late 1979, the Chamber also developed a contingency plan to expel foreign workers at a rate faster than they could be withdrawn. Within a year all workers from Botswana, Swaziland, and Zimbabwe would be gone. Mozambicans and Malawians would follow within three years. By the end of five years all Basotho would be replaced. Neither plan was ever implemented. The Association of Home Countries idea was stillborn though the SALC continued to meet annually. At each meeting, delegates from the frontline states engaged in rhetorical denunciation of the migrant labor system and renewed pledges to recall their labor. Only Zimbabwe made any effort to recall workers. President Robert Mugabe ordered all Zimbabwean miners to leave South Africa in 1981. None of the others did anything effective, either individually or collectively.

A critical review of the operation of the Southern African Labour Commission by the ILO noted that the organization had not delivered on its commitment to change and to improve the welfare of its workers in South Africa.[54] It pointed out that the SALC countries were not pursuing a policy of withdrawal. In his speech to the SALC in 1984, the new chairman, Rui Baltazar, minister of Finance in Mozambique, repeated the ritual condemnations, arguing that "effective ways and means have to be found to enable us to break away out of the dependency on the system of migrant labour."[55] He made no reference to the Nkomati Accord, signed with South Africa earlier that year, or to simultaneous high-level attempts by the Mozambican government to get the South African mining industry to increase the number of Mozambican migrants to 120,000. Representatives from the other countries of the region would have known of their own governments' attempts to deal unilaterally with the South Africans to the same end.

The inability of the front-line states to mount a systematic withdrawal campaign is not simply a function of the organizational inadequacies of the Southern African Labour Commission. A century of migrant labor to South Africa has deeply entrenched the dependency of the supplier states. Even more important, they have been unable to generate alternative industries and jobs for their citizens. Disengagement may be a desirable political goal, but the constraints are many. These operate at two complementary (and often contradictory) levels, as the governments of the region seek to secure the conditions for continued accumulation, while simultaneously pursuing their own internal strategies of legitimation.

Directly or indirectly, most of the surrounding governments depend on migrant remittances for revenue. For them, summary withdrawal from the migrant labor system would precipitate a severe fiscal crisis. The cash flow from South Africa through compulsory deferred pay and voluntary remittances rose sharply from 1975 to 1984. (Table 5.4). With the mine wage increases of the 1970s and 1980s, the supplier states have become more, not less, dependent on this source of revenue. The increase in remittances (and therefore in state receipts from taxation and interest on deferred pay) coincided with a decline in alternative revenues, particularly with falling commodity prices on world markets and civil war. Foreign migrants to South Africa have been increasingly squeezed out of other sectors of employment. These trends have deepened the region's dependence on migrant income from the gold mines.

The dependence of governments is mirrored in the position of the families that supply the labor. Thousands of rural households throughout the region depend on mine income for survival. To order the return of migrant workers, without providing those households with an alternative source of income, would be politically hazardous. None of the supplier states are anxious to confront their own working class in this way. Even their attempts to exert greater control over migrant workers have met resistance. In Lesotho, the government's effort in the mid-1970s to increase the rates of compulsory deferred pay, which would be paid into the state bank, provoked widespread rioting and the desertion of 15,000 Basotho miners.[56]

Since then, Basotho miners have devised various strategies to circumvent these restrictions. Many of the workers who return home each weekend do so simply to draw their deferred pay from Lesotho banks before returning to the mines. This represents a considerable loss of revenue to the government and an unnecessary expense to the miners themselves. In 1986, hoping to put a stop to this movement, the Lesotho authorities declared that miners could be paid only in local currency. Almost immediately, scores of informal money-changers began to operate outside banks and recruiting offices. Once again the miners had bested their government in the struggle for control of the mine wage.

Disengagement from the migrant labor system would require, at the very least, the provision of new employment opportunities at home. With rising domestic unemployment, and limited job creation rates, these enabling conditions simply do not exist. The ILO's cartel proposal of the late 1970s called for a program of international assistance to make repatriation a feasible strategy. This has been ignored. One possible conduit for aid, the Southern African Development Co-ordination Conference (SADCC), has consistently refused to place the migrant labor question on its agenda. It denied the repeated requests of the Southern African Labour Commission for incorporation. It is not clear to outside observers why SADCC has taken this line but most are agreed that until there is a change of heart, the commission will remain ineffectual.[57] Even then, it would probably have little leverage.

Table 5.4 Mine Deferred Pay and Remittances by Country, 1975-1989 (R million)

	1975	1976	1977	1978	1979	1980	1981	1982	1983	1984	1987	1989
Lesotho	16.8	20.4	20.2	31.0	31.4	34.9	52.0	111.5	154.2	186.3	216.4	408.4
Botswana	5.9	9.6	8.2	13.1	10.8	13.6	17.1	20.0	24.0	23.6	21.6	19.6
Swaziland	3.1	4.4	5.2	6.8	6.2	7.8	9.6	9.2	11.1	11.4	15.0	16.1
Malawi	22.4	2.1	1.0	10.6	9.2	13.5	14.9	18.9	23.6	26.2	46.7	17.0
Mozambique	33.1	40.3	25.9	28.7	29.3	32.9	52.8	51.1	59.3	70.2	109.9	114.3
Zimbabwe	0.0	0.7	8.5	9.5	6.5	6.3	5.9	0.0	0.0	0.0	0.0	0.0

Source: Adapted from Mining Survey 274 (1986), p. 38; and Chamber of Mines Review (1987-1988, 1989). Data for 1985, 1986, 1988 unavailable.

The idea of labor sanctions against South Africa has always had greater appeal in the corridors of the UN and the ILO than in the region itself. The South African mines and the supplier governments still share a common interest in sustaining the flow of labor across the international border. The dependence is mutual or symbiotic; but it is far from equal. The employment of foreign workers by the mining companies has become increasingly discretionary. One of the fundamental principles of the entire migrant labor system is to always provide the mine owners with a variety of choices. Choice provides leverage, the ability to play one individual off against another, one country off against another. And leverage creates unequal dependence. For a short time in the 1970s, a series of disasters befell the mining houses and it appeared that the supplier countries could exert real leverage themselves. There is no sign that they seriously recognized the possibility of colluding against the Chamber until it was too late. But even if they had, they will never be truly free of the drawing power of the Rand until they can create alternatives, providing revenue and jobs in their own country.

6

Mine Labor Mobilization
in South Africa, 1974–1980

In October 1970, the Native Recruiting Corporation's man at Tugela Ferry joined recruiters throughout South Africa complaining of the difficulties of getting South African blacks to work in the mines: "My personal feeling is that the NRC is losing ground in the area because of the loss of personal contact between the representatives and many areas in the district. The output from this office is at a very low ebb and I am finding it difficult to fill my time. My mind is definitely slowing down and stagnating as a result of lack of work."[1] His personal problems may have been real; but his analysis of the reasons for them was not illuminating.

During the 1960s and into the early 1970s, most South African workers could find far less dangerous, more remunerative employment than the gold mines could offer. The rapid expansion of job opportunities and widening wage differentials in other sectors provided many migrant workers with employment choices unknown since the early years of the century. The establishment of state-run labor bureaus in the midst of traditional mine recruiting areas and widespread contracting of labor outside the law broadened the opportunities still further.[2] The average number of South African miners fell inexorably from 144,000 in 1962 to about 69,000 in 1972 and seemed certain to continue to fall. The NRC's immense administrative machinery lay largely idle and grew rusty with disuse.

Only a few years later, the story had changed completely. In July 1978, the recruiter at Tugela Ferry reported that: "Rural workseekers in the district flood the office daily looking for work. Some from other (more distant) districts phone the office daily looking for work. Some arrive here and choose to wait at the office for days waiting for open mines."[3] After 1977, field reports from all districts emphasized: the large crowds of unemployed sleeping outside mine recruiting offices; the long distances

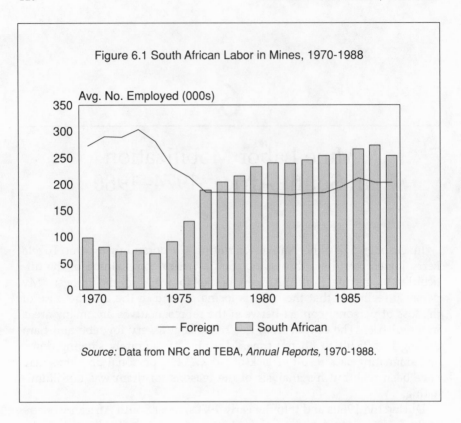

Figure 6.1 South African Labor in Mines, 1970-1988

— Foreign   South African

Source: Data from NRC and TEBA, *Annual Reports*, 1970-1988.

traveled and the patient waiting, often for months; the desperate appeals by relatives of aspirant miners; the imaginative attempts to bribe officials and forge documents; the willingness to work even on some of the worst mines; and the preference for better-paying underground over less-dangerous surface mine work.

The turnaround transformed mine recruiting figures. Between 1973 and 1977, the number of South African recruits jumped from fewer than 90,000 to 366,000. After 1977, the annual number of South African recruits began to fall again. This decline was offset by increasing contract length. Consequently, the total number of South Africans in mine employment continued upward to its 1987 figure of around 265,000 (Figure 6.1). This expanded reserve of domestic labor willing to accept mine work was the direct result of demographic change, economic stagnation, structural unemployment, and state policy. The forced resettlement of hundreds of thousands of blacks and the foisting of "independence" on black reserves ruled by petty and pliable black tyrants, together with substantial mine wage increases, all combined to radically increase the flow of South

African blacks to the mines. The Chamber of Mines tapped this labor through an intensive publicity and recruiting drive. Traditional mine labor supply areas yielded many additional workers, and the recruiters bundled new regions into the system. Yet, the industry did not have everything its own way; in some parts of the country, it made few inroads.

The mutual dependence of state and industry became very intense during the 1970s. Their common interest in expanding South African mine employment promoted closer cooperation. Influx control had captured millions of migrant workers and held them in the bantustans for South African industry, including mining. The policy predated the 1970s and was not designed to serve mining interests alone. Yet the renewed availability of domestic labor was a windfall to an industry whose foreign strategy had recently faltered. Only with the crisis of 1974 did the mines begin to appreciate the significance of this situation. The Chamber of Mines now argued that the state should abandon its protection of farm and urban labor and open the entire South African labor market to their recruiters, which evoked an ambivalent response. The government supported recruitment of urban labor but hesitated on the politically sensitive demand for access to the "white" countryside. In the end, the mounting surplus of labor in the reserves provided a sufficient supply and eased the potential conflict over seigneurial rights to black farm labor.

Attracting Domestic Labor

The level of black unemployment in South Africa is a vexed issue. Official statistics invariably underestimate the problem compared with even the most conservative estimates by independent analysts. All agree, however, that high unemployment levels predate the 1970s. In the 1960s, general unemployment coexisted paradoxically with acute domestic labor shortage in the mining industry.[4] Many of the unemployed were not eligible for mine work because they were women, too old, too unhealthy, or simply feared working underground. But workers also frequently thronged government labor bureaus while adjacent mine recruiting offices were deserted. The chance of a better-paying and less-dangerous job in secondary industry made the wait—even in deprived circumstances—preferable.

The number of jobless blacks rose sharply in the 1970s (Table 6.1).[5] A cyclical downturn in the South African economy after 1975 aggravated structural weaknesses and pushed estimated unemployment from nearly 14 percent in 1975 to almost 21 percent in 1979. Job creation failed to keep pace with the estimated 300,000 new workers entering the job market annually. Mass retrenchment in construction and transportation increased the jobless rolls. Most of the new miners in the 1970s had

Table 6.1 Black Unemployment in South Africa, 1970-1981 (000s)

	Labor Supply	Employed	Unemployed	% Unemployed
1970	7,112	6,274	838	11.8
1971	7,312	6,383	929	12.7
1972	7,519	6,414	1,105	14.7
1973	7,729	6,701	1,028	13.3
1974	7,938	6,901	1,037	13.1
1975	8,150	7,033	1,117	13.7
1976	8,368	7,113	1,255	15.0
1977	8,588	7,125	1,463	17.0
1978	8,811	7,096	1,715	19.5
1979	9,039	7,173	1,866	20.6
1980	9,276	7,351	1,925	20.8
1981	9,497	7,493	2,004	21.1

Source: Adapted from C. Simkins, "Structural Unemployment Revisited," South African Labour and Development Research Unit, University of Cape Town, Fact Sheet No. 1 (Cape Town, 1982), p. 6.

Table 6.2 Proportion of Miners with Previous Employment Experience by Sector, 1976

	Zulu	Xhosa	Tswana	Total
White Agriculture	29.1	24.0	22.4	25.2
Other Mining	6.5	9.3	4.8	6.9
Manufacturing	26.8	15.6	23.9	22.1
Public Utilities	9.7	1.8	8.8	6.8
Construction	40.0	21.3	32.1	31.2
Commerce	19.7	3.9	15.5	13.0
Hotelling	16.2	2.7	8.2	9.1
Transportation	15.0	9.0	10.3	11.5
Banking	1.8	-	1.2	1.0
Services	24.7	13.2	8.2	15.4

Source: Unpublished data from the late Professor J. Nattrass, University of Natal, Durban.

previously worked in other sectors: over 30 percent in construction, 25 percent in commercial agriculture, and 22 percent in manufacturing (Table 6.2).[6] In the early 1980s, severe drought in the countryside added thousands to the jobless queues. Until early 1977, any new worker who wanted to try the mines could do so. Thereafter, the vacancies dried up, recruiting-office line-ups lengthened and the drop-out rates from the mines fell. The mines became correspondingly more selective.

Of the many rural unemployed who became miners in the 1970s, most had limited access to alternative means of support. The collapse of agriculture in the bantustans and the resulting widespread landlessness and deprivation meant intensified dependence on migrant income for survival.[7] In the country's new rural slums, families were even more desperate. Forced resettlement, chillingly documented by the Surplus People Project, swept over three million people from white farms, urban areas, and "black spots" (black settlements in "white" farming areas) to these rural ghettos.[8] Over a third of them were farm workers, displaced by mechanization and the abolition of labor tenancy. The state herded them into the grim, hopeless resettlement camps. The mines turned thankfully to these legions of the dispossessed when they needed more South African labor after 1974.

Despite this windfall, the mining industry still needed additional measures to attract black workers. The wage increases after 1972 helped to reverse the earlier pattern, which saw the rural unemployed waiting in penury for scarce industrial work rather than accept an available mine job. The quadrupling of the gold price to US$159 per ounce by 1974 provided the necessary condition, though not a sufficient cause, for higher rates.[9] Initially, wages increased slowly, reflecting resistance from the more marginal producers. They argued that South African workers would not respond until mine wages matched those in manufacturing. The lower-grade mines, they said, could not afford such rates. It took the Malawian withdrawal of 1974, and the threatened disruption in the Mozambican supply, to convince even the poorer mines that they had to change. Between 1973 and 1976, blacks' wages tripled and the ratio of whites' to blacks' wages was cut in half.[10] These increases caused the mines to be flooded with new workers (Table 6.3).

To advertise the news of higher wages and to promote mine work, the Chamber of Mines embarked on an aggressive recruiting and propaganda campaign reminiscent of its last major push in the 1940s and early 1950s. Many of the old-style trading stores had been replaced by chain stores with little capability for recruiting. Under Tony Fleischer's direction, the Chamber adopted a more professional and less paternalistic approach to recruiting (a prelude to the computer control that was to follow). The recruiting budget increased substantially, and the Chamber retained the American public relations multinational firm, J. Walter Thompson, to promote mine work on radio, in the black press, and throughout the rural areas.[11] An analysis of the domestic labor supply potential commissioned by the Chamber of Mines identified the northwestern Transvaal, the western Orange Free State, the eastern Cape, and Natal as potential

Table 6.3 Domestic Sources of Labor, 1970-1978

	Cape Province	OFS	T'vaal	Natal	Transkei	C'kei	Bop'wana	Other
Number of Recruits								
1970	13,090	1,979	1,071	6,187	42,556	3,556	2,013	605
1971	9,469	1,633	713	4,474	34,518	2,380	1,334	435
1972	9,989	1,706	557	4,372	37,615	2,479	1,312	444
1973	13,480	2,177	750	4,834	40,961	3,075	1,890	602
1974	13,986	2,710	539	4,885	40,281	2,904	1,779	584
1975	30,902	3,521	1,794	9,973	65,747	5,476	3,758	1,862
1976	35,117	6,471	3,690	18,866	88,496	13,662	12,156	3,415
1977	39,265	6,458	5,593	32,103	126,894	20,322	18,098	13,938
1978	24,577	9,118	5,666	28,919	113,200	13,199	15,499	13,934
Number of Novice Recruits								
1970	2,892	498	230	1,076	5,348	531	407	94
1971	1,757	450	191	691	4,115	226	243	53
1972	2,209	493	113	722	5,267	319	310	32
1973	3,474	682	235	939	6,093	585	460	53
1974	3,403	951	139	879	5,742	481	451	12
1975	10,850	1,537	910	3,312	14,097	1,359	1,412	181
1976	10,662	2,656	2,162	6,830	18,022	4,603	4,768	481
1977	9,657	2,288	3,208	12,037	23,375	5,817	5,702	5,597
1978	4,209	3,059	3,002	9,303	17,244	2,415	4,204	4,505

Source: Unpublished data from the late Professor J. Nattrass, University of Natal, Durban.

"high-yielding" areas.[12] The NRC (renamed The Employment Bureau of Africa, or TEBA, in 1977) launched a comprehensive recruiting drive throughout all the districts to which it had legal access. During the 1970s, the bureau opened over twenty-five new recruiting offices, the majority in largely untapped Bophuthatswana, the northern Transvaal (seventeen new offices) and Natal (Figure 6.2).

In traditional mine labor source regions, such as the Transkei, the NRC expanded its recruiting net by restaffing old and opening new suboffices run by black clerks. Active recruitment in the catchment areas around the offices dramatically increased. There were some areas, however, that remained inaccessible. Black workers in the so-called "white" farms and towns remained out of reach of mine recruiters despite efforts to remove legal barriers. In the open areas, the bureau adopted new strategies to expand the range of each recruiting office. It augmented the salaried recruiting personnel with black runners who no longer "ran" but spread the news of higher mine wages from Chamber-supplied bicycles, motorcycles, and even horses. The NRC courted the remaining rural traders, both black and white, luring them with capitation fees, and resumed its game of enticing labor from other employers, including its old adversary, the sugar recruiters. Mobile recruiting stations operated in the densely populated resettlement camps. NRC officials made daily visits to district and "tribal" labor bureaus and Bantu Administration Board offices, to magistrates' and "tribal" courts, to chiefs' villages, to rural market places, and to dipping tanks and cattle sales. Everywhere, they distributed "propaganda" and gave impromptu speeches on the supposed attractions of mine work.[13]

As in times past, tribal chiefs became willing allies and regularly assembled their followers to hear the recruiters' pitch. Movie vans roamed the rural areas, showing promotional films at these and other meetings and in the high schools. In one of the films, made and screened for Kwazulu, Homeland Leader Gatsha Buthelezi himself enthusiastically endorsed mine work.[14] At the schools, recruiters addressed the children, handed out sweets and footballs, and distributed brochures to take home. The NRC also used mini-vans to pick up recruits at various "collection points." Recruits who came on their own received reimbursement for their bus or rail fare.

Farmers and sugar-plantation owners responded to the competition as they had in earlier decades when the mining companies confronted them. They refurbished their recruiting organizations or created new ones in order to fight back.[15] In Natal, black runners from rival organizations such as the Sugar Industry Labour Organization disrupted mine recruiting meetings with embarrassing questions about safety and conditions in the mines. Natal was important to the overall strategy because of the large,

134

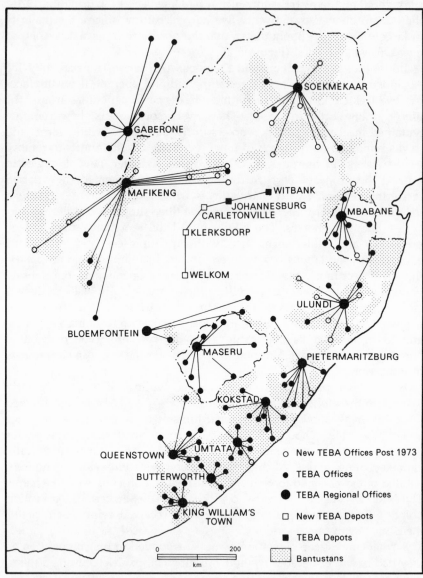

New TEBA Offices Post 1973 ○

TEBA Offices ●

TEBA Regional Offices ●

New TEBA Depots □

TEBA Depots ■

Bantustans

GABERONE

SOEKMEKAAR

MAFIKENG

WITBANK

JOHANNESBURG
CARLETONVILLE

KLERKSDORP

MBABANE

WELKOM

ULUNDI

BLOEMFONTEIN

MASERU

PIETERMARITZBURG

KOKSTAD

QUEENSTOWN

UMTATA

BUTTERWORTH

KING WILLIAM'S
TOWN

0   200
km

Figure 6.2 TEBA recruiting network, 1980. *Source:* TEBA Regional Map, compiled and produced by Map Studio, Wendywood, South Africa, 1982.

untapped store of labor in Kwazulu.[16] Given the long-standing antipathy of Zulu workers to the mines, the Chamber was forced to take special steps to open this source. In the 1960s, the number of Zulu miners, never large, had fallen from roughly 17,000 to below 5,000, a tiny fraction of the available work force. With the onset of the labor crisis in 1974, a Chamber delegation enlisted the support of Chief Gatsha Buthelezi for a major effort to reverse the historical pattern. Buthelezi asked the South African government to remove all mine recruiting restrictions in Kwazulu. Buthelezi, King Goodwill, and other Kwazulu officials publicly urged mining employment upon Zulu workers and made several highly visible mine visits.

In 1975, the mine owners made an important concession. Nine mining companies agreed to accept anyone from Kwazulu for surface work, which was much less unpopular than the underground jobs. The recruiters planned to encourage the recruits to take underground contracts once they arrived in the mines. In an effort to raise participation rates in hitherto underexploited regions, the Chamber routed all orders for surface workers to Natal, Bophuthatswana, and Lebowa and away from the established areas. A few years later the Chamber underlined the importance it attached to Kwazulu by establishing a new regional recruiting office at Ulundi and appointing a fluent Zulu linguist to head the operation.[17]

Except in the Transkei and eastern Cape, black workers in South Africa were generally slow to respond to the initial wage increases of 1971–1973 (Table 6.3).[18] The much larger wage increase of 1975 was critical. Between 1974 and 1975, in response, labor from almost all domestic source areas more than doubled. The Transkei provided the largest absolute number of new recruits. Between 1975 and 1976, the labor from Natal/Kwazulu, the Ciskei, and Bophuthatswana doubled again as layoffs elsewhere continued and workers had to look to the mines, if only temporarily.

A new constituency of worker emerged. In established areas such as the Transkei, the proportion of novices rose to between 20 and 30 percent of new recruits. In the newer recruiting zones, however, the proportion of novices reached 40 to 50 percent. Most of these men were new only to mining, not to wage labor. The largest increase in migrants from the Transkei came in 1976 and 1977, when an extra 38,488 miners joined (fewer than 20 percent novices). When Transkei received its bogus independence from Pretoria, Transkeian migrants found it harder to find alternative employment.[19]

The mines' internal labor market divided into three distinctive spatial zones: traditional suppliers of domestic mine labor, which experienced a major resurgence in the 1970s; areas opened up to the mines on a significant scale for the first time; and those parts of the country where the mines met concerted resistance to their recruiting drive. The thirty magisterial districts of the Transkei, each with its own mine recruiting office, all fell into the first category. Bizana, Engcobo, Lusikisiki, and Matatiele each supplied over 5,000 recruits in 1976 (more than the entire Transvaal). Other areas included the Ciskei, the corridor between the Ciskei and the Transkei, southern Natal, and the Ingwavuma district on the Mozambican border. In southern Natal, a depression in construction and retrenchment in the Durban-Pinetown-Pietermaritzburg manufacturing complex created many new miners (see Figure 6.3).[20]

The mines gained access to several new sources in the 1970s. The flow of mine labor from virtually every district of white and black South Africa increased during the period 1975–1977. The most important new areas included previously untapped bantustans, small urban centers and some white districts bordering the bantustans, and the rural resettlement areas. The internal labor frontier pushed into the northern Transvaal bantustans, Bophuthatswana, Lebowa, Gazankulu, and Venda and penetrated the "white" districts bordering the Ciskei and the Transkei. In central and northern Kwazulu, a similar trend developed. The flow of recruits doubled between 1974 and 1975 and again between 1975 and 1976.

In 1977, the mines hired over 30,000 recruits in Natal with the promise of more to come. The importance of Buthelezi who promoted mine work is uncertain. Without the sharp wage increases, however, even Buthelezi's exhortations would probably have meant little. Like so much else, the Buthelezi connection coincided with increasingly favorable labor market conditions of depression and growing unemployment. Large numbers of workers from more remote labor reserves elsewhere in the country had even less labor market choice than those in Natal. That, coupled with forced resettlement, guaranteed that when mine wages increased, workers would be available.

The number of miners from the sprawling resettlement slums rose appreciably. Witsieshoek in the QwaQwa bantustan north of Lesotho increased its mine labor force from fewer than 150 in the early 1970s to 4,000 by 1978 (and topped 7,000 in late 1985).[21] At Thaba Nchu, in the central Orange Free State close to the dumping ground of Botshabelo, mine recruits rose from less than 1,000 in 1972 to over 4,500 in 1978 (and to more than 20,000 by 1985).[22] Other resettlement areas experienced smaller but still significant increases: Nqutu in central Natal (from less than fifty miners in the early 1970s to 900 by 1982); the Swazi bantustan of Kangwane, which saw a major influx of families forcibly removed from "black spots," white farms, and small towns in the eastern Transvaal (from less than 500 recruits in the early 1970s to nearly 5,000 in 1984); and the Winterveld area north of Pretoria.[23] In the 1980s, mine orders

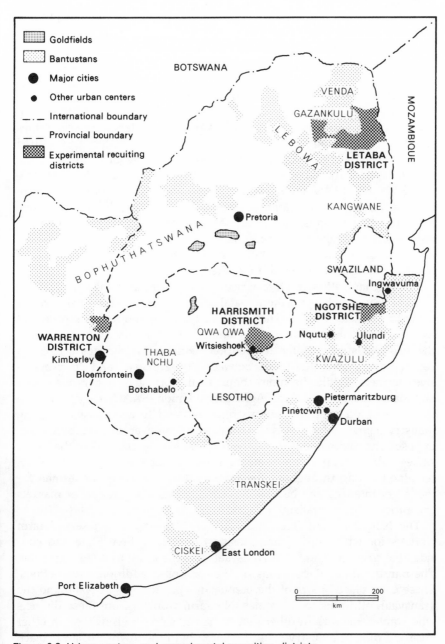

Figure 6.3 Urban centers and experimental recruiting districts

directed specifically to the resettlement areas continued to rise, while those to most other rural areas fell. Without question the mines profited from the teeming resettlement slums created by state policy.

The Conflict Resumes

The mining industry met most resistance in the white-owned farming areas and in the towns. Opposition from farmers and the reluctance of urban workers explains this resistance. Conflict over labor between mines and farms has a long history.[24] The nature of the conflict had shifted considerably by the 1970s, however, mainly because of changes in the composition of the labor force in commercial agriculture itself. During the 1950s and 1960s, the growing capital-intensity of white agriculture led to technological innovation, consolidation of farm units, and the move toward a smaller, semiskilled, more permanent farm labor force.[25] Farmers drew additional labor, on a seasonal basis, from the bantustans or from neighboring "black spots." During harvest time, they sent their trucks into the bantustans to round up workers.

The mechanization of white agriculture was slow and uneven, however. In some areas, such as northern Natal and parts of the Transvaal, farmers clung to obsolete controls (such as labor tenancy) and defied central and local government efforts to hasten change. Labor tenancy continued during the 1970s, despite its official abolition. Differential changes across the country aggravated the divide between "progressive" and "unprogressive" farmers. While the more commercially oriented owners may have dominated the South African Agricultural Union (SAAU), they refused to ride roughshod over the "unprogressives" and to acquiesce to mining industry demands for access to farm labor. Moreover, many progressives opposed the mining companies themselves, fearing the loss of their own skilled labor. Support for protectionist state labor methods, therefore, remained strong throughout the farming sector, even if spokesmen for the larger interests had become fervent advocates of "free labor markets and progressive capitalism" in agriculture.[26]

The Native Labour Regulation Act of 1911 had long reserved farm workers for white agriculture, closing the Orange Free State and considerable tracts of Natal, the Transvaal, and the Cape to mine recruiting. The Bantu Labour Regulations of 1965 imposed additional restrictions. These even placed parts of the bantustans, particularly in Natal and the Transvaal, off limits to the mines. Nonfarm workers from these districts who wanted to work in other sectors had to sign on elsewhere. In other areas the mining industry could recruit only in the townships and "black spots," and not from the resident farm-labor population. In any case, no black farm worker could leave a farm without the farmer's written per-

Table 6.4 Districts of Origin of South African Mineworkers, 1970

	Open Districts		Closed Districts		Total	
	Number	%	Number	%	Number	%
Bantustans	66,373	73.5	2,313	2.5	68,686	76.0
White Areas	12,946	14.3	8,690	9.7	21,636	24.0
Total	79,319	87.8	11,003	12.2	90,322	100.0

Source: Unpublished data from the late Professor J. Nattrass, University of Natal, Durban.

mission. It was an offense for other employers to engage workers without such letters of permission.

During the 1960s and 1970s, the state became firmly committed to agricultural modernization and to ridding the white countryside of "excess" black labor. By endorsing the abolition of labor tenancy, the government merely put itself on the side of the economic forces eroding this long-established system. Officials wanted white agriculture to make more efficient use of black labor and began to use influx-control measures to clamp down on "illegal" employment on the farms.[27] During the 1960s, the state began to consider withdrawal of protection of the farm-labor supply but, fearful of the political consequences, the first real steps did not come until later. From 1971, all employers, including the farmers, had to register their labor with the new Bantu Administration Boards. It followed that unregistered workers would be evicted from farms. Farmers resisted registration, as did many workers. In a more intrusive measure, which failed in the end, local Labour Control Boards were legislated to oversee registration, rationalize the allocation of black farm labor, and ensure the productive employment of resident farm labor.[28] In comparison with previous policies, these were radical measures.

Into this apparently favorable climate, the Chamber of Mines inserted a formal request in 1974 for abolition of farm-labor protection. Convinced that its target of 50,000 additional South African workers was unattainable, the Chamber of Mines turned to the other obvious internal pool. Marshalling the government's own statistics and the reports of its own research organization, the Chamber argued that farmers wasted their labor and had too much of it.[29] The underemployed included squatters, labor tenants, and residents of "black spots." The Chamber claimed that state policy excluded the industry from 85 percent of available farm labor. In the early 1970s, less than 13 percent of South African miners came from districts closed to recruiting (Table 6.4). To get to the mines, these workers had to leave the farms illegally to sign on at mine recruiting offices elsewhere.

Farmers continued to resist invasion of their labor preserve, and the government continued to listen to them. Between 1971 and 1974, farmers' complaints forced the closure of several rural districts, including Herschel in the Transkei to mine recruiting.[30] Piet Koornhof, by then minister of Mines, accepted the Chamber of Mines' analysis in mid-1974. But the Department of Mines lost out consistently to the Departments of Bantu Administration and Agriculture, which responded to the farmers' unions. Nobody ever won a parliamentary seat on the votes of mine owners. Koornhof advanced the Chamber's argument that the labor crisis was severe, that government mining revenues were at risk and that state support for the industry's local sourcing drive was therefore in the "national interest." He called for an interdepartmental feasibility study to determine whether and how the mines could recruit farm workers on short contracts during seasonal lulls in farming activity. The proposal excluded the South African Agricultural Union, and perhaps for this reason it never got off the ground.[31]

In September 1974, the Chamber of Mines approached the minister of Agriculture, Hendrik Schoeman, who brought together the Chamber and representatives of SAAU and the Transvaal Agricultural Union. The SAAU flatly rejected the Chamber's time-sharing proposal. It said that a farm labor surplus existed only in very limited areas, such as the Transvaal lowveld, and pointed out that the farms themselves relied on seasonal labor from the bantustans. Second, the SAAU argued that with rapid mechanization, farms now used their labor efficiently, productively, and continuously. Third, the union complained that if the mines recruited farm labor on short contracts, white farmers would have to provide for their relatives, still resident on the farms. In the face of this intransigence, the Chamber of Mines dropped its labor-sharing proposals and abandoned the frontal assault on resident farm labor. It turned instead toward the other, less controversial parts of the labor supply in the white areas: nonfarm workers, residents of "black spots," squatters on absentee farms and government land, and inhabitants of small townships in farm towns and dorps.

After more badgering from the Chamber, and pressure from elements in the state, the SAAU finally agreed to identify limited farming areas for experimental recruiting as a test of the surplus labor hypothesis. Local white farmers' unions opposed even this move, pointing to the probable adverse effects and warning of the disruption of farming operations. Events in the Orange Free State served to underscore these fears. In early 1975, farmers caused an uproar when they discovered that several hundred farm laborers had signed on at the mine recruiting office at Thaba Nchu. A delegation to Pretoria protested vehemently and also complained of the incessant mine publicity over the radio. The SAAU quickly withdrew its support of the experiment. It asked the NRC to pull out completely from the Free State and not to send recruiting agents into white districts without farmers' permission. Confident of its own political leverage, the union also asked the Chamber to deal directly with the Department of Bantu Administration on all future labor matters. To the irritation of the mining industry, that department showed ever-greater sensitivity to the farm lobby.

In mid-1975, Bantu Administration formally advised the mines to concentrate on urban recruiting and leave the farmers to themselves. In the field, the Chamber submitted applications for recruiting licenses in more than twenty closed districts in the Cape and the Transvaal. Local officials ignored or refused them all. In Natal, the Bantu Affairs commissioner simply informed the Chamber that there was no point in even applying since it faced automatic rejection. In the Orange Free State, the flow of farm labor dried up when the commissioners refused to attest recruits. Officials sent back young farm workers who streamed into the NRC office at Thaba Nchu. Defending this position, Pretoria announced that laborers with legal obligations to farmers had to honor them and could not go to the mines.

After more representations, the Chamber finally put its case to the South African Cabinet in July 1975. It stressed the importance of increasing the proportion of South African mine labor. Protection of the farm labor supply encouraged waste, gave farmers no incentive to improve working conditions, and therefore contributed to labor shortages in some districts. The mines also claimed that the introduction of competition might rescue floundering official efforts to force white farmers to register their farm labor. Whatever the support for these arguments amongst the politicians, the state made few actual concessions. Farmers were voters, and the rural vote helped sustain the National party. The government simply agreed that Bantu Administration should convene tripartite meetings with mining representatives and the SAAU to arrange a carefully controlled experimental recruiting campaign in selected white farm areas, the same scheme that the Chamber had tried to negotiate privately with the SAAU.[32]

Officials wanted to see the evidence that mine recruiting would simply mop up "surplus" labor in white rural districts. Minister M. C. Botha declared that "the recruitment of Black workers in the white area—in urban areas and on the *platteland*—must take place within the framework of existing labor control; it should be concentrated on seasonal workers (and) unemployed or surplus workers."[33] The state accepted the proposition that controlled competition from the mines would force farmers to register their labor with the administration boards and discourage the widespread use of "illegal" labor. By barring the Chamber from recruiting *registered* farm workers in the experimental districts, the administration boards could pressure white farmers to protect their labor by registering it. In early 1977, the SAAU finally supported registration and declared that all white farmers should comply with the law. Many still refused, but they could not expect their union to defend them. The administration boards now got tougher and began to prosecute farmers in areas such as northern Natal who still refused to register their labor. Nevertheless, resistance from farmers to the experimental recruiting campaign continued.

The SAAU and the Chamber of Mines worked out the terms of the experiment, and the union insisted successfully on tight controls. The Chamber asked for access to at least eight districts but got only four, including Letaba in the northern Transvaal and the Louwsburg section of Ngotshe district in northern Natal (see Figure 6.3). In the Free State, the Chamber remained excluded from the farming heartland, and had to be content with the Harrismith area. In the Cape, it completely failed to gain access to the white countryside. In the chosen district of Warrenton, near Kimberley, the state initially permitted recruiting only in the black township. The farmers insisted the mines were not to recruit registered (or even unregistered) farm workers in any of the districts. The Chamber reluctantly agreed on condition that the local Bantu Administration Boards make a serious effort to register all farm labor.

As for farm workers themselves, only those who had written permission from their landlords could proceed to the mines. To restrict the mines still further, each experimental district was overseen by a local committee comprising representatives from mining, farming, and the Department of Bantu Administration.[34] Not surprisingly, the mine recruiters had to return any wrongly recruited, registered workers. They agreed not to send publicity vans or black runners onto or near white farms. Even so, the local farmers' unions in the four experimental districts accepted the campaign reluctantly and only after securing additional safeguards from the administration boards.

Two years of protracted negotiation between the Chamber, the state, and the SAAU had yielded only this unimpressive experiment, and the mines remained excluded from the white countryside. By the time the experiment began, however, the labor shortage in the mines had eased considerably. The industry had recovered almost completely from the loss of the Malawians and was running again near full complement. By the beginning of 1977, recruiting offices throughout the country began turning away labor for the first time since the early 1960s. The sense of urgency, so marked two years before, vanished. The Chamber president, R. S. Lawrence, tried to throw in the towel, stating that the battle with the farmers was more trouble than it was worth. Yet the Chamber persisted with its campaign. Bureaucratic momentum helps to explain this persistence, as does continuing uncertainty about the foreign labor flow from Mozambique and, to a lesser degree, Rhodesia and Lesotho. In addition, the drive to expand the labor supply had become a crusade against the whole notion of state protection of white agriculture. The Chamber redefined its project to accommodate this shift in emphasis.

The earlier focus on short-term recruiting results gave way to an attempt to secure a long-term change in policy. The Chamber now aimed to conduct a benign, low-key recruiting effort without antagonizing local farming committees or disrupting local labor patterns in any way. If this could be achieved, the industry believed it could disarm the farmers and make the case for the abolition of protection. In pursuit of this goal, the mining industry ran its experiment very much by the rules. At local planning meetings, officials even offered to impose a strict monthly quota on the number of workers recruited.

When the state proposed dropping the experiment for lack of results, the Chamber resisted, claiming that failure in a specific area did not invalidate the objectives. For the first time, the mining industry had access to labor areas from which it was formerly totally excluded. Its aim now was simply to show that the mining and agricultural sectors could live together. The easing of the shortage meant that the industry could afford a more statesmanlike approach. As competition lessened, the farmers could also mute their opposition. Recruiting figures for the four experimental districts confirmed that the campaign was not successful in delivering much new labor. Of the nearly 1,000 workers recruited at the four experimental recruiting offices between May 1976 and December 1977, less than 5 percent came from white farms; the rest were from small urban townships and neighboring bantustan areas. The results of the "experiment" were inseparable therefore from normal bantustan recruiting.

In the Ngotshe district of northern Natal, an area of beef farming and irrigated agriculture, the local labor scene was particularly complex and delicate.[35] A large number of absentee landlords "farmed" African squatters rather than the land. There were also at least three "black spots" recently amalgamated to form a new district of Kwazulu. White farmers in the district still depended on labor tenancy despite its formal abolition in Natal in 1970. Many of these "unprogressives" had failed to register their labor, and the local Bantu Administration Board only began to prosecute them after the mines had wound up their experiment. Since local officials were reluctant to confront the farmers, the NRC was very unlikely to make any inroads in the district. So it proved.

At Harrismith, a stand-off between white farmers and the Bantu Administration Board over registration crippled the experiment, which meant that TEBA could only recruit within Harrismith township.[36] Over the entire period, TEBA managed to recruit fewer than twenty-five men from the white farms of the district. The remainder came from the township or the resettlement camp at Witsieshoek in neighboring QwaQwa. Following the end of the experiment in late 1977, TEBA ran this office until 1983 when it transferred all recruiting to Witsieshoek.[37] In the Warrenton district, TEBA never secured access to the agricultural hinterland. The experimental office confined itself to unemployed township residents.

After the campaign to open the experimental areas ended, the Chamber of Mines declared it a "success," even though it had delivered so few laborers. First, it had operated in all four areas without any formal opposition from the farmers. This lack of opposition can be explained by TEBA's extraordinary caution and near invisibility in the districts. Most farmers remained totally unaware that it had moved in. When the organization tried to expand the experiment in Ngotshe, the local farmers' union woke up and demanded to know who had allowed TEBA into the district in the first place. The Chamber recruiters backed down immediately. Second, the Chamber expressed satisfaction that in at least two of the districts it managed to establish a permanent urban recruiting office. Third, its officials thought that the experiment had begun to break down the idea of protected recruiting zones.

Changes in state policy in the 1970s had meant that blanket protection of farm labor gave way to a functional approach, prohibiting other employers from engaging registered farm workers.[38] Farm residents wanting to work in the mines had to resettle first in the bantustans. As recently as 1984, the SAAU reaffirmed its stance that "no sector should be allowed to recruit black labor on the farms and in rural areas, but that all recruitment should be channeled through labour bureaux."[39] The state was no longer listening. Direct mine recruiting in most white farm districts remained formally illegal for only two more years when the influx-control laws were repealed under the government's "orderly urbanization" policies.

With the winding down of active mine recruiting in the 1980s, it slowly dawned on the state that the mines had ceased to be much of a threat to the farmers. High unemployment in the bantustans provided abundant labor for everyone. In addition, farm workers who did move from white farms could no longer count on being recruited for a mine (or any other) job.[40] One nineteen-year-old former farmworker, interviewed for this study, observed:

> I spent most of my younger years working in a white man's farm for our payment for being squatters. We did fieldwork, tilling and planting. I was not being paid. I only got R10 a month. I finished that contract after five

years and then we went to Nqutu [a resettlement area]. I came to look for work at the factories but now that I can't find it I've decided to go to the mines. It is better at the mines than no job at all. To me it makes no difference.[41]

Considerations such as this powerfully inhibited farmworker mobility. The more backward parts of white agriculture continued to benefit from a "captive" labor force that now had even fewer options. The more progressive farmers were operating with a smaller, better-paid, and more-skilled work force. They, too, had less to fear from the mines. At the height of the drought in 1984, farmers in parts of the Orange Free State even encouraged their workers to take mine contracts. The SAAU received permission from the state that registered farm workers could seek off-farm employment without having to resettle in the bantustans. When the state finally withdrew its legal protection in 1986, therefore, there was no great outcry from the farmers.

Wedded to the Factories

The second major source of labor that the mining industry attempted to exploit in the 1970s was urban South Africa.[42] In 1974, the Chamber of Mines opened new recruiting offices in several black townships. They intented to lure urban residents to the mines but felt they could also capture workers living illegally in the towns.[43] Analysts differ sharply on what happened next.

Two ILO consultants later pronounced "the recent drive to recruit urban Blacks" as a "dismal failure" but advanced no substantial evidence in support of this position.[44] In a rejoinder to the ILO, the Chamber of Mines called the campaign a success after comparing the number of recruits engaged at urban recruiting offices and those secured in many of the rural agencies.[45] The number of urban recruits in seven of South Africa's largest urban centers rose to 40,674 by 1977, although only 17 percent were officially resident in those urban centers (Table 6.5). By 1979 the annual intake from these same urban offices had fallen to 15,198 (and to 9,980 by 1982). The fall-off was particularly dramatic in East London where the numbers dropped from 11,601 at their peak in 1977 to 4,344 in 1979 (and to 2,668 in 1983). However, at some urban offices, the number of recruits did jump dramatically in the 1970s and has continued to expand since. Bloemfontein is a good example, although most of the 4,000 workers engaged there in 1985 came from the neighboring resettlement area of Botshabelo.

In contrast to its equivocation on the farm labor issue, the state quickly lifted the ban on urban recruiting, for two reasons. First, the state was

Table 6.5 Urban Recruits, 1975-1982

	Total Recruits[a]	Resident No.[b]	Urban Recruits % of Total
1975	21,898	8,268	37.8
1976	39,357	13,035	33.1
1977	40,674	6,870	16.9
1978	23,798	4,239	17.8
1979	15,198	2,211	14.5
1980	14,551	2,790	19.2
1981	12,001	954	7.9
1982	9,980	1,044	10.5
Total	177,457	39,411	22.2

[a]Recruits in 8 major urban centers (see Table 6.7).
[b]Recruits with rights of urban residence under influx control regulations.
Source: Unpublished data from Chamber of Mines of South Africa, Human Resources Laboratory.

becoming increasingly nervous about the growing army of urban unemployed, swelled by economic depression and illegal migration to the cities. Second, unlike the farmers, urban employers had no need to fear the mines. Opening the townships to mine recruiters was an uncontentious issue politically. Some of the main urban centers had already been opened either officially or unofficially: mine recruiting in East London, for example, had gone on since 1971. In Port Elizabeth, too, the mines recruited covertly. By contrast, recruiting at the Durban office stopped in 1968 and the company had to refer all workers to the Pietermaritzburg office.[46] In September 1974, however, several Bantu Administration Boards opened or reopened their urban townships to the mines. Others followed so that by mid-1975, the mining industry had access to most major urban centers.

Rather than spread itself through the smaller towns, the Chamber focused on the larger centers: the Witwatersrand, Greater Durban, the Cape peninsula, East London, Port Elizabeth, Bloemfontein, and Kimberley. In an important development, which removed one major deterrent for the potential urban recruit, the state decreed that urban recruits with Section 10 entitlements (under the Native Laws Amendment Act of 1945) would not lose their rights of urban domicile if they accepted temporary mine employment in another district. In each of these centers, the NRC followed the same recruiting procedure, setting up temporary offices adjacent to the administration boards. From there, recruiters and runners made daily sweeps into the townships in mobile vans, distributing publicity, talking to workers, and transporting recruits to the board offices

Table 6.6 Urban Recruiting by City, 1973-1984

	CT	PE	EL	Kim	Bloem	Durban	P'burg	PWV
1973	230	543	1,403	0	1,881	0	1,034	93
1974	241	559	2,196	0	823	0	1,553	1,809
1975	596	1,740	6,092	876	694	0	3,909	7,991
1976	1,493	3,379	9,208	1,565	3,070	2,618	5,017	13,007
1977	1,500	2,948	11,601	1,952	3,522	3,926	4,811	10,414
1978	0	1,234	5,298	1,340	3,946	2,761	3,110	6,109
1979	0	638	4,344	819	2,597	1,719	1,936	3,145
1980	0	0	4,294	482	2,175	1,485	1,827	4,288
1981	0	0	4,134	409	2,413	1,449	1,810	1,786
1982	0	0	3,070	429	1,323	1,220	1,837	2,101
1983	0	0	2,668	496	1,961	885	1,313	3,478
1984	0	0	2,538	663	3,194	1,006	1,386	3,486

Note: CT, Cape Town; PE, Port Elizabeth; EL, East London; Kimb, Kimberley; Bloem, Bloemfontein; P'burg, Pietermaritzburg; PWV, Pretoria-Witwatersrand-Vereeniging.
Source: Unpublished data from the late Professor J. Nattrass, University of Natal, Durban.

for attestation.[47] Major recruiting points included the Aid Centres of the administration boards, urban labor bureaus, and the informal gathering places of the urban unemployed.

The Aid Centre visits underlined the close collaboration of the recruiters and local officials. The centers were actually collecting points from which the Bantu Administration Boards endorsed influx-control offenders out to the bantustans. The boards allowed the NRC to recruit freely among these "illegals" on condition that the mines returned the workers to the rural areas after completion of a mine contract. In Durban, for example, the Port Natal Administration Board was boarding out 700–1,500 "illegals" per month in mid-1975, and it gave these workers the option of a mine contract. Officially, the NRC could recruit only unmarried men; in practice the boards did not enforce this restriction. To consolidate these local alliances, the Chamber of Mines accepted an invitation in mid-1975 to nominate its own representatives to sit on the boards.

All of the major South African urban centers had some increase in the number of recruits after 1974 (Table 6.6). Many of these recruits were not those the mining industry had targeted: actual residents of the urban areas (Table 6.5). Most were recent arrivals from rural districts who had either come looking for work in other sectors or who had lost their jobs in town. Only in East London, where the densely populated Mdantsane township supplied many recruits, did the recruiters make significant inroads on the "urban reservoir." Recognizing the poor results, TEBA wound down the urban recruiting campaign, particularly on the Witwatersrand. The general manager of TEBA commented, "We have had to close down our Soweto office because it simply didn't produce the results we had hoped for. Urban men are wedded to the factories."[48] In 1978, it closed the Cape Town office; Port Elizabeth followed in 1981. The numbers recruited, while not insignificant, were very small when compared with the size of the unemployed urban population.

For most unemployed urban residents, improved mine wages were an insufficient incentive. The social and economic support network built into township life, informal sector activity, and casual labor made it possible for the jobless to "wait" without starving. Like urbanizing poor whites in the period between 1900 and 1930, many poor blacks despised manual work and mine work in particular. The regimentation and migrant culture of the compounds was also unattractive to most. Of the urban workers who did sign on, few stayed very long. Mine officials disparaged the urban recruits as "loafers" who caused trouble in the compounds, refused to submit to mine authority, and rarely worked when required.[49] In addition, contract breaking was frequent with many working for less than a month before deserting. As a result, some mines refused any urban recruits. In 1977, for example, Vaal Reefs abandoned an attempt to use recruits from Guguletu and Nyanga in the Cape, claiming that they were undisciplined, detribalized urban "tsotsis" (or hooligans). In the early 1980s, the number of orders received from the mines by urban recruiting offices fell steadily; many orders specified rural recruits only.

As in the past, rural dwellers did not generally come to the city to look for mine work and only went to the mines as a last resort. Of these, the majority went directly to the mine rather than to a mine recruiting office because their illegal status was less prone to discovery this way. In the late 1970s, the pool of urban labor declined severely with the tightening of influx control, following the grant of "independence" to several bantustans. After 1977, Transkeian "citizens" could not be recruited except in the Transkei itself. In 1976, over 60 percent of the industry's Johannesburg recruits had been Transkeian. Four years later in 1980, the state declared that no workers from neighboring countries or any of the bantustans, whatever their political status, could be recruited at either the mine gates or at urban offices. In Durban in 1983, over 400 Transkeians, most retrenched from manufacturing, were refused employment in the mines for this reason.

In the 1980s, recruiting offices in Johannesburg, Pretoria, Bloemfontein, Kimberley, and Durban remained open despite falling demand. These centers could undoubtedly have drawn many more workers from the throngs of unemployed who regularly congregated outside the TEBA offices. In Durban, for example, only 1,000 workers were forwarded to the mines in 1984 (down from a high of 3,700 in 1977). In early 1984, however, TEBA was turning away 200–250 unemployed workers each month and estimated that with a "free run" it could recruit 7,000 miners in Durban.[50] To some extent the fall-off was a result of the more general tendency toward long-term mine employment among the existing mine work force (see Chapter 7). Many mines also exercised the option provided by the structural labor surplus not to employ urban recruits.

The mines' inability to hold urban workers cannot simply be attributed to the peculiar circumstances of the 1970s. In the mid-1980s several mines again tried to increase their recruitment of local labor from neighboring townships. The results confirmed the earlier experience. Rand Mines' East Rand Proprietary Mines (ERPM) near Boksburg was typical. In 1981, ERPM announced plans to increase the size of its work force by 6,000–7,000, and immediately became embroiled in a dispute with neighboring white residents over the location of the new hostels. The company wanted them close to the mines, but whites in adjacent residential areas complained. The Nationalist M.P. for Boksburg argued that "a further 6,000 men in a hostel in the town would be detrimental to the town's way of life." Local whites proposed that the company bus in the workers from townships 15–20 km away. They also demanded that the number of foreign workers at the mine be reduced and offered to supply local unemployed workers to replace them.

Management claimed that this would cost an extra R5 million per annum in transport costs and impair mine efficiency. A spokesman explained that "nowhere in the South African mining industry are workers housed remote from their shafts. Long hours underground in hot humid conditions—together with varied shift times—dictate that workers be housed adjacent to the shaft." In an attempt to compromise, management announced in November 1985 an effort to increase its recruitment of urban blacks so that "locally recruited workers could live with their families, unlike migrant blacks who are housed in single-sex hostels on the mines." TEBA began recruiting throughout the townships of the East Rand, aiming at township residents not new arrivals. Clive Knobbs, chairman of Rand Mines, saw this as a pilot project for the industry: "We will start with ERPM and when we see what happens after the Government's proposed influx-control changes we will extend the campaign to other mines in the group." Unsurprisingly, in view of ERPM's reputation as a hard and dangerous employer, the experiment failed; it would probably not have been much more successful at any of the other mines.[51]

It is not yet clear whether the enlarged urban population, which will inevitably result from the abolition of the pass laws in 1986, will deliver urban workers more amenable to mine employment. Mining officials clearly hope that it will, and their support for the ending of influx control must be seen in this light. As one official pointed out: "They [black workers] imagine that the ending of influx controls will be all beneficial. What they don't realize is that it will also benefit us. It means more workers going for the same jobs and that means lower wages."[52] Most mines are not, of course, located close to existing black townships. Of those that are, the same kinds of constraint identified in the ERPM experiment still apply. The production requirements that dictate housing workers close to the shafts cannot easily be overcome without major restructuring of the labor process. Future urban recruits will therefore have to either submit to the inhospitable compounds or (possibly a more attractive proposal) go into new married accommodation on mine properties or in special township developments. They may also decide to relocate to the proliferating squatter camps in the vicinity of the mines.

Crown Mines, Johannesburg, South Africa's largest producer of gold before the 1950s. Photo courtesy of Africana Museum, Johannesburg. (*top*) Black miners drilling gold reef in narrow underground stope, ca. 1920s. Photo courtesy of Africana Museum, Johannesburg. (*bottom*)

Black miners with white supervisor in stope, ca. 1920s. Photo courtesy of Africana Museum, Johannesburg. (*top*) Miner at stope face. Photo courtesy of Africana Museum, Johannesburg. (*bottom*)

Turn-of-the-century mine compound on the Witwatersrand. Photo courtesy of Africana Museum, Johannesburg. (*top*) Inside a mine compound, ca. 1920s. Photo courtesy of Africana Museum, Johannesburg. (*bottom*)

William Gemmill, the Chamber's "labor czar." Photo courtesy of Africana Museum, Johannesburg. (*top*) Beginning in the 1950s, a fleet of WLNA DC-3s was used to maintain a regular service for picking up migrants from throughout the northern zones. Photo courtesy of Chamber of Mines, Public Relations Department, Johannesburg. (*bottom*)

Mine compound at Harmony Mine, Orange Free State, built in the early 1950s; the distinctive panopticon characterizes many compounds of the period. Photo courtesy of Chamber of Mines Library, Johannesburg. (*top*) Modern mine hostel complex, Elandsrand Mine, built in the 1970s. Photo courtesy of Chamber of Mines Library, Johannesburg. (*bottom*)

Modern Johannesburg, with mine headgear in foreground. Photo courtesy of Chamber of Mines Library, Johannesburg. (*top*) Life President Hastings Banda of Malawi addresses five thousand Malawian miners at Western Deep Levels Mine on a visit to South Africa in 1971. Photo courtesy of Chamber of Mines Library, Johannesburg. (*bottom*)

Unemployed workers wait for mine jobs outside a fortified recruiting office in rural Natal. Photo courtesy of Chamber of Mines Library, Johannesburg. (*top*) Part of a crowd of fifteen thousand miners gathered at the Jabulani Amphitheatre, Soweto, for the 1987 Annual Congress of the National Union of Mineworkers. Photo courtesy of *The Star,* Johannesburg. (*bottom*)

A delegate to the 1987 NUM Congress remembers the 1946 mine strike. Photo courtesy of *The Star*, Johannesburg.

Defiant miners dismissed during the last days of the 1987 strike. Photo courtesy of *The Star*, Johannesburg.

NUM leaders (*from back*) Marcel Golding, Cyril Ramaphosa, and James Motlatsi at a press conference during the 1987 strike. Photo courtesy of *The Star*, Johannesburg.

7

The Social Impact of
Labor Stabilization, 1980–1990

In early 1984, a bus from the TEBA depot at Carletonville arrived at a mine recruiting office in Nongoma in Natal. On board was a miner, Philemon S., carrying more than R8,000 in deferred pay. Most of his fellow travellers had no more than R200–300. The white recruiting officer drove him home. When they arrived, there was no sign of his homestead, or of his wife and children. This was, perhaps, not surprising. He had last been home thirteen years earlier, in 1971, when he accepted the mine contract that took him away. Since then, he had worked continuously for the same mine in Johannesburg in defiance of influx-control regulations.[1] Migrant miners often ignored the regulation that limited their stay to one year at a time, and the companies connived at this skirting of the law. Nevertheless, few miners have cut their rural links as completely as Philemon S. He is, however, very much the prototype of a new kind of black miner in South Africa.

Over the past decade, the gold mining industry has finally achieved one of its most consistently elusive goals: a regular, predictable flow of labor between the mines and the rural reserves. A new element of stability has come to migrant behavior at all levels of the job hierarchy. Previously this was the case only with the foreign component of the work force and a few longer-serving South African migrants (see Chapter 3). The difficult work of mining is no longer a temporary expedient for the army of the unemployed, waiting for easier, better-paid jobs in industry. Those jobs have disappeared; mining has become a career. With the emergence of the career miner-migrant has come increased rural stratification, breeding new tensions in the countryside. The men are now continuously absent; the old pattern of lengthy leave periods between mine contracts no longer applies. This situation has further eroded already weakened rural production and family life.

The main reason for these changes lay in altered labor-market conditions, which severely restricted the flexibility and choice available to rural workers. The changes were also a product of a shift in the geographical and social composition of the mine work force, as the proportion of miners from South Africa's impoverished bantustans increased rapidly in the 1970s. Greatly lengthened contract periods and the resulting short periods at home—now weeks instead of months—have had mixed effects. The companies gained greatly from the emergence of a new miner: more proletarian, less concerned with the farm calendar and long-term security in the reserves. Many of the fluctuations in labor strength associated with the migratory labor system have disappeared; productivity has increased; and (with the introduction of computer technology) management can engage in an unprecedented degree of manpower planning and control. These are all advantages normally associated with a permanent labor force, and it is true that at first the pressures on the mining houses to stabilize their labor diminished somewhat. But it also provided new reasons why stabilization might in fact be desirable.

First, the workers themselves paid heavily. As employment periods lengthened, the incidence of alcoholism, sexually transmitted diseases, and occupational diseases, such as tuberculosis, surged.[2] The well-documented hardships of migratory labor and compound life were felt even more keenly by a work force employed continuously in the mines. Second, and as a result, these workers were far more responsive to the appeal of unionism as a way of improving those conditions. Unbroken mine work proved to be a fertile environment for union organizers. The militancy of South Africa's black miners in the 1980s forced management to view housing delivery increasingly as an industrial relations strategy.

Instability Within the System: The 1970s

The rapid withdrawal of foreign labor between 1974 and 1976 exposed the latent instabilities in the migratory labor system. When 170,000 Malawian and Mozambican mineworkers left the mines, they took with them skills, experience, and work discipline. These workers came disproportionately from the industry's upper-wage categories, and their repatriation decimated the most stable component of the work force. Replacing them were new workers, mainly South Africans, with little first-hand knowledge of the mineshafts and compounds, and with very different migratory habits and expectations. Many were drawn to the gold mines by rising wages and pushed there by general economic recession and high unemployment. Initially, they intended their stints in the mines to be temporary and were uninterested in the long contracts of the departing foreigners. Their expectations of life in the mines were formed through many years of avoiding them.

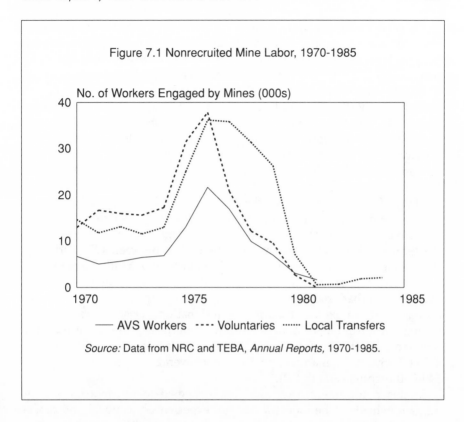

Figure 7.1 Nonrecruited Mine Labor, 1970-1985

No. of Workers Engaged by Mines (000s)

—— AVS Workers   ···· Voluntaries   ······ Local Transfers

Source: Data from NRC and TEBA, *Annual Reports*, 1970-1985.

To attract such workers, the mining industry had to make concessions. The Assisted Voluntary Scheme (see Chapter 2) became popular again; the number of workers engaged directly at the mine gates on flexible contracts jumped dramatically; and the industry restored its six-month contract for recruits (Figure 7.1). In good times, the Chamber of Mines always eliminated the short contract because of the higher recruiting and training costs and the production inefficiencies that resulted from it. Now, times were not good, and the short contract was a price the industry had always paid when it needed more local labor. In 1976, 75 percent of South African workers came in on this contract. Influx controls restricted local migrants to contracts of no longer than a year. Few of the new miners wanted to stay that long, and the average period of continuous service declined dramatically.

These powerful shifts in mine labor demography intensified seasonal fluctuations in manning levels. In December 1974, total industry strength dropped to 75 percent of requirements. Some mines, such as ERPM in Boksburg at 42 percent, were harder hit. The ability to maintain complements varied widely across the industry. Some Free State mines managed over 90 percent in late 1976. More unpopular mines, such as ERPM, Loraine, West Driefontein, and Winkelhaak, had difficulty maintaining 65 percent. For the next two years, the mines again faced year-end shortages of 60,000–80,000 workers. In 1977, labor shortages cost the companies an estimated R30 million in lost production. Mines trimmed labor where they could, demanded that miners work harder, and redeployed workers from development work to active production.[3] They also focused mining activity on the more accessible reefs. Production dipped sharply in 1975 in many mines, but the industry as a whole soon restored production to former levels.

Many of the replacement workers who joined the mines (40 percent in 1976) were first-time miners or "novices." In the mines most affected by the foreign withdrawal, the proportion was higher, about 65 percent of the 1976 intake at ERPM. Many soon absconded. Between 1973 and 1977, the number of contract-breakers rose fivefold to almost 10 percent of the work force. The proportion went to about 25 percent among the smaller number of urban recruits. The mines watched their desertion figures escalate with a mixture of alarm and resignation.[4] Desertion aggravated the high turnover rates that went with short contracts. In 1972, the industry required almost 350,000 recruits to maintain an average work force of 411,000. By 1976, maintaining the same average work force required 544,000 recruits (Figure 7.2).

In this predicament, the managers struggled to regain control over migrant behavior. The industry had not experienced turnover and desertion rates of this magnitude since the anarchical conditions at the turn of the century. In 1975, the Chamber of Mines' research division conducted extensive on-mine interviewing to try to understand the motives and behavior of their new workers. By identifying the workers' motivations, planners hoped to anticipate fluctuations in the size of the labor force and to restore predictability.[5] In belated pursuit of understanding, the Chamber of Mines also turned to academic social scientists with whom its relations had formerly been distant. It offered contract work to various South African and overseas social scientists to investigate the rural dimensions of migration.[6] In the late 1970s, when the migrant labor flow unexpectedly stabilized, the Chamber summarily abandoned the projects.

At the height of the crisis of instability the Chamber of Mines convened an in-house seminar on mine productivity. Its object was to examine ways to reimpose control on migrant behavior and to raise worker output. Participants repeatedly stressed the close connections between productivity, mine mechanization, and labor control through computer technology. While the supply of labor remained so volatile, little improvement could be expected. Hence a year later, the Chamber's recruiting organization

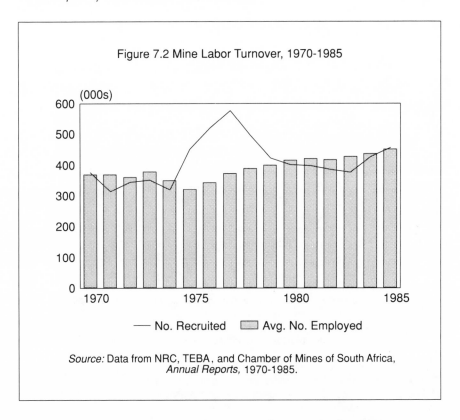

Figure 7.2 Mine Labor Turnover, 1970-1985

— No. Recruited   ▢ Avg. No. Employed

Source: Data from NRC, TEBA, and Chamber of Mines of South Africa, *Annual Reports,* 1970-1985.

defined its primary goals: reduction of wastage and turnover rates, encouragement of "career workers," introduction of standard service agreements, and adjustment of foreign recruitment rates to reduce seasonal fluctuations.[7]

In an effort to control labor flows, the mines resorted to various devices. One of these was the use of the long-established Valid Reengagement Guarantee (or VRG). VRGs carried entitlement to reemployment at the former job rate. To meet the new circumstances of the mid-1970s the industry reformulated the program. The industry began to offer financial bonuses for early return to work after completion of a nine-month contract (early return bonuses). In 1976, capitulating to the preferences of local workers, it introduced a reemployment guarantee for six-month contracts. A very important move was the introduction of a "stabilization bonus" for workers in more skilled positions who returned to a mine on a date specified by mine management. After several years of experimentation, in mid-1979, the companies agreed on uniform reengagement incentives (Table 7.1).

Table 7.1 Categories of Recruited Labor, 1978-1987 (percentages)

	TEBA VRGs				Old VRGs	Total VRGs	Ex-miners[e]	Novices
	461[a]	460[b]	459[c]	458[d]				
1978						30	43	17
1979						47	37	15
1980	35	7	4	3	4	53	30	17
1981	35	10	8	3	0	56	28	16
1982	38	5	10	4	0	57	30	13
1983	28	3	24	5	0	60	30	10
1984	21	1	35	8	0	65	25	10
1985	13	0	24	28	0	65	15	11
1986	1	0	22	52	0	75	15	10
1987	0	0	17	61	0	78	12	10

[a]461: Re-employment Guarantee and Early Return Bonus Certificate. Issued after at least 9 months' service. Guaranteed reemployment in a similar occupation at the same wage rate on the same mine if the worker returned within 6 months of discharge. Return within 3 months qualified for an early return cash bonus (ERB).
[b]460: Re-employment Guarantee Certificate. Issued after at least 6 months' service. Same guarantees as the TEBA 461 provided the worker returned within 2 months of discharge. No ERB.
[c]459: Stabilization Certificate. Initially issued to workers in skilled and semiskilled categories 4-8 after at least 6 months service. Guaranteed reemployment for return on a specified date. Miners who had worked 9 months were eligible for a "stabilization bonus" for early return on date(s) set by management.
[d]458: Leave Certificate. Issued for temporary paid or unpaid leave of absence from the mine. Specified an exact date of return.
[e]Exminers are recruits with mine experience not holding Valid Re-engagement Guarantees.
Source: Data from J. Taylor, "The Pattern and Consequences of Declining Mine Labour Recruitment in Botswana" (Geneva, International Labour Organization, 1986) and the Employment Bureau of Africa.

The new system had two interrelated objectives. First, it tried to standardize migrant behavior across the work force by offering additional cash incentives for longer contracts and shorter home-stays. In this respect, there were continuities with policies dating back to 1912, policies that, in opposite labor-market conditions, South African miners had consistently rejected.[8] Second, the revamped VRG program (unlike earlier schemes) made special provision for skilled and semiskilled workers in upper job categories. The industry wanted to match specific workers with particular jobs, encourage employment continuity, especially in the more skilled grades, and reduce costly training and retraining procedures.

In selling the scheme to black miners, the Chamber of Mines stressed the idea of "career mining," and the lexicon of mine work began to change. "Recruits" became "employees," who were "engaged" not "re-cruited," on "agreements" rather than "contracts."[9] The code concealed a darker side. While the VRG program originated, like its predecessors, as a system of incentives, it also became a coercive device. First, VRG use was discretionary and the mines often withheld them. As one miner observed: "If you don't complete they punish you by sentencing you to a number of months without re-employment."[10] Failure to return to the mine within the time specified on the VRG could lead to temporary or permanent exclusion from the industry. One Basotho miner, interviewed by Guy and Thabane, saw it this way: "You have to make sure that the days of the *bonus* (VRG) don't expire, because if this is the last day, the day you think you should be here at the NRC, they tell you that you have eaten your *bonus* because by the time you get to the mine the *bonus* would have expired." Another described how he had missed his bus back to the mine and eventually arrived there two days late: "When I got to the mine it was said that I had loafed for two days and by then I had been discharged."[11]

In these ways, a system designed to bring predictability to the industry's labor supply produced great uncertainty, insecurity, and fear among the workers themselves. When a mine wanted to reduce its labor force, it simply stopped issuing VRGs. In 1985, Western Areas mine did just this, causing widespread dissatisfaction amongst workers. Similarly, when TEBA closed down its recruiting operations in northern Botswana in 1984, it denied affected workers VRGs. Management also withheld VRGs from workers they did not wish to see again and threatened to do so with those who stepped out of line.

As part of a new blacklisting system, the Chamber of Mines introduced the 463 card (or "blue letter") in the late 1970s. The card specified penalties of varying severity for a variety of offenses. By issuing blue letters, a company could ban further work in the individual mine, in the mining house, or the industry as a whole for variable lengths of time. Recruiters had orders to accept blue-letter offenders only when no other labor was available.[12] After 1982, the term "undesirable" was expanded to include union members and organizers, prompting the NUM to take up the struggle against "blacklisting," arbitrary dismissals, and the disciplinary use of the VRGs. An early success of the NUM was the abolition of the blue letter in 1983. Nevertheless, desertion from the mines became much less common (Figure 7.3).

Stability Within the System: The 1980s

In contrast to the 1970s, the 1980s were a period of unprecedented stability in the migratory behavior of black miners. Most of those processed

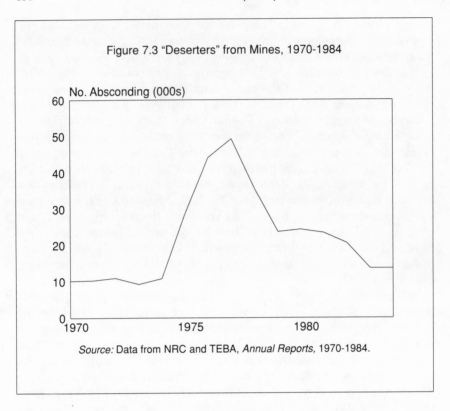

Figure 7.3 "Deserters" from Mines, 1970-1984

No. Absconding (000s)

Source: Data from NRC and TEBA, *Annual Reports,* 1970-1984.

through rural recruiting offices were simply miners with VRGs, returning to work after a brief, and controlled, leave period at home: "We work for these things (VRGs). Without them we lose our jobs. Sometimes I try to return even earlier because we have no money. Now I don't stay at home so much."[13] This complaint was typical: "In the mines there you will work for four months or for six months, get fed up with work, and now feel like a rest. But you find that there is no rest, for when you try and rest this money gets finished and you go back once again. You are going to work in a mine and it is hard work."[14] Both statements showed that the VRG system was affecting behavior but was not the only influence. Economic necessity drove the workers back to the mines, sometimes even before the VRG dates. Increasingly, recruiting offices no longer functioned as recruiting centers. They became transit points from which workers collected deferred pay on the way home and at which they boarded buses on their way back to work. Most miners returned regularly and repeatedly, usually to the same mine and very often to the same work gang and job. The change reflected long-term structural conditions.

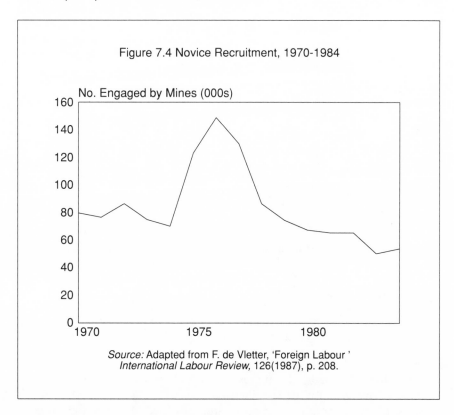

Figure 7.4 Novice Recruitment, 1970-1984

No. Engaged by Mines (000s)

Source: Adapted from F. de Vletter, 'Foreign Labour'
International Labour Review, 126(1987), p. 208.

The mining industry's 1979 VRG program worked very successfully (Table 7.1). By 1985, nearly 70 percent of rural recruits had unexpired VRGs. At some mines the rate exceeded 90 percent. Another 25 percent were workers with mining experience, though without valid VRGs. However, most of these had certificates that they allowed to expire for various domestic reasons. Consequently, over 90 percent of mine recruits were returnees, pushing the annual intake of new workers below 10 percent for the first time (see Figure 7.4).

Additional modifications to the VRG system further reduced the flexibility allowed to migrants. Table 7.1 shows the decline in use of the more flexible 460 and 461 cards (from 45 percent in 1981 to 22 percent in 1985) in favor of the more rigid stabilization and leave certificates (which rose from 11 percent to 45 percent over the same period). Rigid time restrictions, originally designed for workers in more skilled jobs, were now extended throughout the work force. In pursuit of stability, the mines enforced standardized employment periods for all workers, awarding fixed periods of annual paid leave and holding each worker to particular departure and return dates. As one official stated:

Table 7.2 Contract Lengths of Mine Recruits, 1981-1987 (percentage of total)

	26-week	45-week	52-week
1981	22	59	19
1982	18	63	17
1983	14	62	24
1984	9	46	45
1985	3	40	57
1986	3	13	84
1987	3	7	90

Source: Unpublished data from Chamber of Mines of South Africa.

> As we go on and need a higher output from a more sophisticated worker, this is what is desirable for the mines and probably also for the people who are making a career on the mines. This is our way of trying to discipline things. Every worker will come to realize that if this is his job and he goes on leave he must come back on a specific date. This is what's coming. What we're trying to get to is a stable work force where a worker knows he's employed permanently at a mine and only goes home for leave.[15]

From the late 1970s, the mines worked to phase out the six-month contract (Table 7.2). By the late 1980s, almost all miners worked for fixed periods of nine months to a year and returned to their job after a predetermined period of leave. The most obvious effect of such inflexibility is the reduction in the number of new workers needed to sustain mine complements. The total number of recruits needed annually from throughout southern Africa fell steadily from the late 1970s. At the same time, the size of the work force gradually increased (Figure 7.2). The industry's once constant need for large numbers of novices has ended. The main exceptions to this recent development are Bophuthatswana and Kwazulu, where the percentage of novices is greater, because the mines are still developing them as new sources.

From the late 1970s, the mining companies began imposing still tighter controls on black miners. These strategies included abandonment of the VRG system in favor of leave schemes; the abolition of the AVS system and recruiting at mine gates; the busing of workers between home and compound; and the use of computer technology. By the late 1980s rail transport had been virtually replaced by a fleet of mine buses shuttling workers between home and mine, which reduced time lost in transit but also served to insulate miners from the hazards of public transport. In the early 1980s in the Ladysmith area, for example, a gang of women estimated at 100 strong worked the trains, plying returning miners with alcohol and drugs and relieving them of their pay packets.[16]

Large-scale computerization has greatly facilitated management's ability to control migrancy and eliminate worker flexibility (see Chapter 1). In the early 1980s, the Chamber of Mines began to computerize migrancy. Terminals were installed in TEBA depots with on-line connections to a central data base in Johannesburg. A massive program of computer identification (through palm-printing of migrants) was introduced, giving recruiting officers immediate access to the records of miners and exminers seeking employment. The mines supplied data on the physical characteristics, educational qualifications, work history, and mine behavior of all employees for the central record. Computer technology has greatly increased the ability of the mines to identify and exclude "undesirables" from mine work.

To describe continuous employment in the mines simply as a policy success for the industry would be to ignore the importance of favorable labor market conditions. By 1980, mines were operating with full complements, in conditions of overwhelming regional labor surplus, and diminishing alternative employment opportunities. The industrial reserve army, coupled with active recruiting to smooth perturbations in the supply curve, sheltered the industry from the previously frequent fluctuations in the labor supply. Increased security for the managers came at the price of growing insecurity for the workers themselves. In an employers' market, exclusion from mine employment became an everpresent threat.

Most mineworkers conformed, however reluctantly, to the new more rigorous regime. The mining companies always expected workers to be obedient and docile; they now acquired unprecedented ability to enforce servility. Given the general state of the South African economy and the sheer size and rate of growth of the labor pool, these conditions seem likely to persist. For the workers there was more safety in numbers, however, which is one reason why the NUM became so important to them. In the old days, disgruntled miners voted with their feet; not many could now afford this luxury.

By the late 1970s, for the first time in their history, the mines had a captive domestic surplus of labor with practically no stake in the bantustans. Analysts agree that the South African countryside has ceased to provide most rural households even with partial subsistence; migrant wages alone sustain consumption. Within South Africa, including the homelands, there has been "an irreversible erosion of the material basis of temporary migration"; homesteads require constant infusions of migrant earnings.[17] The old pattern in which household income came typically from a combination of the receipts of agricultural production and migrant wages no longer applied to many migrants.[18] This was particularly the case with the millions of families forcibly resettled in rural slums such as QwaQwa and Botshabelo. As the South African component of the work force came to dominate over the last ten years, the proportion of "proletarians" among the miners grew until it transformed the social basis of the mines' labor system.

Like scores of other rural dwellers, numerous South African miners retained a rural base not because they wanted to but because they had no legal option. Because of the immiserization of the countryside, many South African miners would have moved closer to their place of work if regulations and mine policy allowed. In mid-1987, a market research company polled Anglo American's 48,000 married South African mine workers. Almost half said they would, if permitted, immediately abandon the rural areas with their families.[19] Equally significant was the finding that the remainder wished to retain a rural base. Their reasons varied considerably but some at least still had access to land, livestock, and other resources to permit a modicum of rural subsistence. Like First's earlier study of Mozambican miners, this survey suggested that South African mineworkers are part of a differentiated and stratified rural populace. Although many are undoubtedly fully proletarianized, many are not.[20]

Waiting for Work

From early 1977, seasonally at first but throughout the year for most of the 1980s, a highly visible reserve army of unemployed workers appeared at mine recruiting offices country-wide. They included retrenched workers from other sectors, experienced mineworkers unable to get back, blacklisted workers, and large numbers of school dropouts without other prospects. For all of them, the outlook was bleak. In growing numbers, they waited despondently throughout the region.

One recruiter described how his office received a special order for 100 novice underground workers. Word quickly spread: "By the next morning the office was inundated with workseekers of all ages, sizes and sexes . . . and chaos reigned for a few hours." Another expressed his apprehension about the "literally thousands of men sitting around our offices" and the "aggressive mood of the workseeker."[21] A third commented:

Where they hang about I don't know. We don't provide them with accommodation. Under the local regulations we are only allowed to sleep a certain number of people here. They disappear and the next morning they are all back again. I turn a blind eye to quite a bit of sleeping on the property here. They sleep in the garage or under the nearest bushes adjoining the property here. Those are the ones who have traveled the furthest.[22]

At one office in rural Natal, six hundred men were sleeping outside the office every night in mid-1984.

Day-to-day survival, through casual labor, informal sector activities, begging, and depending on relatives made the wait possible. Many live hand-to-mouth at TEBA's door indefinitely. One retrenched worker waiting for mine work described his predicament: "There is no employment. . . . I have worked for one firm for ten years and when it closed down I was left jobless. I have tried all other places but without success. It's the problem of feeding my family that worries me most. I depend on selling candles and paraffin but I do not always make enough and at times I am harassed by the police."[23]

Another described the struggle for survival: "Everywhere I look there are scores of people standing and waiting for jobs. Now I am forced to go to the mines. My child has become very unhealthy and I have started selling some of my belongings like shoes and pants to survive. Before long I will be without anything."[24]

A third noted that he could no longer afford to make the trip from home and had decided to wait at the recruiting office until he was employed: "There are no jobs at home and it is expensive to keep coming from there. I can't find work here because I have no permit. I have been coming for about 7 times. I rely solely on myself and a bit of cardgames while looking for work."[25]

Most had tried other avenues first before turning, in desperation, to the mines:

> I have spent a lot of time without a good job. When I found these other jobs I kept hoping that they would turn out good but every time it's the same end, the job ends. I wasted my time in an Indian's factory . . . only earning R35 a month. I have hardships. They are also suffering at home. So it's the situation. After I lost my last job I came straight here and I am going to keep coming for a long time. I have no knowledge of the mines. I have suffered so much I don't see there is a choice.[26]

The news of a mass firing, as during the 1987 strike, spread rapidly and brought thousands more to join the throng.

Disadvantaged workers in the rural areas took to venting their frustration on the symbols of their exclusion with frequent attacks on recruiting offices and personnel. In the eastern Cape, according to one recruiter, "the men who congregate at the offices have become aggressive and insolent when they hear there are no vacancies. Staff members have been subjected to verbal abuse while selecting labour and at times fear for their safety when confronted by hundreds of desperate and unruly workseekers."[27] TEBA built security fences around many of its rural offices;

they now resemble police stations. Interviews with unemployed workers, however, suggest that despair rather than aggression is the dominant response of the chronic unemployed, particularly in major supply areas where mine labor is firmly entrenched and alternatives completely lacking. This is the human price of economic conditions that secure for the mines practically "unlimited supplies of labour."

In their desperation, workers do what they must to secure mine contracts. Bribery and currying favor with black clerks at TEBA offices are common: "We discovered that unless someone bribed the clerks we would wait for some days at TEBA before getting what we need. If someone is late and pays some money to bribe a clerk then things will be smoothly arranged."[28] Work seekers at some offices fill their pockets with stones in anticipation of the weight-check part of the mine medical examination. Recruiting clerks are onto this and force them to turn out their pockets before stepping up to the scales. A large clandestine trade in forged VRGs sprang up after 1979. Books of the certificates regularly went missing in the mines themselves. Recruits holding forged certificates, many of them novices, came from as far away as Malawi and Mozambique. One worker described how he acquired a forged VRG:

> I had never worked on the mines. I accompanied my brother when he went to seek employment. I met a clerk at one mine when I went there to ask for employment. He told me he could find me a job on the mine as he had reengagement certificates. He asked me for R250. I paid him this money on that same day. Then I went home. Later I took the 'bonus' to TEBA. After I got a contract I tore it up.[29]

Workers leaving for home with VRGs also played the system to their own advantage. On payment of a bribe some mine clerks would stamp incorrect dates on the VRGs, giving workers a longer period at home than otherwise allowed. In the face of massive abuse of the VRG system by workers, managers introduced tight security to guard their documents. In September 1984, for example, a black clerk at West Rand Consolidated received fines of over R2,200 on seven counts of fraud for selling VRGs to Mozambicans for R450 each.[30] By the late 1980s, however, computer identification had greatly reduced the opportunities for workers to "play" the system in this way.

Labor recruiting South Africa style was always a no-frills business. When recruits became plentiful, the recruiters put cost-cutting even higher on their agenda. In 1984, TEBA's extensive network of recruiting offices drew in less than 50,000 new workers. None of these workers was recruited; they were simply taken "off-the-doorstep" as needed to fill orders from individual mines. TEBA no longer recruited very actively anywhere. It maintained its network for insurance reasons. TEBA officials in the field became muscle pinchers and doormen, while acquiring new skills such as computer literacy. In 1988, TEBA's Orange Free State manager, Mike Hobson, introduced a pilot project there to facilitate selective recruiting and to ease the congestion at recruiting offices. Work histories and personal details of all prospective miners were fed into a computerized data base in Welkom. TEBA undertook to contact workers at their homes if appropriate jobs became available.

In other areas, compared with the mid-1970s, the recruiting network is now a shell. TEBA has closed many offices and dropped whole regions from the system. When the Chamber shut down its expensive operation in northern Botswana in 1983, it reluctantly agreed, following protests from the Botswana government, to maintain a presence at Francistown for the few northern miners kept on. These men now pay their own expenses to and from Francistown. In southern Botswana, TEBA closed five offices in 1985, leaving only a few in the towns to serve surrounding rural areas. It implemented similar cost-cutting measures throughout the periphery.

Unemployed workers everywhere had to pay for their own transport to TEBA offices. This arrangement was at the expense of those who lived furthest away, particularly if they tried to maximize their chances by coming regularly to wait. The delay is always long, and workers return many times. Some are hired, encouraging others to make the daily trek: "It all depends on luck. Some have been employed on their first visit; some after months are still unemployed Although certificates are sold I do not have enough money to buy it. It costs between R150 and R200. Maybe I'll have to borrow money from relatives to buy."[31]

Even then, for some the call never comes. The contraction of the network carries a price for the industry also. As one official complained: "Our activities are becoming limited to an ever-decreasing circle around each office. The source of labour is confining itself into a smaller and smaller area with the increasing possibility that no matter how selective we try to be the material we select from is falling off in quality."[32]

Since individual mines could draw their labor from anywhere in the network, they became much more fussy. Orders routed to a particular reserve (for instance, a designated district of the Transkei or rural Kwazulu or a named resettlement area) often specified the age, physique, educational level, work experience, and rural origins required. In the field, TEBA followed "selective" policies to identify what it calls "the pick of the bunch." In parts of the Transkei, the selection of workers took place outside the beleaguered depots, and only then did officials admit the chosen through the "security hatch" in the fence.[33] Would-be miners in the countryside, once courted by the recruiters in the 1970s, tended to become faceless, computerized labor units in the 1980s.

As TEBA scaled down its activities in some areas and withdrew completely from others, its ability to guarantee future labor supplies was at risk. To offset this, the recruiters tended to concentrate on particular areas, especially the northern Transvaal, Transkei, and Kwazulu. TEBA works them carefully and uses its propaganda in the schools to "keep the flag flying," as one official put it. Reliance on the Zulus, in particular, is controversial, however, if only because most make no secret of their aversion to mine work. Several Gencor and Rand Mines companies built up their Zulu strength in the early 1980s but have recently reconsidered. At Rand Mines' ERPM, nearly 80 percent of Zulu novices broke their contracts, and in late 1983 at Gencor's Winkelhaak Mine, Zulu workers departed en masse. Following this incident, the mine cancelled an order for 500 workers from Kwazulu.[34] Nevertheless, Zulus appeal to management because of their conservative reputation and presumed immunity to modern labor radicalism.

Because the number of new workers required each year is now so small, it has become fashionable in the industry to question the need to retain TEBA. One mine, St. Helena, has opted out of TEBA altogether. Others will surely follow. Some mines in the Orange Free State briefly set themselves up in competition by issuing application forms to the men for use by their relatives. This tactic produced more than 10,000 applications for one mine in 1984. TEBA heard of this and condemned the violation of the monopsony through which the industry has maintained its common system for more than eighty years. It seems that few in the industry are ready for anything as drastic as phasing out the recruiting system. However, the individual companies and groups are becoming restive under the restrictions that a common policy necessarily involves. Following a major review in 1985, management decided to preserve TEBA intact, but its future is uncertain. The monopolistic recruiting system that sustained the industry throughout its first century is becoming an appendage at the beginning of its second, replaced by a streamlined bureaucracy based on the computer. TEBA's future survival probably depends on its ability to transform itself into a more general employment agency for other industrial sectors. There are strong indicators that the organization is now moving in this direction.

At the supply end, the social implications of continuous mine employment still await proper examination. Spiegel suggested that in Lesotho the mineworker insiders (though mostly absent) may become dominant in their communities through their command of wage remittances and ability to purchase control of rural resources.[35] Murray concluded that it is "easy today to identify a relative elite of professional mine labour migrants on the one hand, and on the other hand an entire generation of young and middle-aged men engulfed by a surging tide of structural unemployment."[36] Such rural differentiation will nevertheless have important consequences for the supplier communities. Generally, the negative effects of the migrant labor system, now well documented in the literature, only intensified in the 1980s as a result of these fundamental changes in the nature of migration. Longer and more continuous employment periods, and shorter homestays further undermined already fragile conjugal, homestead, and kinship ties.

For miners on the job, the "sanction of the sack," once a not particularly powerful weapon for management, has taken on new significance. As noted above, individual contract-breaking and desertion, while far from eliminated, now carry severe penalties, including permanent exclusion. A recruiting officer noted: "If they don't complete a contract they don't get a second chance since there is plenty of untried labor to go to."[37] Worker protest, when it assumes this form, carries a heavy penalty, one reason that the mineworkers have turned increasingly to collective action. The experience of the NUM suggests that "safety in numbers" is far from assured, but collective protest carries less risk than the individual act of defiance.

The existence of an increasingly stable migrant work force has provided the National Union of Mineworkers with unprecedented opportunities for worker organization, but with several unemployed workers waiting for every job, the union leadership must move with extraordinary care. Workers in the gold mines have begun to fight, in E. P. Thompson's famous phrase, "not against time, but about it."[38] The union directed its attack against the disciplinary uses of the VRG system by the mines, called for improved leave conditions, and, most recently and radically, began to urge fundamental reexamination of migrancy itself. It used both the annual contract negotiations and arbitration in the Industrial Court to press its case.[39] These developments came at the same time as important elements in mine management were also looking critically at their long-established labor supply system.

Toward Stabilization

During the 1970s, a debate began within the mining industry on the feasibility of a shift toward a more permanent work force settled on or near the mines. Serious discussion of these questions had lapsed since the early 1950s. At that stage, the industry passed up an opportunity offered by the opening of the Free State mines to develop an alternative system there (see Chapter 3). The new willingness to think seriously about stabilization arose from several developments. Large wage increases

Table 7.3 Skill Levels of Black Miners, 1960-1990 (percentages)

	1960	1970	1980	1990[a]
Skilled	2.3	4.5	6.6	8.8
Semiskilled	21.7	26.7	31.6	36.4
Unskilled	67.8	60.4	53.1	45.7
Unclassified	8.2	8.4	8.7	9.1
Total	100.0	100.0	100.0	100.0

[a]Estimates.
Source: Adapted from P. Pillay, "Future Developments in the Demand for Labour by the South African Mining Industry," International Migration for Employment Working Paper, No. 34 (Geneva, International Labour Organization, 1984), p. 7.

for black miners in the 1970s called for corresponding improvements in productivity. This led, in turn, to a new emphasis on mine mechanization as a way of reducing labor needs in the unskilled categories, particularly. Effective mechanization required a more stable, skilled, and committed component in the black work force. The proportion of skilled and semiskilled jobs grew in the 1970s, though still constrained by the Color Bar (Table 7.3) (see Chapter 4). As the number of skilled and semiskilled workers increased, managers came to doubt that short-contract migration could deliver such workers reliably.

At this stage, few mining executives considered abolition of migrancy even as a distant goal. In evidence to a government inquiry in 1975, during the upsurge in mine violence, the Chamber of Mines accepted the "intrinsic sociological shortcomings" of oscillating migration. The statement insisted, though, that it arose from unavoidable political, economic, and geographical realities. Thus, for "pragmatic reasons" the Chamber said labor migration must continue for the foreseeable future. The Chamber concluded its evidence by arguing that because continued reliance on migrancy was inescapable, all concerned shared an interest in the restoration of "order and control."[40]

Most of the R300 million spent by the mining industry on black accommodation between 1975 and 1980 went on upgrading hostels for single workers, not on family housing units.[41] This investment was a response to the explosion of protest in the mines after 1973. At the time, at least one observer attacked the policy as an exercise in "straitjacketing the future."[42] Compounds could not accommodate families; improving old ones and building new ones simply entrenched the established way of mobilizing labor. In response to critics, the defenders of migrancy answered with the old argument about the benefits it brought to the supply regions.[43] More concretely, they focused on improvements made possible by the more stable migrant patterns that were emerging rapidly. By recruiting closer to home, the Free State mines began to encourage "weekend commuting" to Lesotho and the nearby bantustans, Thaba Nchu and QwaQwa. Almost half of Basotho miners work in the Orange Free State (Figure 7.5). The mine owners hoped that these "commuter migrants" would be less resentful of the bleak working and living conditions, if they could escape from them more often.

In the 1970s, some executives began to promote the idea of a two-tier black work force in which an increased number of black miners (the exact number was not agreed upon) would become stable, proletarianized workers. They would have higher wages, paid leave, and pension schemes and live permanently with their families on or near mine properties. The remainder would continue to be transients but locked into stable patterns of migratory behavior. According to this view, the labor force was a pyramid in which the top 10–15 percent would constitute the permanent elite. Committed to mining as a career, given a definite stake in the system, and accompanied by their families, they would be the guarantors of industrial peace.

In 1978, Tony Fleischer outlined the thinking behind this model in some depth.[44] He identified the barriers to stabilization. First, there was the political obstacle of the state's 3 percent restriction on family housing. Even if government yielded on this, economic and social considerations would still prevent any rapid move away from migrancy. On the one hand, the cost of providing family housing and social services for most of the workers was too great. On the other hand, he saw that the mines did want to achieve greater social stability among black employees, to build up a cadre of more productive career workers, and to reduce costly training and retraining. Over ten or fifteen years the industry could increase to about 10 percent the number of resident workers. This goal was modest but, as events showed, surprisingly hard to achieve. Managers with substantial numbers of older, low-grade, properties thought 10 percent was too many. To them, even limited restructuring was unnecessary—a waste of money.

As these ideas were debated internally, the Chamber of Mines began negotiating with the South African state. The Chamber wanted more flexible limits on stabilized labor, particularly in coal mining where mechanization had gone furthest. However, most of the gold mines had not come close even to the long-standing 3 percent limit. A survey of forty mines in early 1974 revealed that the proportion of the black work force in married quarters was not even 1 percent, with an additional tiny number housed in municipal townships. Anglo American, Anglo Vaal,

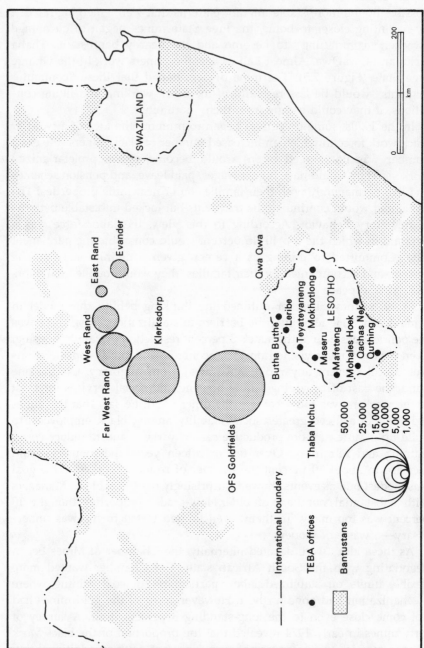

Figure 7.5 Places of employment of Basotho mineworkers, 1985. *Source:* Compiled from unpublished Chamber of Mines data.

Table 7.4 Married Accommodation Units, Anglo American Mines, 1975-1985

	1975		1980		1985	
	No.	%a	No.	%	No.	%
Elandsrand	132	1.89	153	2.05		
Freddiesb	59	1.33				
FS Geduld	96	1.12	284	1.54	287	1.18
FS Saaiplaas	6	0.15	30	0.64	30	0.29
Pres Brand	163	1.16	201	1.30		
Pres Steyn	140	1.16	164	1.02	216	1.07
Vaal Reefs	186	0.64	1,100	3.05	1,100	2.69
Welkomc	146	1.64	229	1.45		
Western Deep	100	0.79	332	1.97	389	2.01
Western Holdings	143	1.60	219	1.45	452	1.86
Total	876	0.87	2,653	1.95	2,828	1.86

a% = proportion of work force housed in married units.
bFreddies was merged into FS Geduld in 1978.
cWelkom was merged with Western Holdings in 1982.
Source: Unpublished data from Anglo American Corporation, Gold Division.

and JCI all reported fewer than 1 percent in married quarters. On most Gencor and Goldfields mines, the proportion was even lower.[45]

In 1975, a Chamber of Mines delegation met with the ministers of Mines and Bantu Administration and pressed for an increase in the legal quota of married quarters. The politicians rejected this proposal but did agree to some modest concessions. Mining companies could build family housing for married employees who qualified for urban residential (Section 10) rights, and individual mines could apply on an ad hoc basis to go above 3 percent, if there was no township nearby to take the workers. In a submission to the Riekert Commission in 1977, the Chamber argued that senior career miners should not be migrants and said the mines, not the state, should determine the level of stabilization.

Some mines did begin to use the latitude existing regulations permitted them to build married accommodation for skilled black workers, but progress was slow. The 3 percent limit was not breached anywhere, except marginally on Anglo American's Vaal Reefs. A few others began to approach it. Between 1975 and 1980, Anglo American increased the number of married housing units from 876 to 2,653. In the next five years, however, the company built only 191 new units, and the proportion of the work force in family accommodation fell slightly (Table 7.4). The other mining houses moved even more slowly. The Rand Mines group had only

431 family units on gold mines in 1985, still less than 1 percent. This mirrored figures for the industry as a whole, which showed 4,902 married quarters in 1984, housing slightly over 1 percent of the labor force. If the industry was implementing the 10 percent model, its progress was glacial. There were several reasons for this slow pace.

First, the state remained wary. It made a few concessions but hedged these around with conditions and qualifications. It agreed, for example, to distinguish between three types of mine: conventional underground mines (most of the gold mining industry), highly mechanized conventional mines, and open-cast mines. In the first group, much the largest, it decreed no concessions at all; the 3 percent rule would apply. In the second category, the highly mechanized mines, the companies could accommodate up to 8 percent in family housing, if the actual number of units did not exceed 120 on any one mine. For the third category, the state devised an elaborate formula, providing leeway, particularly for the coal mines, while apparently adhering to the 3 percent rule. By 1984, the coal mines had 4.4 percent of their work force in married housing. A few companies went much further. Rand Mines' Rietspruit colliery soon had 45 percent of its work force in married accommodations.[46]

Second, bantustan "independence" in the late 1970s directly contradicted the industry's plans to develop a more permanent labor force at least at the top of the employment ladder. The application of the policy to the Transkei (which supplied 30 percent of the work force by 1980), Bophuthatswana, the Ciskei, and Venda made their citizens foreign workers without rights in "white" South Africa. Underlining this situation, the government stated that its family housing policies included only workers with permanent rights to live in urban centers or "white" rural areas. Workers from the homelands need not apply.

Third, many of the most experienced and skilled black miners, those that the mines most wanted to stabilize, came from outside South Africa (see Chapter 5). Practically no one in government and few, if any, in the industry intended to stabilize this group:

> The economics of mining and the demands of productivity will inevitably compel the industry to increase the number of stabilised, trained black workers and these should come from within the borders of the Republic as far as possible. While the industry may wish to stabilise Mozambique Shangaans, for instance, this would have to be avoided. Cyclic employment . . . could continue provided there are no political barriers to such movement.[47]

In any case, the governments of the supplying states would have opposed it because their economies depended fundamentally on migrant remittances.

Fourth, the emergence of "career" mining in the late 1970s reduced the immediate pressure for permanent stabilization. Many of the advantages that the industry wanted from a permanently resident work force—employment continuity, reduced training and retraining costs, and improved manpower planning—proved to be achievable in this less costly way. In addition, despite a substantial investment in research and development, the barriers to mechanizing deep-level mining remained intractable. Thus, the demand for skilled black workers, those whom the industry wanted most to stabilize, has grown more slowly than seemed likely in the 1970s and very slowly compared with the coal mines.

Despite this situation, planners refined but did not abandon the stabilization project. Worker militancy in the 1980s explains why the issues of permanent work and family housing remained high on the agenda. Once given access to the compounds, the NUM found it an ideal organizing environment. In time, the union began to mount a fundamental challenge to management control. For management, the delivery of family housing became an important industrial relations strategy.[48]

During the early 1980s, the Chamber of Mines continued to press the government for more flexible housing policies, stressing the different needs of individual mines. In 1983, it asked the Department of Co-operation and Development to abandon any fixed rule on married housing. In 1985, the Chamber reiterated this position. It stressed once again that, as the skilled black work force increased, housing them on mine property would ensure that the costs of training were not lost.[49]

One year later the state did act decisively. In a move that was not directly related to the mining industry but to the simple collapse of influx control throughout the country, it repealed the pass laws, intending to replace them with a new form of restriction, euphemistically styled "orderly urbanization."[50] Urban rights would depend on access to state-approved housing and regular employment. While stemming from wider considerations, the new approach did have major implications for the mining industry. At a stroke, it removed most of the legal barriers to family housing. The Chamber's arguments over the previous decade may have had some influence on policy makers. The new dispensation certainly favored management's plans. The authorities quietly waived the old 3 percent rule for workers who lived in black townships. In some areas this would mean creating new townships; elsewhere mine housing units could be built in established townships where these are close to the mines.

In 1986, Anglo American commissioned a survey of black miners' attitudes on stabilization (Table 7.5). Over 40 percent of the South Africans sampled said they wanted to settle at or near the mines in family accommodations within five years. Among foreign workers the proportion was only 29 percent.[51] In any case, Anglo intended to exclude them from its

Table 7.5 Attitudes of Mineworkers Toward Stabilization, Anglo American Mines, 1986

	Would Settle		Would Not		
	No.	%	No.	%	Total
Married/S. African	24,948	47	28,271	53	53,219
Single/S. African	20,478	44	26,474	56	46,952
Foreign Workers	20,922	29	51,313	71	72,235
Total	66,348	38	106,058	62	172,406

Source: Unpublished data from Anglo American Corporation, Gold Division.

housing schemes. Included, though, were workers from the "independent" bantustans who have had their South African citizenship restored. The survey of Anglo's "target group," the married South African miners living in single-sex compounds, showed that 47 percent wanted to bring their families to live with them. Of these, 63 percent said that their move would be permanent. Almost 80 percent of this group said they were interested in owning a home at the mine or in a neighboring township within three years.

Anglo American used these figures as a basis for planning and in its negotiations with the state. Amid much fanfare, the corporation announced plans to move up to 24,000 miners into family housing at four locations.[52] Earlier, in meetings with the minister of Constitutional Development and Planning during 1986, company officials gave two reasons for their approach.[53] These reasons turned out to be simply a restatement of what the more forward-looking labor analysts had been saying for at least a decade. On the one hand, they said that family housing was appropriate to the sophisticated work force. On the other, the chronic problems of violence and disorder in the compounds pointed to the need for change. Anglo American decreed that initially as many as 7,000 employees would participate in homeownership schemes and stressed that the figure would eventually go much higher.

In April 1987, Anglo American announced plans to build up to 16,000 housing units for purchase by married black employees in Welkom's black township, Thabong.[54] The Thabong development was the first of several new townships and township extensions envisaged under Anglo's homeownership scheme. In Carletonville District, there are plans for significant expansion of Wedela Township. At Klerksdorp, the existing municipal township, Kanana, will get new development. During 1987 and 1988, three other mining groups—JCI, Rand Mines, and Gencor—announced homeownership schemes for black employees.[55] Not surprisingly, Gold-fields expressed little interest.

The high costs of providing family housing have long constrained the mining industry from moving more rapidly on stabilization. Even in the mid-1980s, the companies were not willing to bear the full cost themselves. Workers will pay for family housing through subsidized mortgage schemes. Managers have accepted the political and labor-relations arguments for black homeownership. They aim to make the housing affordable for certain groups of workers by providing a variety of housing units in different price ranges.

By 1989, however, progress was slower than the industry leader in this area, Anglo American, anticipated. The flood of workers expected to sign up for homeownership plans had not yet appeared, and the government continued its dithering and foot-dragging.[56] At the end of 1989, only 2,000 workers (1.1 percent of the black work force) had signed up for Anglo's homeownership scheme. The mining companies expected the state to assume the immense cost of providing services for the new townships. Given continuing fiscal crisis and the competing demands on shrinking state revenues, that is not going to happen. Little progress can be expected until some form of cost-sharing emerges from current discussions between the industry and the government. Many workers appeared to be taking matters into their own hands and moving their families closer to the mines regardless of official plans. The ubiquitous squatter camps are already growing in the mining areas, as throughout urban South Africa.[57]

These problems notwithstanding, the gold mining industry has finally begun to abandon its almost exclusive reliance on migrant labor. The skilled black miner will be living on the mine property or in a nearby township in subsidized family housing. The mining companies' target figure of 10 percent is still some years off. Achieving it will depend on costs, the proportion of South African workers in skilled categories, the rate of housing development, and the pace of mine mechanization. Some workers will remain excluded. In particular, foreign workers, who still dominate the upper skill and wage categories, are ineligible for permanent residence. They will continue to be migrant workers for as long as the mining industry wants to employ them and they are willing to come. Accommodating the differing needs and interests of migrants and stabilized workers will become one of the major challenges confronting the National Union of Mineworkers.

8

The Struggle for
Black Miners' Rights, 1973–1990

For most of its history, the South African gold mining industry has
opposed trade union rights and collective bargaining for black workers.
Although it introduced many changes in health, living conditions, and
even wages before the 1980s, the industry rarely negotiated any of them
with the workers themselves. It consistently refused to recognize popular
worker leaders or to provide credible institutional mechanisms for real
negotiation. Coercion, while always threatened and frequently used, was
not by itself a basis to manage a work force of this size and complexity,
however. When workers rose in protest, as they frequently did, against
their supervisors or in opposition to bad working conditions and low
wages, an element of negotiation and informal grievance resolution was
sometimes involved.

Relations between workers and low-level management in the mines
themselves were often governed by an implicit moral contract.[1] This
unwritten contract specified a set of informal rules that set limits on the
coercive treatment of the work force. It also allowed workers a measure
of latitude to regulate their private lives with regard to technically illegal
practices such as alcohol production and consumption. Violation of the
bounds of this contract could precipitate moral outrage and collective
action by workers. Until the 1980s, however, black miners were completely
without formal legal recognition and representation. Like all black workers
before the 1970s, they were excluded from the definition of employee in
the state's industrial conciliation legislation. The Chamber of Mines worked
assiduously to maintain that policy.

During the Second World War, for example, when the Smuts government was considering a limited form of union recognition for blacks, the
Chamber of Mines sided with those in government and in the opposition
National party who rejected the idea. The draft legislation to recognize
black unions did not become law. Rejection of workers' rights was even

more strongly evident in the reaction to the African Mine Workers' Union, which attracted impressive support before the 1946 strike. The companies closed the hostels and compounds to union organizers. They launched reprisals against union members and, working with the police, effectively crippled the union in the months before the strike. When 70,000 workers nevertheless carried off their protest, the mining companies responded with unrestrained aggression. The union, unable to weather the assault, was crushed and the mining companies' despotic regime of labor control survived intact for another three decades.

Both in law and in day-to-day practice black miners remained without collective bargaining rights. The Chamber of Mines and mine management made labor policy with scant regard for the wishes of the work force. Virtually the only channel through which workers could route their grievances was the "induna system." Black supervisors, often figures of tribal authority, were appointed by management to govern the compounds in association with white compound managers and black "police-boys."[2] Whatever the successes of this system in handling individual grievances, its primary purpose was compound control.

For twenty years following the repression of the late 1940s, the mines were remarkably quiet. Collective protests by workers were sporadic, unorganized, and short lived.[3] Broader black political struggles in the 1950s had little impact on a mine work force which was, in any event, becoming increasingly non–South African in content. For many foreign workers (over 80 percent of the work force by the late 1960s) mine work constituted a real opportunity given the dim employment prospects at home. These workers tended to have a limited commitment to the mines— working periodically and episodically, always looking for alternative opportunities, and retiring early. A migrant career was successful insofar as it allowed a man to establish his own rural homestead and to build his holdings of land, livestock, and equipment.[4] These factors, together with the rigid control of labor in the mines, help account for the general absence of militancy in the 1950s and 1960s.

In contrast, beginning in the early 1970s, the mine compounds experienced frequent disturbances, including attacks on mine property and severe violence between workers of different ethnic origin. These struggles were diverse in form and complex in origin, but they exposed major defects in existing structures of control. Management spent heavily on compound upgrading but this failed to address the more fundamental social roots of unrest. In the early 1970s an independent black trade union movement emerged and grew rapidly in South African manufacturing industries.[5] Initially, the movement had little obvious impact on mining. Endemic unrest in the compounds, however, pushed some mining houses to recognize their need for a new system of centralized collective bargaining to contain the outbreaks of violence. Differences in philosophy and practice between the various mining houses were given formal expression in the Chamber of Mines' split-submission to the Wiehahn Commission in the late 1970s. In late 1982, following another upsurge of black protest at several mines, the Chamber of Mines announced its intention to allow black miners to organize and to bargain with any unions that emerged. That decision belatedly recognized the failures of a century-old paternal and coercive system of control.

To facilitate unionism among black mineworkers, the Chamber and the state removed the major legislative and institutional obstacles to unionization. Management allowed union organizers onto mine properties and even gave them offices on some mines. Organizers were permitted to recruit new members and some companies established payroll deduction schemes for union dues. Even then, in common with many in the labor movement, management held the view that migrant miners would be hard to organize. Migrancy and unionism were widely held to be incompatible. The conventional wisdom failed to take account of changes in the social composition of the mine work force since the early 1970s. Most commentators focused on the dramatic geographical changes in sourcing patterns; they failed to recognize that these changes had also produced a more proletarian mine work force.

If the Chamber of Mines imagined that these concessions would produce a "sweetheart" union or an end to endemic mine conflict, it badly miscalculated. Perhaps the single most important development in labor relations in the mines since the white worker upheavals in the early 1920s has been the rise of the National Union of Mineworkers. The emergence and dramatic growth of the NUM confounded the predictions of most observers. The Chamber of Mines and the constituent mining houses initially attempted to confine collective bargaining to a narrow range of issues, primarily wages. The NUM pressed for negotiation across a much broader spectrum of concerns affecting the lives and welfare of the membership. The concessions wrung out of the industry through bargaining and industrial action were hardly revolutionary, but they probably seemed quite dramatic to workers denied a voice for so long. In 1987, the NUM felt confident enough to pull its membership out on what turned into the longest and costliest strike in the history of the industry.

The story of the NUM calls for a reexamination of the conventional argument that migrancy and union organization are necessarily incompatible. The more tolerant attitude of sections of industry and the state toward the existence of black unions was a necessary precondition for the union's success. But this does not explain the NUM's rapid growth or the unprecedented militancy of black workers in the 1980s. This chapter focuses on the character of the NUM as a migrant union. It argues that basic changes in the nature of mine migrancy in the 1970s are an important element in any explanation of the growth and appeal of mine unionism in the 1980s. Further, it suggests that the early success of the NUM lay precisely in its ability to harness the institutions of migrancy—particularly the compound system—to its own ends.

A Crisis of Control, 1971–1982

The new industrial relations era in the mines began, not in 1982, but nine years earlier in Anglo American's Western Deep Levels mine in Carletonville. In September, the police crushed a strike of 200 machine operators over wage grievances. The police occupied the mine for a week and left behind twelve dead miners.[6] During the months that followed, unrest spread to other mines and other areas. A government inquiry in 1975 documented fifty-four major upheavals at twenty-two mines by April 1975. Several years later, at the end of 1979, the number of incidents had risen to eighty, with an estimated 205 black deaths and 1,168 injuries.[7]

A recent study of mine conflict distinguishes three forms of mass worker protest during this period: conflict arising from tensions associated with changes in the employment status of workers from the major foreign supplier countries; internal conflict between different groups of workers (or "faction-fighting"); and industrial action over wages and working and living conditions.[8] In practice, the three types of protest were often intertwined, as were their causes. Mine and government officials inevitably interpreted the violence in terms of their own ingrained racism. This attitude was very clear in the evidence to the commission of inquiry into mine conflict in 1975. Echoing the views of government ethnologists and other "experts," the mining industry submitted that "tribal" antagonisms were rooted in "the inclination of many Blacks to become violent at the slightest provocation." Not surprisingly, these views found their way into the official report. It traced the origins of violence to primordial "tribal" fears and cited "expert" opinion to attribute to the entire southern Nguni group a propensity to violence and to "fighting as a form of recreation."[9]

Outside critics saw more clearly; some of the better informed tried to comprehend the structural basis of the unrest. One attributed the violence to the existence of migratory labor and the "boredom of a monotonous, barrack-like existence" within the compounds.[10] These conditions had prevailed for decades and do not themselves explain why workers should have responded so angrily in the 1970s. Much of the initial violence in the mines stemmed from the changing political environment of the mid-1970s, which included actions taken by the home governments of foreign migrants. Portuguese decolonization and the quickening of guerrilla war in Rhodesia aroused expectations of rapid political transformation and intensified discontent in the mines as elsewhere in South Africa's black communities.

As the mining industry's subcontinental labor system began to shake under the ramifications of political transformation spreading across its northern tier, some of the effects spilled inevitably onto mining property in the form of escalating violence and confrontation. In late 1974, for example, there was an upsurge of industrial conflict involving Malawian workers due for repatriation. At one mine two weeks of sporadic rioting followed a seemingly trivial incident, which led to a strike of 3,500 Malawians, fighting between Pondo and Basotho, several deaths, and a running battle with management.[11] Despite the persistence of racial and ethnic stereotyping in official accounts of mine violence, independent analysis began to uncover the close connections between ethnic cleavages within the work force, racially based strategies of domination, and faction fighting. Struggles over access to prostitutes and liquor and work conflict over jobs, wages, and privileges aggravated these divisions.[12] They could erupt suddenly and disastrously, as in the 1974 clashes between Sotho and Xhosa mineworkers near Welkom, which left thirty-five dead and 315 injured.[13]

It appears that the coincidence of ethnic and occupational divisions contributed significantly on this occasion to the buildup of tension in the months before the violence.[14] Basotho control of higher-paying, skilled, and supervisory positions created resentment among new South African recruits. The huge influx of new workers in the period 1974–1976 (when faction fighting peaked) exacerbated the tensions between established (mainly foreign) and new (mainly South African) workers. Almost from the beginning of gold mining, individual mines had promoted and used ethnic divisions and rivalries to control miners through segregated living and working conditions and the promotion of ethnically based cultural activities. Now, in the changed circumstances of the 1970s, these policies produced a harvest of violence and destruction.

Sometimes the causes of worker discontent related to conditions in the supplying areas. In 1975–1976, Basotho workers agitated repeatedly and violently against their government's demand that they defer 60 percent of their earnings to Lesotho. Management imposed the demand without consultation and took the blame for acting for Leabua Jonathan's deeply unpopular government. The Chamber of Mines eventually agreed to send joint management-worker delegations to Lesotho to negotiate with the administration.[15] Basotho miners were staunch supporters of the opposition Basutoland Congress party and the struggles over deferred pay gave them valuable experience in mobilizing against unpopular policies. Militant workers from Lesotho came to the forefront in the early days of the NUM, utilizing the political structures and resources of the party to recruit members for the union.

After 1976, the incidence of faction fighting declined sharply but other forms of worker resistance continued. Between 1972 and 1982, the miners launched over 100 wildcat strikes and many other confrontations with management over mine wages, terms of service, and working conditions. Strikes often led to extensive damage to mine property and to renewed attacks on subordinate black mine officials, notably the indunas. In sharp contrast to the earlier round of faction fighting, the strikes involved coordinated action between workers from different areas and could even include nonminers, such as gangs of Basotho youths who called themselves "Ma-Rashea" (or Russians).[16] The indunas were unable to contain the conflict. Several strikes occurred at mines where rates of pay had slipped below those of neighboring mines and only ended when management came back to the workers with wage increases. The use of the strike weapon to secure wage increases set a pattern of informal, but direct, negotiation between workers and management.[17]

During the 1970s, management and the state usually responded to mine violence with still greater coercion. In the closed world of the compounds, mine security forces were beyond media scrutiny. They supplemented bullet, baton, and sjambok with the use of armored vehicles and helicopters. Even these tactics failed to stop the unrest. The mining companies began to appreciate the need to address underlying causes, nothing short of which could prevent further, and possibly long-term, deterioration of production and profitability. After the 1973 strikes, Harry Oppenheimer observed that "managements are more and more feeling the grave disadvantages of there being no effective leaders with whom to negotiate in times of difficulty or conflict."[18] TEBA established a Liaison Division to monitor industrial action and provide centralized information on mine conflict. The individual mining groups sent delegations to Europe, North America, and the Far East to investigate the operation of industrial relations systems in those areas. They established industrial relations divisions and hired labor relations consultants, as did the Chamber of Mines in 1977. Investigations of mine violence became frequent, though their findings, like those of the official inquiry in 1975–1976, were generally not made public.

The Inter-Departmental Committee of Inquiry into Riots on the Mines (the Du Randt Commission) reported in 1976.[19] In the report, Du Randt tried to come to terms with the unrest. While focusing on interethnic conflict and "tribalism," he tended to see "communist agitators" everywhere and endorsed greater repression. He proposed that mine discipline be tightened, an effective "blacklisting" system developed, worker protest filmed to identify "ringleaders," news about mine unrest rigorously suppressed, and well-trained security forces deployed in every mine. Du Randt did concede that the root cause of the troubles lay in the migrant labor system, however. This admission was one of the reasons why the report was not made public. Accepting that there was no prospect of its abandonment, Du Randt called for upgraded compound accommodations. He proposed uniform pay scales on all mines and accepted the mining industry's own argument for more married quarters.[20] Concerning industrial relations, the Du Randt Report called for more direct lines of communication between management and workers, including an industry-wide system of liaison committees.

In response to the commission, and the violence itself, there was a widespread move in the mining industry to abandon ethnic segregation in the compounds, which discredited the long-held view that faction fighting originated in primordial "tribal" attachments.[21] The induna system also came under serious scrutiny. Some mines opted to extend the powers of the indunas and their police boys. Others tried to democratize the system by allowing for the election of indunas. The more astute managers worked to develop better ways of monitoring grievances. Black "personnel officers" appeared in some mines, and works committees emerged with a limited form of worker representation.[22] In the established way, management made its plans and imposed them. The works committees had no say on policy and little on work practices and conditions. Nevertheless, the moves toward a consultative system, though partial and hesitant, were important. The reforms showed workers that they could bring changes to the long-standing authoritarian system, and provided a basis for the NUM's more fundamental challenge to management after 1982.

Aware that grim living conditions aggravated work-related grievances, mine managements began to improve compound accommodations. A survey in 1978 revealed upgraded facilities, provision of smaller, more comfortable living spaces, and extra privileges to more senior black personnel. Concrete bunks gave way to beds and mattresses, and normal privacy appeared in the toilets in place of open-row, latrine seating. The new hostels included improved dining and recreation facilities and more privacy for senior workers.[23] These improvements applied mostly to newer and wealthier mines and to those hardest hit by industrial unrest, but the sums of money involved were significant. Between 1973 and 1978, the mining groups budgeted over R300 million on compound upgrading. Management clearly believed that improved living conditions and leisure facilities for some would help to control unrest.

With the decline in faction fighting in the late 1970s, industrial action focused on workplace issues became more important. Yet the mines still resisted direct negotiation with their workers. Union organizers made dramatic progress in secondary industry in the late 1970s, as management sought to accommodate and co-opt the new union movement. In the mines, officials continued to ban them. By 1978, works committees were already being phased out in manufacturing as the independent union movement gathered strength, but the Chamber still hoped to avoid even this modest concession.[24] However, the costs of the failure to develop some established means of negotiating with the black miners were mounting year by year. Zac de Beer, an Anglo American director, in 1977 noted, "If the aim is to preserve the free enterprise system in South Africa . . . then surely joint institutions must be created which will enable the two parties to become aware of their common purpose."[25]

Not everyone in the mining industry shared such sentiments. As the 1970s progressed, there were clear indications of a lack of consensus within the Chamber of Mines. At the time of the Wiehahn Commission in the late 1970s, most outside analysts were predicting that mining would be among the last economic sectors (along with agriculture) to organize. The Chamber's split-submission to Wiehahn was clear evidence of this, though it was also the first of many divisions that started to open up at the end of the 1970s in a previously monolithic industry.[26] In the first part of the document—supported by Goldfields, Anglo Vaal, Rand Mines, and the Union Corporation/General Mining (later Gencor) group—the Chamber argued that union rights should only be extended to permanently industrialized black workers. The concession was virtually meaningless given that over 98 percent of the black work force consisted of migrants deemed ineligible for unionization. In a much longer and considerably more sophisticated minority submission, Anglo American and JCI forcefully argued that union rights should be extended to all black workers irrespective of whether they were migrants or not. Buying into the conventional wisdom, Anglo added the rider that the vast majority of black migrants had "neither the capacity nor the desire" to unionize. The split heralded several years of policy wrangling within the Chamber of Mines as Anglo sought to win acceptance of its minority position, rather than going it alone.

Following the publication of the initial Wiehahn Report, the Chamber issued guidelines for its members that amounted to a rejection of most of Wiehahn's recommendations. It urged the groups not to recognize or to bargain with unregistered unions. The union leadership was often reluctant to register because of the controls over organizing, collective bargaining, and strike action under the Industrial Conciliation Act.[27] Yet the guidelines, which amounted to total rejection of the independent union idea, turned out to be the last cry of the old era. At the urging of Anglo American, and internal industrial-relations experts such as Johann Liebenberg, the Chamber revised them several times, and each revision moved closer to acknowledging the need for a fundamental change in labor policy.[28]

There were structural reasons that may help to explain why Anglo American and JCI led in efforts to establish collective bargaining arrangements in the mining industry. JCI is controlled by Anglo American. Anglo is primarily a holding company with very substantial industrial interests. Top management had been forced to come to terms with independent black unions in their industrial enterprises. For them, it was a small step to extend these ideas to their gold-mining operations. Anglo had also been dealing with unions on the Zambian Copperbelt mines for decades, and some top executives had first-hand experience in Zambia. In the 1970s, these mining men were joined by local university-trained intellectuals who were not wedded to the established labor practices of the mining industry, and who saw the need for radical change.[29] In addition, top management at Anglo American coveted international respectability and acceptance for their corporation. Continued denial of union rights for black workers in the mining industry patently contradicted this "internationalist" image. The South African holdings of Goldfields and Gencor were predominantly or exclusively in mining. Local executives in these groups mostly lacked the breadth of industrial experience of their counterparts in Anglo.

Anglo projected a growing need for more-skilled and better-trained black workers to staff their more-modern and more-mechanized mines. The group perceived that independent union rights, and established means of collective bargaining and conflict resolution, would be particularly important for the type of career-oriented, more-skilled black work force that the company wanted to develop. The corporation was also arguing for higher wages, particularly for workers in the more-skilled categories. Rejecting this approach, the more conservative groups pointed to rising unemployment in the bantustans and argued that it was folly to pay more.[30] Although by no means as liberal and moderate in labor matters as the public relations people made it appear, Anglo's top management was at least able to plan more creatively for the probable future development of the mining industry and the type of black labor force that would be needed.

It seems that breadth of interest and local industrial experience within management were thus more important than whether the corporation was local or based overseas in explaining the differing standpoints of the various groups. Anglo American is a local conglomerate, run by South African managers and funded by local capital. It is true that Gencor represents Afrikaner capital in the mining industry, and is aligned with the government, which some saw as sufficient explanation of its initially reactionary approach to labor matters. However, Goldfields, the leading conservative among the major gold producers, was part of an international mining operation in which the London parent retained a significant stake. Some have suggested that the groups with lower-grade, marginal mines were also less predisposed to countenance the unionization of black workers. This may be true of Rand Mines (whose coal division has been far less hard-line), but cannot account for Goldfields's stance. Goldfields numbers two of the wealthiest and most productive mines—Driefontein and Kloof—in its portfolio. It was, and is, much the least liberal of the mining houses on labor issues.

Institutionalizing Conflict

Between 1978 and 1981, the frequency and severity of mass action on the mines waned. The reasons for this decrease are not altogether clear though it was probably related to the initial damping effects of a mounting surplus of labor in the countryside and the increased risks of industrial action. Some managers saw it as a victory for their strategies of compound upgrading and believed the crisis resolved. More perceptive commentators argued that the easing of unrest could only be temporary and that the Chamber should introduce reforms before conflict flared again. They stressed the advantages that might accrue through unionization and the recognition of independent union leaders who could speak for their members. The Wiehahn Commission was now moving in the same direction; its sixth report, in 1981, supported a limited form of unionization in the mines.[31]

Wildcat strikes in 1981 and 1982 led to more rioting and heavy property damage at several mines. The 1981 outbreak was significant for two reasons. First, the work stoppages and rioting, which mainly affected five mines, apparently resulted from worker rejection of a new death-benefit scheme, one which improved the benefit but included an insurance element, requiring workers to pick up part of the cost. The decision by workers to protest even improvements in conditions not negotiated with them was a new development pushing the Chamber toward collective bargaining.[32] Second, the riots, which involved a growing number of attacks on senior and better-paid black employees, revealed that other tensions were brewing within the work force.[33] In the late 1970s and early 1980s, the Chamber consistently awarded larger percentage pay increases to more-skilled workers. The growing wage differential between unskilled and skilled workers produced another set of grievances for those at the bottom.

Further serious work stoppages and rioting occurred in mid-1982.[34] Ten mines experienced outbreaks, mainly Goldfields and Gencor properties, involving perhaps 70,000 workers. Again, there were several deaths and extensive damage to hostels. The immediate cause on this occasion was the Chamber's wage increase for 1982, the lowest in real terms since 1976. Gencor and Goldfields had stuck with the original proposal after Anglo and the other groups decided to improve it. Renewed mine violence finally convinced the hold-outs within the Chamber of Mines that, on wage issues at least, some form of centralized bargaining was now necessary. This realization led to the recognition that limited union rights should be extended. All of the groups agreed that management's bargaining power would be seriously compromised if they dealt independently with any unions that might emerge. By agreement, the groups now added industrial bargaining to the long list of centralized activities performed for members by the Chamber.[35]

The National Union of Mineworkers emerged in mid-1982 through the initiative of the black Council of Unions of South Africa. Another five black unions had also begun to organize in the mines in 1982–1983. The first to secure Chamber recognition (in September 1982) was a registered artisans' union, the Federated Mining Union, a "parallel union" linked to the (white) South African Boilermakers' Society. That union had also won recognition at De Beers in Kimberley and elsewhere.[36] By mid-1984, the union had recognition agreements with three gold mines, involving possibly 6,000 members, far fewer than the NUM at that stage. Even at the outset, none of the other unions constituted much of a threat to the NUM.

As an established confederation of mainly black unions, the Council of Unions of South Africa had a good record of successful organization in secondary industry.[37] Many in the independent union movement recognized that bringing in the roughly 500,000 gold and coal mineworkers would be fundamental to long-term success. Organizers argued that efforts to unionize mineworkers should concentrate first on other sectors of the mining industry where workers were more accessible, turning to the gold and coal mines only after securing a foothold elsewhere. The NUM reversed this strategy. By October 1982 the union was recruiting with Anglo's permission at several mines in the Free State. At the time of its first congress in December 1982, the NUM claimed 14,000 members. Eighteen months later it had recognition agreements with a number of Anglo mines and one Goldfields mine.[38]

NUM's membership growth far outstripped that of its rivals. By late 1985, the NUM had a membership of 200,000 (100,000 paid up); one year later, the figures were 320,000 (and 180,000). In July 1984, it had only eighteen recognition agreements with mines; by the end of 1985 it had fifty-two, and by September 1986, seventy-two. By 1987, it had organized over half of the total labor force. From the outset, it worked for an accommodation with the Chamber of Mines and the Anglo Amer-

Table 8.1 Recognized NUM Membership by Mining Group

	Total Workers	NUM Members		% Distribution of NUM Members
		No.	%	
August 1985				
Anglo American	163,000	66,000	40.5	83.2
Gencor	97,000	485	0.5	0.6
Goldfields	69,500	8,270	11.9	10.4
Rand Mines	68,200	2,387	3.5	3.0
Anglovaal	26,800	2,198	8.2	2.8
March 1987				
Anglo American	186,699	107,175	57.4	71.3
Rand Mines	74,083	2,398	3.2	1.6
Goldfields	80,436	6,489	8.0	4.3
Gencor	91,763	26,580	29.0	17.7
JCI	24,605	7,681	31.2	5.1

Note: Figures are for paid-up membership as recognized by mines. Signed-up members on mines or job categories where the NUM is not recognized are excluded.
Source: Unpublished data from Chamber of Mines of South Africa.

ican Corporation. Not surprisingly, the union made its most rapid gains at those mines to which organizers were given access, where the union was granted facilities, and where it was able to obtain recognition agreements. By mid-1985, over 80 percent of the NUM's paid-up membership worked on Anglo American mines (Table 8.1). By early 1986, NUM had recognition agreements with every Anglo mine, and on most of those 40 to 60 percent of the black work force were recognized union members (Table 8.2). Despite the growing popularity of the NUM, it made only modest gains where management remained resistant (Figure 8.1).

The response of the different groups to the NUM phenomenon remained divided.[39] Anglo American Corporation and JCI led in asserting the advantages to management of an effective system of collective bargaining. Other companies, notably Goldfields and Gencor, were hostile. The chairman of Goldfields, Robin Plumbridge, made no apology for the hard-line attitude: "Our reputation with the unions is tough. . . . The union leaders know exactly where they stand. . . . We have a conservative image. So be it."[40] A deposition by the management of Goldfields' Kloof Gold Mine in the western Transvaal revealed how this attitude was reflected at mine level:

Table 8.2 Recognized NUM Membership in Anglo American Mines

| | 1986 | | | 1988 | | |
| | | NUM Membership | | | NUM Membership | |
	Work Force	No.	%	Work Force	No.	%
FS Saaiplaas	10,485	6,400	61.0	13,764	7,846	57.0
Pres Brand	17,106	10,184	59.5	18,657	13,975	74.9
Western Holdings	24,039	13,460	56.0	17,918	11,543	64.4
Pres Steyn	20,962	10,314	49.2	18,819	10,905	57.9
Elandsrand	7,772	3,767	48.5	8,449	5,416	64.1
Western Deep	23,481	11,010	47.9	23,913	8,440	35.3
FS Geduld	24,694	9,934	40.2	14,902	9,217	61.9
Vaal Reefs	43,417	9,593	22.1	41,722	18,831	45.1
Total	171,956	74,662	43.4	158,144	86,173	54.5

Source: Unpublished data from Anglo American Corporation, Gold Division.

These people are mostly illiterate and uneducated. They are hundreds, if not thousands, of miles from home. They are superstitious and fearful. They are a tinderbox waiting only for the appropriate spark to send them into a surging flame of unrest and devastation, spreading even to other mines with consequences too horrific to contemplate. Every mine management is alive to this . . . its only weapon is an effective and speedy disciplinary procedure that strikes quickly and efficiently at agitators who make it their business to promote these evils.[41]

Goldfields took a highly legalistic approach to labor relations, adopted the narrowest interpretation of the recognition agreement between the Chamber and the NUM, and denied union organizers access to the hostels or workplace.[42] Indunas appointed by management continued to administer ethnically divided compounds on many Goldfields mines.

The NUM was initially able to exploit the divisions within the industry and to strain the industry-wide monopsony that had successfully fixed wages at a low level for nearly a century. Yet, the divisions between the mining groups were not fundamental and narrowed through the 1980s. One mining house, Gencor, began to move closer to the Anglo position on union issues after a change in management in 1986. NUM membership on Gencor mines immediately began to climb (Figure 8.2). Despite the obstacles, union membership also grew at Goldfields (from 6,500 in early 1987 to 16,500 a year later) where the NUM has recognition agreements

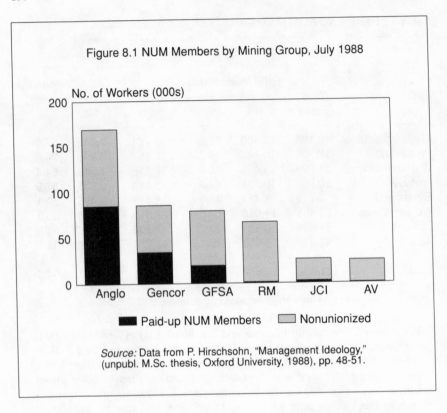

Figure 8.1 NUM Members by Mining Group, July 1988

Paid-up NUM Members ▢ Nonunionized

Source: Data from P. Hirschsohn, "Management Ideology,"
(unpubl. M.Sc. thesis, Oxford University, 1988), pp. 48-51.

with four mines. After several tolerant years, however, Anglo adopted a far less conciliatory approach during, and after, the 1987 strike.[43]

Access to mine property and recognition were the necessary preconditions, though not the sufficient cause, of rapid mine unionization. Any explanation of the NUM's growth must also take account of two interrelated factors: first, the organizational strategies of the NUM, and second, its status as an explicitly migrant union. Industry recognition rules specified that a union could represent workers in a particular job grade once it had organized "a significant proportion" (33 percent on Anglo American mines) of workers in that category. Initially, the NUM had concentrated on organizing skilled supervisory and clerical workers. One reason for this was the recognition rules. The NUM, which needed quick results, focused on those categories, the more-skilled grades, where the numbers were fewest and recognition could come quickest. This strategy had the expected payoff in increasing the number of mines recognizing the union but the disadvantage that it threatened to associate the NUM more with the upper strata of black workers and the black supervisors than with the rank and file.

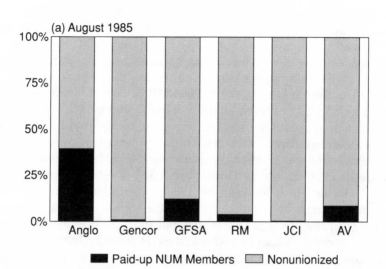

Figure 8.2 Proportion of NUM Members by Mining House

(a) August 1985

■ Paid-up NUM Members ▨ Nonunionized

(b) July 1988

■ Paid-up NUM Members ▨ Nonunionized

Source: Unpublished Chamber of Mines of South Africa data.

The NUM also focused much of its initial organizing effort on team leaders. The supervisory role, privileged position, and significantly higher wage levels of these workers tended to set them apart from the rank and file, however. Labor unrest in 1981–1982 had, if anything, widened the gap between team leaders and the mass of underground workers. The union risked identifying itself with the upper strata of the work force to which many miners were hostile. By 1984, the NUM organizers had switched their attention to the skilled machine operators. Unlike the team leaders, the machine operators "are at the top of the rank and file, but they are *of* the rank and file."[44] The NUM's success with this group tended to help also with the ordinary miners, who mostly aspired to the status and privileges of the machine operators. As more machine operators joined the union, they in turn drew in lower-ranked workers.

As the NUM sought strength in numbers to force its demands more effectively, it launched a systematic drive, in 1984–1985, to recruit semiskilled and unskilled workers. By 1986, a distinctive pattern of membership by occupation had emerged, with the highest rates of unionization occurring in the upper job categories but the bulk of union supporters occupying semiskilled and unskilled posts (Figure 8.3). In mid-1988, over 85 percent of the union's recognized members in Anglo American mines were in the four lowest job grades. The union's mass base among less-skilled workers tended to ensure that it remained responsive to grassroots concerns. The NUM has, for example, consistently refused to accept Anglo American's differential wage increase policy, which favors skilled workers.

The Chamber of Mines initially thought it might be able to confine collective bargaining with the NUM to issues such as the annual wage negotiations. The NUM, however, soon began to press for debate on a much broader range of issues. Safety in the workplace became a major rallying point for workers and enhanced the appeal of the union.[45] Despite long-standing emphasis on safety by both the Chamber of Mines and the individual companies, accident death-rates remained high. Although estimates vary, it appears that by 1984 at least 20,000 workers, most of them black, had died in mine accidents since World War II (Table 8.3). In 1983, 604 mineworkers died and in 1985, 539. From the outset, the NUM leadership had begun to emphasize mine safety. The leadership asked for the recognition of shaft safety stewards, for the right to refuse to work in unsafe conditions, for the right to participate in accident investigations, and for safety clauses in collective agreements. At West Driefontein in 1982, the newly formed union took management to an industrial tribunal over the dismissal of seventeen workers who refused to go into an unsafe workplace. This dispute ended ambivalently. Several months later NUM attorneys appeared at a routine inquest following the

Figure 8.3 NUM Members by Job Grade,
Anglo American Mines, July 1988

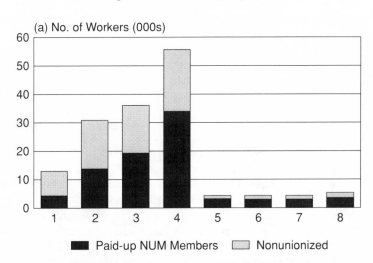

(a) No. of Workers (000s)

Paid-up NUM Members   Nonunionized

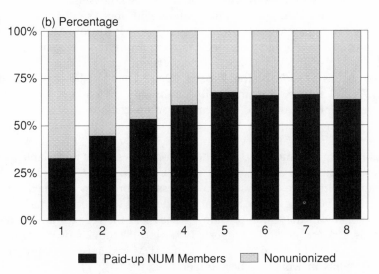

(b) Percentage

Paid-up NUM Members   Nonunionized

Source: Unpublished Chamber of Mines of South Africa Data.

Table 8.3 Mine Mortality by Cause of Death, 1945-1984

	Disease	Accidents	Assaults	Total
1945-1949	4,093	2,326	308	6,727
1950-1954	2,873	2,576	463	5,912
1955-1959	3,307	2,783	670	6,760
1960-1964	2,921	2,773	923	6,617
1965-1969	2,804	2,655	792	6,251
1970-1974	2,973	2,429	800	6,202
1975-1979	2,566	2,530	1,406	6,502
1980-1984	2,481	2,718	1,498	6,697
Total	24,018	20,790	6,860	51,668

Source: Unpublished data from Chamber of Mines of South Africa.

Hlobane Colliery disaster. The inquest heard evidence suggesting negligence by management. Criminal prosecutions followed.

A primary goal of the union was to secure worker rights to refuse to work in dangerous conditions and to have access to mine records on worker safety. As part of the campaign, the NUM emphasized safety training for its members. Its first national safety conference took place in March 1985 and brought together about 350 shaft stewards from the principal mining areas.[46] During 1986, at Gencor's Kinross Mine at Evander, 177 miners died and a further 235 were injured in a disastrous mine fire.[47] The NUM acted quickly, using eyewitness accounts to contest management's version of the disaster. On 1 October, between 250,000 and 275,000 miners (together with thousands of workers from union affiliates) stopped work and participated in special services.

The union subsequently held several safety congresses and formed regional and national safety committees. In July 1986, the Chamber of Mines had argued that safety and health issues were not negotiable. After the Kinross disaster and the mass protest that followed, it became more accommodating. The NUM secured concessions on safety during the wage bargaining of October 1986. Several Anglo mines have recently negotiated agreements with the union on safety issues and the recognition of safety stewards.[48] A recent study suggested that local struggles over workplace safety (backed up by the vigilance of NUM officials) was producing improvements in work practices underground.[49]

The NUM as a Migrant Union

The shift in attitude at the highest levels of the mining industry and the state toward black unionism in the mines was a necessary precondition for the emergence of the NUM. And the NUM leadership's bargaining skills and legal victories help to explain the legitimacy and loyalty it began to enjoy among workers. Yet over 97 percent of the mine work force (and most NUM members) are still migrant workers, oscillating periodically between the mines and distant rural reserves. Established wisdom suggested that migrant workers would be extremely difficult to organize. They were more marginal to the labor market, their access to wage employment was tenuous and intermittent, and they were easily displaced and replaced. Participation in union activities exposed them to costly reprisals and their marginality made them more willing (and desperate) to scab. Lack of employment continuity, high labor turnover, and job mobility undermined organization and "shop floor" camaraderie. In the mining industry, the compounds effectively insulated the work force from outside organizers and helped to perpetuate forms of ethnic loyalty and identification inimical to worker solidarity.[50]

In the mining industry, many of these inhibiting factors ceased to apply in the 1980s. Though the mine work force remained migrant, a steadily increasing proportion of black miners were becoming "career" miners, employed in the mines on an almost continuous basis (see Chapter 7). As workers began to spend more and more time working in the mines, and less at home, their sensitivity to unacceptable working and living conditions was heightened. An environment that was endurable for a few months could become intolerable as employment periods lengthened and as they could see no prospect of finding employment in other sectors. For some, such as Mozambicans and Malawians, this experience was not altogether new. These workers had always worked long contracts and spent the greater part of their working lives in the mines. For many South Africans, however, this was a new and unwelcome development. The new generation of South African miners had shown a marked preference in the mid-1970s for short contracts, mines with a better reputation, and other forms of employment when these were available. Together with miners from Lesotho, they were also more proletarianized than their northern counterparts.

After 1982, the NUM's organizing efforts were therefore directed at a work force that experienced the mines as a permanent and continuous source of employment and that was responsive in a new way to the potential of formal organization. As a more-proletarian work force, with at best grossly inadequate access to rural sources of income, miners became more sensitive to wage levels. In a situation of obvious labor oversupply the penalties for individualized forms of protest became more severe. The appeal, and protection, of mass action was enhanced accordingly.

Much of the leadership and energy that went into the NUM at the outset came from younger, educated men from the eastern Cape and

Table 8.4 Recognized NUM Membership by Geographical Area, Anglo American Mines, 1988

	Members	Non-members	Total	% Unionized	% of Ttl. Members
Foreign					
Lesotho	31,021	18,180	49,201	63.0	33.8
Mozambique	3,541	6,704	10,245	34.6	3.9
Botswana	2,028	2,352	4,380	46.3	2.2
Swaziland	1,467	3,381	4,848	30.3	1.6
Malawi	133	601	734	18.1	0.1
Ttl. Foreign	38,190	31,218	69,408	55.0	41.6
S. African					
Transkei	26,038	18,848	44,886	58.0	28.4
OFS	9,760	10,627	20,387	47.9	10.6
Ciskei	2,265	2,120	4,385	51.7	2.5
Cape Province	2,261	1,897	4,158	54.4	2.5
QwaQwa	1,658	2,072	3,730	44.5	1.8
Bophuthatswana	3,051	3,504	6,555	46.5	3.3
Kwazulu	2,563	4,807	7,370	34.8	2.8
KwaNdebele	2,407	1,750	4,157	57.9	2.6
Transvaal	1,716	3,332	5,048	34.0	1.9
Lebowa	948	1,159	2,107	45.0	1.0
Natal	281	463	744	37.8	0.3
Gazankulu	246	796	1,042	23.6	0.3
Venda	235	237	472	49.8	0.3
KaNgwane	109	219	328	33.2	0.1
Total S. African	53,538	51,831	105,369	50.8	58.4
Total	91,728	83,049	174,417	52.6	100.0

Source: Unpublished data from Anglo American Corporation, Gold Division.

Lesotho. The general membership of the NUM was also dominated by workers from these two areas (Table 8.4). In these areas, job opportunities were few, which bred dissatisfaction among workers with high aspirations but no choices open to them except, if they were fortunate, low-wage unskilled work in the gold mines. Furthermore, the eastern Cape has had a long tradition of independent black unionism and of community radicalism. Workers from Lesotho were also centrally involved in the wave of worker protest in the 1970s and early 1980s. Particularly in the Orange

Free State fields, militant Basotho workers led in the mobilization of rank-and-file support for the NUM.

Since 1982, the NUM has amply demonstrated that the compounds also offer important opportunities for mass organization. In a hothouse environment where tens of thousands of male workers are packed together in barracks accommodations, union activities were bound to be more successful. Moral and physical suasion enhanced union recruiting drives, ensured mass attendance at union meetings, and helped to enforce solidarity during industrial action.[51] In the period since 1984, for example, a series of boycotts of mine stores, bars, taxis, and sports facilities have been rigorously enforced and policed by the union. These were often called to protest against price-gouging widely practiced wherever there were local monopolies. The first major action was a five-week boycott of liquor stores run as a management monopoly at Anglo Vaal's Hartebeestfontein mine. Union boycotts quickly spread across much of the western Transvaal, though not without vigorous opposition from nonunionized miners.[52]

In the run-up to the 1987 strike, the mine compounds continued to be the site of severe, often brutal, conflict between workers and management and among different groups of workers. The level and intensity of mass action did not tail off in the way that the mining industry hoped it would with the granting of recognition to the NUM. Instead, resistance became more coordinated and focused. Apart from the conflict arising directly from wage bargaining, the mines continued to experience more limited forms of action. Between January and September 1986, for example, there were over 100 "illegal" work stoppages in the mines, not all of which were supported by a union leadership sensitized to complex legal procedures.[53] During the early stages of the 1987 strike, at mines where the union was strongest, militant union strike committees attempted (with mixed success) to seize control of the compounds and enforce strike discipline on wavering colleagues.[54]

Apart from grievances over wages and working conditions, the NUM has sought to displace the ruling hierarchy within the compounds. After 1982, rejection of the induna system and the works committees became more systematic and organized. During mine conflicts, attacks on indunas and mine police became more frequent.[55] At the NUM's 1987 annual congress, again reflecting grassroots militancy, the union called for the abolition of the induna system. A spate of attacks by union members on nonunionized team leaders (both before and during the strike) prompted management to begin removing team leaders to separate upgraded accommodations. Management also viewed the segregation of workers and supervisors, and the granting of extra privileges to the latter, as a way of diffusing support for the NUM.

Migrancy and Mass Dismissals

Underlying the NUM's post-1987 demands for the abolition of migrant labor and the compounds was a realization that for all its organizational possibilities, migrancy was still a powerful weapon in the hands of management. One indication of this power was management's increasing resort to mass dismissals as an industrial relations tactic.

In February 1985, for example, several hundred workers struck work at the East Driefontein Gold Mine. Their concerns were safety-related and shared by the team leaders involved, many of them NUM members. The company went to the civil courts, secured a judgment against the strikers, and had them forcibly evicted. Because they were migrants, their right to remain in the urban area depended entirely on continued employment. Once fired by the company, they were subject to summary eviction and deportation.[56] An even more telling case occurred at Anglo American's giant Vaal Reefs mine. Several months of trouble in early 1985—including boycotts, go-slows, and wildcat strikes—culminated in the dismissal of 14,000 workers in April. Worker grievances included wage demands, the persistence of the Color Bar, and claims that management was thwarting NUM organizers. More violence and dismissals followed.

Cases such as these clearly demonstrated the potential of mass dismissals as an effective strike-breaking strategy in the context of a migrant labor system. Once workers were dismissed and removed from mine property, they had no legal right to remain in the area. Back in their home areas they were widely dispersed throughout the region with very little communication with each other or with the union leadership. TEBA's network of rural recruiting offices then played a key role in the rehiring process. There is no indication that management wanted to, or could afford to, rusticate its entire work force permanently. On most occasions when the tactic was used, the vast majority of workers were rehired. Mass dismissals were simply intended to chasten the work force, to deal with the immediate threat of industrial action and to purge the work force of "undesirables." As Bobby Godsell of Anglo American observed after the Vaal Reefs dismissals, "Our former employees will have preferential treatment for re-employment. We have specified two pre-conditions. We will hire according to operational requirements and we will consult employment records of employees."[57] The computerized tracking system operated by the Chamber of Mines greatly enhanced TEBA's ability to exclude those individuals (often union shaft stewards and activists) whom the mines wanted to get rid of. This action, performed surreptitiously in some remote rural recruiting office, was difficult for union organizers to monitor, much less contest through legal means or further strike action. Perhaps the most successful use of the dismissals weapon came during the 1987 strike, however, when 50,000 miners were sacked by Anglo American and JCI in a bid to break the strike.

One commentator described the 1987 strike as "the most important trial of strength" between management and a union in the history of the country.[58] The NUM had been working up to it for at least three years. Buoyed by the evidence of worker solidarity and a rapidly expanding membership, the union determined to shift its bargaining strategy in the 1987 wage negotiations. It began with a wage demand of a 55 percent increase and refused to reduce it below 30 percent, keeping a gulf between its figure and the Chamber's offer too wide for Anglo to cross. In previous years, as the NUM moderated its demands, Anglo had improved its offer and secured a settlement, which in turn tended to encourage compromise. In mid-1987, the union executive had decided to face a major test of strength with the gold industry as a whole. Something of the same sentiment seemed to develop in management circles. Undoubtedly, the leadership of the Chamber of Mines had become more concerned about the union's growing support. Management probably decided that since a decisive test with the NUM was inevitable, it was better that it come sooner rather than later, before the union became an even more formidable opponent.

> We thought that this was not only a strike about this year's wage but a strike about future bargaining patterns. We had lived for a couple of years with what I could call bargaining by brinkmanship. We thought we had to go through a strike experience at least once in order to indicate that the threat of a strike was not always going to move us where NUM wanted us to be.[59]

Moreover, the mining groups held most of the key cards and they knew it. Membership in the union remained uneven across the industry. Even among members the level of support for a prolonged strike could be expected to be small. The union did not have a strike fund. The savings of most workers were known to be slight or nonexistent. Furthermore, depressed economic conditions and high unemployment across southern Africa meant that there were scores of unemployed miners or novices eager to replace every striker. Evidence that the companies had decided to confront their black workers came in the rejection of the union's offer to send the wage issue to mediation. Although unique in its scale, intensity, and degree of organization, the strike should be seen in the context not only of the two major strikes earlier in 1920 and 1946 but also of the growing solidarity among workers in the 1980s. The depth of the union's organizational structure and the extent of worker loyalty to it remained untested when the 1987 strike broke out. The gains that the NUM had made since 1982 were mostly those it was permitted to make, either by the acquiescence of the companies or by the union leadership's use of the few openings that the law allowed them.

The Chamber of Mines expected a short strike with support for the union dwindling with each passing day. Instead, the NUM managed to bring out over half the mine work force and keep most of them out for more than three weeks. The independent Labour Monitoring Group, which surveyed six of the principal mining areas, estimated that 330,000 workers were out at the height of the strike. By the fourth day, the financial cost of the strike overtook the annual cost of granting the NUM's 30 percent wage demand. At that point, the conflict intensified. The NUM claimed that its officials were denied access to mines and that workers were prevented from holding general meetings and threatened with dismissal. Management retorted that strikers were illegally preventing non-strikers from returning to work and using violence to intimidate nonunion workers. Meanwhile, police arrested the entire NUM regional committee in the Klerksdorp area. Shaft stewards and strike committee members suffered detention in other areas. Despite these actions, and the looming presence of the police, the workers stayed out.

On this occasion, however, militancy was not sufficient to bring victory. The strike ended after three weeks when further talks failed and Anglo American and JCI dismissed over 50,000 strikers. These companies proceeded simultaneously to hire strikebreakers, usually experienced miners recruited from many of the same villages as the dismissed workers. At the end of the strike, the companies initially refused to take back many of the strikers. The strike had been about wages, and the workers went back with no concessions on that front whatever. While the three-week work stoppage was an impressive demonstration of how far the NUM had come, in the end it was the power of the companies that told. In the face of mass dismissals, the strike could not continue, and the union leadership recognized this fact very quickly.

In this way, the companies dealt the NUM a sharp lesson on the limits of its power. NUM General Secretary Cyril Ramaphosa commented after the union had called off the strike that he thought he had known how tough the companies could be, but that he had underestimated them. The action was far from a complete defeat for the NUM, however. The Chamber certainly did not reckon on the power of the union to bring out the workers and keep them out. The leaders of the mining houses had been hoping for a much earlier collapse of the strike and a humiliating defeat for the NUM. This did not happen. The strike confirmed the very widespread support that the union enjoyed among the workers in those mines where it has recognition. During the prolonged struggle, the commitment of workers to the union was firm. In the aftermath of the strike, however, that loyalty was again severely tested by the strikers who were not rehired and who doubtless blamed the union for what may well be their permanent exclusion from mine employment. An out-of-court settlement between Anglo American and the NUM in 1988 saw all but 6,000 workers reinstated. While this helped to defuse some of the pressure, many NUM shaft stewards and organizers were frozen out for good.

The manner of the strike's ending revealed that the mining industry and the state retained the capacity, which they had hardly begun to use, to destroy the union. Destroying the union was not the intent in confronting the NUM in 1987, and the industry and government are unlikely to resort to anything so drastic, barring the coming to power in Pretoria of a far-right counterrevolution. Any convincing analysis of the events since the mid-1980s from the industry's standpoint would be bound to stress the benefits rather than the costs that the union has brought. In the months following the strike the companies were able to reimpose control over many of the compounds most heavily affected during the strike. Management also dramatically curtailed the access of union organizers and personnel to mine property.[60] On the defensive, the NUM was forced to begin a long rebuilding process.

Since the mid-1980s, the struggle for power in the compounds has evoked varied responses from different sections of the industry. These responses are perhaps best exemplified by the differing stances of Goldfields, Gencor, and Anglo American. One policy is to rely on traditional authoritarian methods. A Goldfields spokesman recently declared that "hostel administration is not a union matter."[61] The disciplinary code at Goldfields' wealthy Kloof Mine stated that "the maintenance of discipline on a mine is the prerogative of management and a union has no role to play."[62] In contrast, Gencor has recently shifted its position. It expressed a willingness "to talk to the NUM about how workers would want to participate in managing hostel life."[63] This new stance could lead to unprecedented worker participation in structures designed to exclude that possibility. It also throws up a fundamental contradiction. If the industry concedes to black miners (through the NUM) a greater and greater say in the running of their own lives, a major benefit, authoritarian control of the labor force, of the compound system, and of migrant labor, falls away. Aware of this possibility, planners in the Anglo American Corporation are moving forcefully in the third direction: toward a partial abandonment of the compound model and the industrial conflict associated with it since the early 1970s (see Chapter 7).

Even with the backing of the NUM, black mineworkers will remain vulnerable as long as they remain migrants. Their right to stay in an urban area now depends on their continued employment and access to state-approved accommodations. Dismissal followed by deportation are ever-present threats. Worker rights are unlikely to be secured simply by the further entrenchment of collective bargaining in the industry. Also required will be the dismantling of the compound system and its replacement by stabilization in which the miners live with their families at or close to the mines. In 1987, this condition emerged as a central platform in the NUM's demands, despite the contradictions inherent in this position.

Depopulation of the compounds and the end of migrancy, however gradual, are likely to pose as many challenges to the NUM as their perpetuation. Stabilization of part of the work force will drive an inevitable wedge between a "labor aristocracy" of permanent, more-skilled workers in owner-occupied accommodations, and unskilled and semiskilled workers still living in the compounds. If more workers move out of the hothouse organizing environment of the compounds, the NUM would have freer access to its members but shaft stewards and strike committees would find it more difficult to organize mass meetings, enforce solidarity, and police strike activity. Finally, over 40 percent of the mineworkers (and an even higher percentage of the current NUM membership) come from outside South Africa and must, according to current law, continue to be migrant workers. How to balance the claims and interests of stabilized and migrant workers, and those from inside and outside the country, is the next major challenge for the NUM. If it fails these tests, there will inevitably be serious erosion of the unity and solidarity displayed in the union's first few years of operation.

9

Conclusion

A real sense of impermanence has plagued the South African gold mining industry throughout its one-hundred-year history. Volatility has always characterized the main factors determining success: the proven reserves of payable ore; the availability of miners, machines, and money to extract the gold at a profit; and, in recent decades, the internationally determined price of gold. These factors will continue to be central in the 1990s, but some things have changed.

By the beginning of the 1990s, industry spokesmen were beginning to argue that the industry would probably have to shrink quite drastically to ensure its future.[1] Owners were closing marginal and loss-making mines and cutting costs determinedly in surviving ones. This is nothing new. The gold industry has implemented similar measures in virtually every crisis over the past century. The employers have always skillfully used the problems of the marginal mines in their efforts to cut costs throughout the industry.[2] No doubt they will continue to do so.

Although there is much continuity within the industry and its labor empire, there is also a great deal of change. Traditionally, reducing black wages was a major means of cutting costs, but in the 1990s different responses have begun to emerge. In the eighteen months preceding January 1991, the gold mines eliminated 80,000 jobs from a labor force of about 505,000.[3] Gold mining labor, although still migrant, has clearly become similar in many ways to unionized labor in industrial countries elsewhere.

In 1972, the first major study of South African migratory labor to appear in a generation was published.[4] The book described a labor system that seemed unshakeable, having endured apparently unchanged in all of its main features for more than fifty years. It rightly pointed to the profound impact that mine migrancy had had on the wider society. After 1948, apartheid's social engineers had tried to entrench migrancy as the central feature of modern racial domination. Territorial segregation and the hiving of blacks into labor-exporting enclaves variously called reserves, bantustans, and then homelands were certainly not new in 1948. Under Hendrik Verwoerd, first as minister of Native Affairs and then as prime minister, however, they became the defining elements of official race policy and a cornerstone of grand apartheid. From the perspective of 1972, six years after Verwoerd's assassination, both the migrant labor system and the racial domination that it underwrote seemed more durable and permanent than ever. In fact, though there was little sign of it, the mining industry and the country were poised on the edge of upheaval.

The first explicit signs of significant change came in 1973 when a tide of black industrial action and worker protest began to sweep the country. Simultaneously, after two decades of relative calm, violence and disorder spread across the gold fields. Chronic black labor unrest in the mines led to dozens of deaths, hundreds of injuries, and major property damage. Disorder in the mines had its counterpart in the wider society when the Soweto uprising in 1976 launched a decade of recurrent township protest against the structures and symbols of apartheid. Although the state was never seriously challenged, even at the height of the crisis in 1984–1986, these dramatic events starkly demonstrated that the timing and structure of change in South Africa was no longer at the discretion of the white minority and its leadership. The decolonization of Angola, Mozambique, and Zimbabwe reinforced this lesson, as did the legalization of the African National Congress, the South African Communist party, and other banned organizations in 1990. Political transformation in the subcontinent suggested that the mining industry's labor empire was now at risk. Before 1973, there had been little indication of any of this.

Gold mining is not, however, an industry that experienced decades of uninterrupted stability and then fell suddenly and without warning into two decades of turmoil. The upheaval of the 1970s and 1980s was only the latest in a long series of crises that have periodically threatened the labor system. Historically, the mining companies have demonstrated and continue to demonstrate an unrivaled capacity to manage and overcome recurrent political, economic, and social turbulence while maintaining intact the main features of their labor system. Mine migrancy in its present form was born in crisis. The South African War and its aftermath put the very existence of large-scale gold mining at risk. Yet, aided by the state, the mining companies succeeded in restoring and expanding their labor system and providing the basis for renewed prosperity. It was the response to the crisis at the turn of the century that entrenched migratory labor in its present form.

First, in the period between 1902 and 1940 the increasingly interventionist state entrenched a system of labor controls and pass laws that were far more effective than anything the feeble colonial governments of the Victorian era had contemplated and certainly beyond anything they could have enforced. Without this state-mandated regimentation of labor resources, expressed in intensive bureaucratization and regulation of labor markets, the mining industry's labor system could not have endured for very long. Although weak compared to the modern system at its most authoritarian in the 1960s, the labor controls of the early decades of the twentieth century constituted, at that time, a revolutionary extension of government authority. Equally, the state acted to guarantee order in the mines themselves and intervened repeatedly to suppress the chronic outbreaks of black (and white) labor militancy. The growth of state power was slow and uneven and was not at first enough to bring black labor back to the mines in sufficient numbers after the War of 1899–1902. Recognition of this fact came with the decision to import Chinese workers in 1904.

The second element in the reconstruction of the migrant labor system became evident following the repatriation of the Chinese after 1907. The mining industry slowly but successfully began to mobilize black labor on a subcontinental scale, to bureaucratize the recruiting system, impose central control, cut costs, and drive out or absorb private recruiters. Authoritarian state controls on labor mobility and a centralized approach to worker mobilization by the employers became two of the essential pillars of the mining industry's domination of the subcontinent.

The third defining element of South Africa's mine labor system was the social and political interests in the supplier areas that benefited from the perpetuation of the system. These interests included the revenue-hungry colonial administrations in the British and Portuguese territories of the region, rural African notables such as chiefs and headmen, and even many migrant homesteads themselves. Migrancy's disruptive impact has been well documented, but for large numbers of migrants the gold mines were still the best of the available options. Desperate for cash to pay for taxes, bridewealth, agricultural implements, and consumer goods, they poured onto the Rand. Colonial administrations enacted legislation to ensure that the migrants and their wages did not remain there. They also intervened periodically to stem the flow of South Africa–bound migrants and redirect them to labor-starved enterprises in their own countries.

The defining characteristics of the labor system were tested a second time in the 1940s, when the mining industry faced another prolonged period of economic difficulty, labor turbulence, and political uncertainty. Rather than raise wages, modernize labor relations, and rethink the fundamentals of the migrant labor system, the mining groups took steps to entrench more firmly their traditional methods. The measures, which restored stability in the late 1940s and early 1950s, were essentially similar to those used successfully half a century before. Backed by the state, the industry broke the 1946 strike. Under William Gemmill, the Chamber of Mines turned again to geographical expansion of the system, drawing in workers from as far afield as Tanzania.

The events of the mid-1970s bore a striking resemblance to earlier periods of crisis. Rising worker militancy and loss of control over particular labor markets prompted the usual response. The industry first attempted to crush worker opposition and to seek out new sources of labor. The state, recognizing its own symbiotic dependence on the mines, took an active role in the campaign to restore order and find labor. The disruption of the northern labor frontier in the 1970s precluded further outward expansion, however. In mobilizing 300,000 South African migrants in only three years to replace the foreigners who left or were withdrawn in 1974–1976, the mining industry sustained production levels and restored a semblance of order to the system. By the end of the decade, the mines were again running at full complement, with foreign labor in a much-reduced role, and the industry as a whole was awash with labor. Compared to earlier upheavals, the labor shortage crisis of the 1970s was relatively shortlived, easily overcome, and much less costly.

There were a number of reasons for this situation. The sudden crisis in the labor supply resolved a growing industry debate over the merits of raising blacks' wages. The mines could not afford to wait for the impersonal forces of demography and rising unemployment to solve the labor shortage. Flush with the profits of a booming gold price, the companies raised wages quickly and substantially after 1974. This tipped the balance of long-standing resistance to mine work among many black South African workers. The rural unemployed began to besiege recruiting offices, demanding better-paid underground work in preference to safer surface work. The impact of higher wages reverberated throughout the region. In every supplier state unemployed migrants clamored for jobs in the South African mines.

South Africa's domestic unemployment among rural and periurban workers had increased dramatically since the 1960s. The economy plunged deep into recession after the Soweto uprising, with accompanying mass retrenchment and soaring unemployment. High unemployment certainly predated the recession but before the mid-1970s many South African workers preferred to wait for more congenial work rather than turn to the mines. Recession and retrenchment dried up alternative employment opportunities, erasing this important element of freedom and choice for many.

State intervention greatly facilitated the mining companies' search for labor. Apart from diplomatic efforts to cultivate the remaining foreign suppliers, the state lifted long-standing legal restrictions on domestic recruiting and even put its own labor bureaus at the disposal of the mining industry. More generally, the mining industry in the 1970s took advantage of a decade or more of vigorous state planning to spread the use of migrant labor throughout the economy. The millions of poor resettled in the rural slums of the bantustans in the 1960s and 1970s formed a ready labor supply for the mines. The state had long wanted the mining industry to give precedence to South Africa's rural dispossessed over workers from neighboring countries. The industry, facing critical supply problems abroad, finally obliged. "Independence" for the Transkei, the Ciskei, and Bophuthatswana in the late 1970s meant it became harder for migrants from those areas to get nonmining jobs in South Africa and easier for the mining companies to recruit them. State support was not unconditional, however, particularly when white farmers voiced objections. Through the late 1970s, white farmers successfully resisted unrestricted labor recruiting in the "white" countryside. When they withdrew their opposition in the mid-1980s, the mines no longer needed the labor of the *platteland*. Although the state did everything it could to direct urban-based workers to the mines, most remained unpersuaded by the companies' new wage policy. The Chamber's urban recruiting drive produced unimpressive results.

Subcontinental expansion had rescued the migrant labor system in the past; this time the expansion took place within South Africa. However, the conditions that ensured the perpetuation of labor migration to the mines were also the preconditions for its transformation. The freeing of world gold prices in the 1970s injected new vigor into a stagnating South African industry, quickly returning the metal to a preeminent position in the South African economy. Buoyant prices also allowed the mines to hire more expensive domestic labor when their foreign sources were threatened. Black mine labor was no longer "cheap" labor (in the classic sense that migrants were only partially reliant on mine wages for subsistence). In turning inward for labor, the mines began to face a very different kind of worker: more proletarian, often with previous industrial experience elsewhere, and alive to broader political struggles against apartheid. New labor market realities, which forced mineworkers to return continuously or forfeit their jobs, merely heightened resentment of the cheerless conditions of mineshaft and compound.

The intense conflict that erupted in the compounds after 1973 was related, in complex ways, to the inward reorientation of the migrant labor system. Initially, management and the state responded with greater doses of force. A round of heavy expenditure on compound upgrading followed. Neither strategy had the desired effect. Finally, after several years of wrangling within the Chamber of Mines, a more modern system of industrial relations emerged. Official acceptance of the inevitability of black mine unionism marked a decisive break with the past. The rapid growth of the NUM between 1982 and 1987 would have been impossible without the watchful tolerance of the state and sections of industry. Once access was granted, however, the work force proved ripe for unionism and the compounds offered an ideal organizing environment.

As the material and political supports of the migrant labor system eroded, employers, employees, and the state began increasingly to question the future of migrancy itself. In the mid-1980s, the South African state finally acknowledged the failure of its forty-year campaign to stem permanent black urbanization and to allocate labor through an elaborate bureaucratic system of pass laws, labor bureaus, and restrictions on urban residence. It announced the end of influx control and introduced a policy of "orderly urbanization" designed to control the pace and direction of (but no longer prohibit) black urbanization. The new policies, still not fully in place, lowered the barriers and led to a rush for the cities.

A well-known caveat about forecasting suggests that it is like driving along the road while watching the rear-view mirror: It only works well when the road is straight. As the history of South Africa's migrant labor system reveals a road that is far from straight, it seems somewhat hazardous to be categorical about the future. There is considerable evidence, nonetheless, that the old pattern of long-distance contractual migrancy has now entered a phase of radical, though undoubtedly protracted, transformation. The continuing erosion of the migrants' rural bases means that the increasing urbanization of the mine work force is irreversible. This does not mean, however, the early demise of migratory labor and its single-sex barracks. Structural and fiscal constraints on state and industry make that extremely unlikely. Instead, a process of "trifurcation" is producing a more differentiated work force with three main components.

The first group in the new black work force will be a growing proportion of stabilized, skilled production workers, artisans, and supervisors living in owner-occupied housing on mine properties or in neighboring townships. Since the mid-1970s, the industry has shown renewed interest in creating such a group. In the 1980s, the stabilization of migrant miners became far more than a simple technical requirement of the changing skill profile of the black work force. Housing delivery and homeownership are now important components of an industrial relations strategy aimed at depopulating the compounds, segmenting the work force by function and geographic region, and incorporating skilled black workers. This group will compete directly with members of the white Mine Workers' Union and is already making deep inroads into previously white-only job categories. The MWU is an industrial, not an artisan, union and is reliant on an apartheid-imposed closed shop. It does not have a bright future.

Though this group of black mineworkers will grow rapidly and be of crucial importance, it should be emphasized that it will remain a small part of a very large labor force. Support for stabilization varies across the industry and even the most optimistic estimates do not foresee more than 10 percent of the black work force in family housing by the year 2000. The heavy costs associated with large-scale family housing, together with the major expenditures on township infrastructure required of the state, suggest that movement toward stabilization will be slow. Mines run out of ore eventually and the fear of ghost towns is a real one. New mining operations will undoubtedly make far greater provision for genuinely stabilized labor, but on existing labor-intensive mines it will simply be uneconomical to replace compounds with family housing on a large scale.

A second, and much larger, group of workers in the emerging black labor force will be "commuter migrants," living while at work in the compounds but commuting on a regular monthly or weekly basis from family homes in adjacent resettlement areas, rural reserves, or (in the case of Lesotho and the Orange Free State mines) foreign countries.

The final group in the new, trifurcated labor force will more closely resemble traditional labor migrants: long-distance, allottable, contract labor from mainly foreign, but some local, sources. Unlike traditional migrants, most will be career miners returning to the same mines and the same jobs for much of their working lives. Although many of these, particularly the Mozambicans, will fill the skilled artisan-type positions, they will be excluded from supervisory jobs. The majority will be used to provide the still considerable demand for unskilled labor and to staff the more dangerous, marginal, and unpopular mines. The industry's efforts to eliminate unskilled workers through mechanization and technological advance will intensify. It therefore has little reason to move the latter two groups out of the compounds.

As long as the mining industry wants to employ foreign workers (and there are various strategic reasons to do so) something approximating old-style migrancy will persist. Whether migrancy would survive the transition to majority rule in South Africa is another question; a post-apartheid state would undoubtedly feel the pressure to use the mines to ease domestic unemployment even more intensely than the current white-ruled South African state.

In the short term, foreign workers from the inner crescent of suppliers—Botswana, Lesotho, and Swaziland—are close enough to the major gold fields to allow them to participate in the form of "commuter migrancy," which has become increasingly commonplace within South Africa. Domestically, with the abolition of influx control in 1986, the proportion of commuter migrants in the mine work force is likely to expand dramatically as many workers relocate their rural homesteads and families closer to the mines.

The possibility of significant stabilization, and mineworker urbanization, over the next two decades raises issues that both management and
labor have barely begun to confront. On the one hand, management
clearly subscribes to the argument that residential segregation, family
housing, and homeownership will give workers a stake in stability and
turn them away from radicalism. The reality may be quite different. The
NUM, on the other hand, will have to deal with the different, and perhaps
conflicting, demands of various sections of an increasingly stratified work
force. The institutions of migrancy are both the greatest source of a
migrant union's strength and its greatest weakness. The depopulation of
the compounds, and radical changes in the social and spatial order in the
mines, is a desirable goal, but, paradoxically, it may also severely weaken
the union's power.

The social and geographical segmentation of the work force will thus
pose enormous challenges to the National Union of Mineworkers, which,
since the early 1980s, has had considerable success in organizing migrant
miners. As the interests of the different components of the work force
diverge, the ability of the NUM to speak for both stabilized and migrant
workers will increasingly be tested. So will its ability to continue to
represent the interests of both foreign and local workers in a situation of
chronic unemployment. Nevertheless, the early successes of the NUM
marked the development of a vibrant industrial and political culture among
the migrants. Despite the setbacks experienced in the 1987 strike, the
centrality of the black miner in the transformation of modern South Africa
is assured. The achievements of the union are the product of complex and
sometimes contradictory phenomena, the result not only of the consciousness and will of the workers themselves but also of the tacit (and frequently
active) support from employers and the state. The union's gains, while
considerable, remain essentially fragile. Whatever the future of the NUM,
the black miner will play a central role in shaping the future of black
political and industrial mobilization, of gold mining, and of the country
itself.

Ultimately, as in the Zambian case to the north, the strength and power
of black unionism in the mines will depend as much upon the nature of
the post-apartheid state as on the changing mine environment. The
incorporation and co-optation of organized black labor, paralleling a
similar process experienced by white labor in the 1920s and 1930s, could
certainly happen in a nonracial South African state.

There is another possibility. If the South African state follows a corporatist model—the tripartite rule of big government, big business, and
big unions—then black miners could become a privileged elite, protected
by a closed-shop union. The development of large, centralized migrant
unions could then turn out to be crucial. Notwithstanding the expressed

intentions of both the black mass political movements and the black unions, the corporatist outcome still seems to us to be the more likely.

Unless some new and important discoveries are made, or the metal price increases significantly in the next decade, the production of gold by South African mines is likely to fall gradually but significantly from a level of about 600 tons annually at the end of the 1980s. Reserves remain enormous: In 1990, the Economic Geology Research Unit of the University of the Witwatersrand in Johannesburg identified sufficient proven ore reserves to yield 40,000 tons of gold, nearly equal to the 42,000 tons produced by these mines in the century since large-scale mining began in 1886.[5]

The costs of extraction, however, have risen so sharply—largely but not only because of higher black wages and the increased cost of capital accompanying international economic sanctions—that analysts are predicting losses to annual gold production of between 100 and 325 tons within a generation.

Whether, or to what degree, gold production decreases, does not depend only on the gold price and on new geological discoveries. It depends also on the industry's ability to raise new capital abroad, especially equity capital. Even more importantly, it depends on how the migrant labor system in the mines develops. Gold mining will probably remain a major source of foreign exchange and employment, as it has been throughout the modern era in South Africa. It will remain crucial, but the degree to which gold mining continues to dominate the South African political economy is vitally dependent on developments in the migrant labor system. As always, the black miner will be central.

Notes

Chapter 1

1. At the beginning of the 1990s, there were more than thirty producing mines on seven principal gold fields extending across a discontinuous arc of more than 250 miles. The fields run from the Evander field in the southeastern Transvaal, westward to Johannesburg and the East, Central and West Rand fields, on to the Far West Rand field at Carletonville, then southwest to the Klerksdorp field and ending at the Orange Free State field at Welkom (see "Location Map of South African Gold Mines"). The mines are controlled by six large holding companies, called groups or houses, which also have extensive investments in coal mining, manufacturing, agribusiness, banking, and commerce. With over half the annual gold output, the Anglo American Corporation dominates. The others are Rand Mines (a subsidiary of the manufacturing giant Barlow Rand), Goldfields of South Africa (GFSA), the Afrikaner-dominated Gencor (or Genmin) group, Johannesburg Consolidated Investment (JCI), closely linked to Anglo American, and Anglo Vaal. An industry-wide organization, the Chamber of Mines of South Africa (established in 1887), speaks for the industry in its dealings with the state, handles public relations, and runs its labor system. See Appendix, Table A.1.

2. Johnstone (1989: 1–45).

3. Wilson (1972: 141–142).

4. See, for example, Alverson (1978), McNamara (1978), First (1983), Beinart (1987), Coplan (1987), Moodie (1988a), Leger and Mothibeli (1988), Guy and Thabane (1988).

5. Beinart (1982), Low (1986), Crush (1987a). On the destructive impact of migrancy, see Murray (1980), Brown (1983), Stichter (1985: 29–87).

6. Industry practice is to reserve the term "miner" for those who have a blasting certificate. In other words, there are no black miners, only black mineworkers. Even the NUM has implicitly accepted this distinction in its choice of name. In this book both terms are used interchangeably.

7. Johnstone (1976), Lacey (1981), Jeeves (1985).

8. Delius (1983: 62–82), Turrell (1987: 19–31), Worger (1987: 54–109).

9. Bundy (1979), Beinart and Bundy (1987), Keegan (1987).

10. Jeeves (1985: 121–186).

11. Historically the recruiting organization was divided into two branches responsible for different geographical areas. The Witwatersrand Native Labour Association (WNLA) recruited in areas to the north of South Africa; the Native Recruiting Corporation (NRC) took charge within South Africa and in the former High Commission Territories of Botswana, Lesotho, and Swaziland. In 1977, the

Chamber renamed its recruiting organization the Employment Bureau of Africa (TEBA).

12. Harries (1983), Crush (1987a).

13. Lacey (1981), Morrell (1988).

14. The Color Bar refers to a group of labor practices, informal trade union practices, government regulation, and legislation, all of which were developed over time to prevent blacks from competing for certain categories of jobs monopolized by whites. Although sometimes referred to as the "job bar," the Color Bar is a special kind of job bar and is a more accurate description of what we want to convey.

15. Yudelman (1983).

16. Johnstone (1976), Davies (1979).

17. Yudelman (1983: 16–19, 32–33).

18. Marks and Trapido (1979), Harries (1986).

19. Yudelman and Jeeves (1986), Gemmill (1930).

20. Vail and White (1980), Jeeves (1986).

21. Yudelman (1983: 13–42).

22. Simkins (1981a), Beinart (1986).

23. O'Meara (1982), Moodie (1986), James (1987).

24. Hindson (1987), Moodie (1988b).

25. Agency for Industrial Mission (1976, 1985), National Union of Mineworkers (1988), Moodie (1988a), Leger and Mothibeli (1988), Malunga (1988).

26. On changes in domestic patterns of migrancy in the 1970s, see Lemon (1982, 1984), Mabin (1989).

27. Katzen (1964), Wilson (1972), Yudelman (1983: 263–290).

28. Brett (1983), Gowa (1983).

29. The individual mines get financing, purchasing, technical advice, general administration, and accounting services from their respective parent groups, and they must conform generally to group policies as laid down from the center. However, the groups relate to the individual mines in complex ways. A tradition survives of considerable autonomy for the individual mining companies, which are mostly separately listed on the Johannesburg Stock Exchange. Something of the aura of autocratic power that once was associated with ship captains still clings to the position of mine manager.

30. Wiehahn (1982).

31. Interview with David Yudelman, Cape Town, 4 February 1986.

32. Webster (1988).

33. Leger (1986), James and Lever (1987).

34. Wilson (1975: 182) refers presciently but in passing to the growth of the "call-in card system" increasing the likelihood that workers will return to the same employer and to the streamlined administrative machinery of the state and the purchase of computers to make this possible. What has actually happened has been a streamlining of the Chamber of Mines machinery and its computerization to a degree that dwarfs the capability of the state; see also Crush (1987b).

35. According to the Chief Executive of the Chamber of Mines, Tom Main, the Chamber has nine million palm prints on computer file (interview with David Yudelman, Johannesburg, 11 January 1990).

Chapter 2

1. For further details, see Jeeves (1986).

2. See for instance the Report of the Royal Commission on Rhodesia-Nyasaland (Bledisloe Commission), 1938–1939, paragraphs 283–284; and Chanock (1977: 229–232).

3. See Greenberg (1980), Lacey (1981), Lipton (1977, 1985).

4. Public Record Office (PRO), CO 525/166/44053/3, Pt 1, Secretary, U.K. High Commission to Malcolm MacDonald, 10 May 1937; CAD, NTS 2247 603/280, 4, SNA to Union High Commissioner, London, 22 February 1952; NTS 2247 603/280, 4, WNLA statement to the ILO, 27 September 1951; NTS 2247 603/280, 3, *Rand Daily Mail* clipping, 13 June 1951; CO 525/166/44053/3, Pt 1/1937, Memorandum on recruiting for the Rand mines, n.d. [1937].

5. These negotiations are discussed in Jeeves (1986: 73–92).

6. WNLA *Annual Reports*, 1934–1945, on tropical recruiting levels.

7. CO 525/166/44053/3, Pt 1, Minutes by J. A. Calder, 4 February 1937, noting that by 1937 the Rand mines were expecting to draw 70,000 miners per year from the northern territories; WNLA *Annual Reports*, 1935–1945.

8. BNA S S344/10/1, Notes on the northern Bechuanaland organization of WNLA, 21 July 1945; and Wilson (1972: 70).

9. BNA S S344/10/1, "Report of the Commission Appointed by the Secretary for Dominion Affairs to Advise on the Medical Administration in the Bechuanaland Protectorate," 1947. The Chamber's initial grant was shared between the three High Commission Territories.

10. This brief survey of mine medical conditions is based on the following: CAD, ARB 1508, 1103, Secretary for Mines and Industries to the Minister, 21 October 1924; BNA S B437/1/1, NRC memo, 26 June 1928; BNA S S398/6, medical report of 500 men consecutively examined at Molepolole, by P. M. Shepherd, June 1933; BNA S S426/5, Note on British Social Hygiene Council memo, 23 July 1935; BNA S S426/3, R. Reilly, Acting Resident Commissioner to High Commissioner, 3 April 1935; CAD, K 26, 5, Frank H. Brownlee, evidence, 2856-66; NTS 2006 8/280, NRC memo on medical examinations, 2 March 1923; and Packard (1987), Marks and Andersson (1987).

11. *Report of the Witwatersrand Mine Native Wages Commission . . . 1943*. U.G. 21-1944, Pretoria, Government Printer, 1943, paragraphs 43, 114, 122, 200, and chapter VII.

12. Ibid.

13. Report of the Miners' Phthisis Acts Commission, 1941–1943 (Pretoria, U.G. 22-43), cited in Wilson (1972: 51); Marks and Andersson (1987: 180–181), on the National Health Services Commission.

14. This was the conclusion of T. F. Sandford, a senior Provincial Commissioner of the Northern Rhodesian government, when he toured the mines in 1937. He was one of several such officials to make tours of inspection at this time; see CO 525/166/44053/3, Pt 2, Report of T. F. Sandford, 18 November 1937; CO 525/166/44053/3, Pt 2/1937, S. S. Murray to Chief Secretary, Zomba, 8 October 1937.

15. For many years Orenstein was the director of the Rand Mines, Ltd., Health Department and a key pioneer in the development of effective industrial health and sanitation policies for the industry.

16. BNA S S426/5, C. F. Rey to Gemmill, 18 December 1935; Gemmill to Government Secretary, Mafeking, 21 December 1935.

17. BNA S S392/7/1, Report of Sir Walter Johnson on the Medical Administration of the Bechuanaland Protectorate, July 1937, on the high rates of syphilis and tuberculosis among the mineworkers and other population groups in the territory; PRO, DO 35 1182/Y1032/2/1, H. W. Dyke, *Basutoland Annual Medical and Public Health Report for . . . 1942*, 1 May 1943, noting a sharp increase in the incidence of TB, which he attributed partly to increased recruiting rates for the Rand.

18. Packard (1987: 208).

19. CMIC, Rand Mines Health Dept., Annual Report, 1935. The morbidity figures for TB were 11.78 per thousand in 1915 and 2.23 per thousand in 1935.

20. A comprehensive X-ray examination, using miniature radiography, was introduced for the black work force after World War II.

21. Jeeves (1985: 229); CO 525/166/44053/3, Pt 1/1937, Memorandum on recruiting for the Rand mines, n.d. [1937], reporting the views of Orenstein and Chamber officials; CO 525/173/44053/3 Pt 1/1938, "Gold Producers' Committee Memorandum on the Mortality Amongst Tropical Natives," 21 April 1938.

22. CO 525/172/44053/1938 Gore Browne to Malcolm MacDonald, 15 August 1938, in this case, a personal letter, condemning the "deplorable" medical facilities for migrants.

23. BNA S S344/8, Resident Magistrate, Francistown to Resident Commissioner's Office, Mafeking, 12 February 1936; BNA S S344/10/1, E. Baring, U.K. High Commissioner, Pretoria to Viscount Addison, Commonwealth Relations Office, 19 September 1947; and Gemmill (1952).

24. WNLA *Annual Report*, 1939; Hailey (1957: 658–659); ZA, CNC S1561/4, W. Gemmill to H. J. Stanley, Governor of Southern Rhodesia, 15 December 1937.

25. Gemmill (1952: 15–19).

26. On the farm labor scheme see BNA S S344/11, draft agreement between WNLA and the Southern Rhodesian National Farmers' Union, 1942; and S344/11, WNLA Secretary to Government Secretary, Mafeking, 8 April 1947.

27. CO 525/185/44053/1, Pt 2, K. L. Hall to Malcolm MacDonald, 15 February 1940.

28. CAD, MNW 804 2489/25, 3A, Gold Producers' Committee statement to Beyers, Minister of Mines and Industries, 21 June 1928; NTS 2124 230/280, 2, Notes of meeting between Chamber of Mines' representatives and Native Affairs Department officials and others, 1935; NTS 2115 225/280, 9, H. Pirow, Government Mining Engineer, to Secretary for Mines, 9 January 1936; NTS 2115 225/280, 9, P. Duncan, Minister of Mines, to Minister of the Interior, 11 January 1936.

29. Existing controls were anything but trivial and included criminal penalties for breach of labor contracts under long-standing Master and Servant Acts, the ubiquitous pass laws, and a tradition of the unrestrained exercise of employer discipline; NTS 2094, 2095, 2096, 222/280, *passim*.

30. NTS 2247 603/280, 3, Memorandum to the SNA on the Salisbury Conference by F. Rodseth, Under-Secretary of Native Affairs, n.d. [October 1950], quoting the comment of the High Commissioner.

31. The National party and its coalition partner had been returned with a narrow majority earlier in the year; NTS 2247 603/280, 3, Memorandum on the Control of the Migration of Native Labourers in Southern Africa, n.d. [1950]

32. NTS 2247 603/280, 3, contains a complete transcript of the conference.

33. NTS 2247 603/280, 2, Points Made [at the Salisbury Conference, October 1950]; NTS 2247 603/280, 3, Memorandum to the SNA on the Salisbury Conference by F. Rodseth, Under-Secretary of Native Affairs, n.d. [October 1950].

34. NTS 2247 603/280, 3, Secretary for External Affairs to the High Commissioner, Salisbury, 14 July 1951.

35. *Rand Daily Mail*, 13 June 1951, clipping in NTS 2247 603/280, 3.

36. NTS 2247 603/280, 4, WNLA statement to the International Labour Office "Dealing with the Restrictions Placed on the Spontaneous Flow of African Migrant Labor," 27 September 1951.

37. Ibid.

38. Ibid.

39. *Rand Daily Mail*, 13 June 1951, clipping in NTS 2247 603/280, 3.

40. NTS 2247 603/280, 4, S. R. Fleischer to Secretary for External Affairs, n.d. [1952], N. C. Havenga to R. A. Butler, 12 February 1952, Butler to Havenga, 20 March 1952, Union High Commissioner, Salisbury to Secretary for External Affairs, 21 May 1952, W. M. Eiselen to Chamber Manager, S. R. Fleischer, 10 June 1952.

41. NTS 2247 603/280, 3, Report to the Gold Producers' Committee on the Salisbury Conference by W. and J. Gemmill, 9 October 1950, Union High Commissioner, Salisbury to Secretary of External Affairs, May 1952.

42. NTS 2247 603/280, 4, W. Gemmill to Acting Labour Advisor, Zomba, 9 July 1952.

43. NTS 2124 230/280 Union High Commissioner, Salisbury to Secretary for External Affairs, Pretoria, 13 January 1953; Chanock (1977: 259–263), Hyam (1987: 145–172).

Chapter 3

1. Wolpe (1972), Legassick (1977).

2. Knight (1977: 31–48).

3. James (1987).

4. Stein (1978).

5. CAD ARB 1400 1060/23, Pt 1, 19 September 1945, Memorandum—Recognition of Native Trade Unions; ARB 1401, 1063/23, Pt 2, 10 April 1946, Department of Labour, Native (Industrial) Bill, Memorandum; 1946, Explanatory Memorandum Native (Industrial) Bill.

6. Moodie (1986).

7. This brief account relies on the full analysis of the strike in O'Meara (1982), Simons and Simons (1983: 569–578), and Moodie (1986).

8. O'Meara (1982).

9. Moodie (1986).

10. Ibid.

11. This refers to absolute numbers. Owing to the overall growth in the labor force, South African labor remained a much smaller proportion of the mine labor force in the 1950s and 1960s than before the war.

12. O'Meara (1982), Wilson (1972: 81–83, 114–115), Horwitz (1967: 351–372), Nattrass (1981: 154–161), and Gemmill (1947, 1952: 19).

13. Queen's University Archives (QA), Southern African Labour Papers (SALP), Commissions File, Chamber of Mines Statement of Evidence to the Tomlinson Commission.

14. Knight (1977: 41); NRC 357, Mine Recruiting File, Report of a Conference of NRC District Superintendents at Johannesburg, 10, 11, 18 October 1949.

15. This argument stated that wage increases worked to reduce the labor supply because workers responded by contracting for shorter periods on the mines. Their motivation was said to be primitive and limited to a specific monetary target, which, once achieved, resulted in their leaving for home.

16. NRC 357, Mine Recruiting File, Report of a Conference of NRC District Superintendents, 17 December 1947.

17. Ibid.; and NRC 357, Report of 1949 Conference.

18. NRC 357, Report of 1947 Conference.

19. NRC 357, Report of the 1949 Conference.

20. NRC 612, Letter from J. A. Gemmill, 9 February 1956.

21. NRC 612, Memorandum by G. O. Lovett, 28 December 1953.

22. Ibid.

23. NRC 357, Reports of the Conferences in 1947 and 1949; NRC 612, Letter from J. A. Gemmill, 9 February 1956.

24. See Crush (1987a: 90–115) on the background; and Booth (1987).

25. NRC 612, Memorandum on the labor supply situation, n.d. [1953–1954].

26. Ibid.

27. QA, SALP, Commissions File, Chamber of Mines Statement of Evidence to the Tomlinson Commission.

28. Wolpe (1972).

29. UNISA Documentation Centre, Pretoria, Commission on the Socio-Economic Development of the Native Areas within the Union of South Africa, Record of Evidence, vol. XII, 20 May 1952, 612–660.

30. Ibid.

31. NRC 612, Letter from J. A. Gemmill, 9 February 1956; the absolute numbers increased after 1953 but the proportion of the total coming from South Africa remained remarkably constant over the whole period, 1947–1968.

32. Originally recommended by the Fagan Commission, the bureaus were set up under the Native Laws Amendment Act of 1952 as part of the Malan government's expansion of the influx-control regulations. All African work-seekers had to register at a bureau and rural blacks could not legally go to town without the permission of their local labor bureau; see Horrell (1978: 248).

33. NRC 726, Report of an Interview between Chamber representatives, Koch and P. H. Anderson and the Minister of Finance, N. Diederichs, n.d.

34. Knight (1977: 47), Owen (1963).

35. The overall increase in the proportion of workers from Mozambique and the north masked a sharp fall in the number recruited from the tropical areas from a high of 78,893 in 1961 to a low of 41,234 in 1966, before recovering to 83,976 in 1972. Probably this change reflected both the industry's need to pay some attention to government preference for local sourcing as well as the decision of the Tanzanian (1961) and Zambian (1964) authorities to pull out their workers at independence.

36. These figures of tonnage per worker are an overestimate because the total tonnage extracted includes the output from non-Chamber companies, while the figures for the average number employed include the workers employed by Chamber members. But the rate of improvement in productivity over the decade is accurately captured and confirmed by other calculations; see Wagner (1986).

37. Concentrated stoping was important because it reduced the amount of waste rock extracted and sent for sorting, which in turn reduced labor costs and raised the gold yield per ton of ore extracted.

38. Cartwright (1967: 141–172, 1968: 189–190), Gregory (1962).

39. These went back to the early years of the century. Conditions improved dramatically between 1933 and 1939 with the gold price increase but then deteriorated again; see Fraser and Jeeves (1977: 215–219), Cartwright (1968: 209–228, 301–303); and CAD, MNW 804 2489/25, 3A, Gold Producers' Committee statement to Minister of Mines and Industries, 21 June 1928.

40. See Brookes (1951) and Rheinallt Jones (1953: 50–51) praising the new proposals. Oppenheimer was talking about the more skilled categories of underground mining work and those involving the trades. Most of the black mine clerks and senior underground "indunas" and "boss boys" (team leaders in modern, deracialized parlance) were already stabilized in all of the mines. All of them maintained family housing for these workers whose numbers rarely reached the permitted maximum of 3 percent of complement.

41. UNISA, Commission on the Socio-Economic Development of the Native Areas within the Union of South Africa, Record of Evidence, vol. XII, 20 May 1952, W. J. Busschau, 625, James Gemmill, 627; QA, SALP, Commissions File, "Experiments in Stabilization of Labour," Chamber of Mines Statement of Evidence to the Tomlinson Commission.

42. UNISA, Commission on Socio-Economic Development, 625–629.

43. Ibid., W. D. Wilson, 637–638.

44. Gregory (1962: 578–579).

45. In 1947, in evidence to the Fagan Commission, the Chamber of Mines had declared that "the abolition of the present migratory system in favour of stabilized mining communities would be disastrous to the Mining Industry and to the Country"; see Transvaal Chamber of Mines, "Statement No. 10: The Economic Effect on the Industry of any Change-Over from Migratory to Stabilised Labour," Johannesburg, 1947, 10. For further evidence of ambivalent attitudes to stabilization within the mining industry, see Transvaal Chamber of Mines, "Statement No. 8: The Social Aspect of Migratory Labour as Opposed to Stabilized Mining Communities"; University of Witwatersrand (UW), AD 1756, A 44, Native Laws

Commission of Enquiry, Minutes of Evidence, 2891–2989, 3000–3132, 3329–3388; UW, A 394, Rheinallt Jones Papers, "The Housing of Native Mine Workers," 1947; and Gemmill (1947).

Chapter 4

1. Legassick (1977: 187).
2. Fraser and Jeeves (1977: Section III).
3. Johnstone (1976: 93–98), Davies (1979), Lacey (1981: 183–189).
4. Jeeves (1985: 59–84).
5. Moroney (1982).
6. Greenberg (1980: 315), Wilson (1972: 157–158).
7. Yudelman (1983: 190).
8. Lipton (1985: 112–116).
9. Wilson (1972: 110–119).
10. Lipton (1985: 116–117).
11. Yudelman (1983: 264–265).
12. Simons and Simons (1987: 69–72).
13. The Viljoen Commission reported in 1965 against the small crack in the Color Bar that the experiment had opened up.
14. Rafel (1987: 265–291).
15. *Financial Mail*, 17 November 1966.
16. For the struggle to control the white unions during the war, see Simons and Simons (1983: 508–553), O'Meara (1978: 45–72).
17. Sitas (1979).
18. Ibid., 36–42.
19. Ibid., 53–54.
20. Wilson (1972: 116).
21. *Financial Mail*, 7 April 1967, 25 April 1969.
22. Ibid., 16 October 1970.
23. Ibid., 17 July 1970, 4 September 1970, 30 April 1971.
24. Lipton (1985: 59).
25. Rafel (1987: 271–273).
26. Lipton (1985: 207–208).
27. In the end black advancement did not have to wait for the boring machine, which is still not developed.
28. Under the Republic's industrial conciliation legislation this is one of several steps required before a legal strike can take place.
29. "Report of the Commission of Inquiry into the Possible Introduction of a Five-Day Working Week in the Mining Industry," Pretoria, 1977 [Franszen Commission].
30. Leger (1986).
31. Lipton (1985: 204–206). The HNP—Herstigte Nasionale Partie.
32. James and Lever (1987b: 17).
33. Leger (1986).
34. Ramaphosa (1986).

35. Leger (1986).
36. CAD, K26, 8, 7309–7399.

Chapter 5

1. Crush (1986).
2. de Vletter (1987: 214).
3. See Clarke (1977a, 1977b).
4. Yudelman (1987).
5. Yudelman (1983: 265–268).
6. Wilson (1972: 141).
7. Friedman (1987: 37–68).
8. The "maximum average clause" was designed to constrain competition from bidding up wages in order to maintain the recruiting monopsony, while not precluding the payment of productivity bonuses. The rule stated that the individual mines and groups could pay variable wages to black workers for things such as piecework, but that average remuneration rates should not exceed the maximum rate set by the Chamber.
9. Simons and Simons (1978: 3).
10. Association of Mine Managers (1971), McAllister (1974). We are grateful to Pat McAllister for information about the latter report.
11. In 1974, at least seven mines had a work force that was more than 50 percent Malawian; "Mining's Missing Men," *Financial Mail*, 6 December 1974.
12. A. Fleischer, Interview with David Yudelman, Johannesburg, 1984.
13. "South African Move to End Deadlock," *Natal Mercury*, 20 September 1974.
14. Christiansen and Kydd (1983), Kydd (1984).
15. QA, SALP, Malawi File. The numbers employed on the estates increased from 50,000 to 88,000 between 1966 and 1973. By 1976, over 155,000 were employed; Prior and Chipeta (1990).
16. In April 1977, the mines reportedly employed 207 Malawians who had arrived "under their own steam"; "Bad News for Foreign Miners," *Financial Mail*, 10 June 1977.
17. "Banda Steps Down," *Financial Mail*, 17 December 1976.
18. QA, SALP, Malawi File.
19. Ibid.
20. Clarke (1976), McNamara (1985: 149–151); "Ripples in Rhodesia," *Financial Mail*, 27 March 1975; "Southern Comfort," *Financial Mail*, 9 May 1975.
21. McNamara (1985: 151–182).
22. TEBA Official, Interview with Jonathan Crush, Maseru, 1981.
23. For detailed accounts of migrancy to South Africa from the BLS countries and the relations of domination and dependency to which it gave rise, see Murray (1981), Parsons (1984), Crush (1987a).
24. "Bid for Mine Recruits," *Natal Mercury*, 27 September 1974.
25. After 1928, the mines deferred a portion of Mozambican miners' wages (60 percent after 1964) to the Portuguese in gold valued at the official price. After

1969 and the introduction of a two-tier pricing system, the Portuguese received the gold at the official price and sold it at the free market price. Between 1970 and 1974, as the differential between the two prices widened, the Portuguese drew a handsome profit of R40 million. Frelimo inherited the system and made an estimated R150 million in 1975. In 1977, the IMF abolished the system of two-tier pricing providing the mining industry with the excuse to do away with the gold premium. See "Lisbon's Windfall," *Financial Mail*, 11 April 1974; "Gold and Frelimo," *Financial Mail*, 29 August 1975; "Gold Blow for Frelimo," *Financial Mail*, 5 November 1976; A. Fleischer, Interview with David Yudelman, Johannesburg, 1984.

26. QA, SALP, Mozambique File.

27. This would clearly have violated the Mozambique Convention (1964), which stipulated a minimum number of 60,000 Mozambicans in the mines. TEBA's Five Year Plan of 1978 budgeted a figure of 30,000 Mozambicans; see QA, SALP, Mine Recruiting File.

28. First (1983: 58–59). The number of Mozambicans recruited by WNLA fell from 115,309 in 1975 to 32,803 in 1976.

29. Scholars have disagreed over who was responsible, Frelimo or the Chamber of Mines; compare First (1983) with Isaacman (1987). Our argument is that, in a sense, both are correct. If Frelimo had not inadvertently reduced the flow, the Chamber would probably have done it for them.

30. For details of the discussions, see Yudelman and Jeeves (1986: 114–115).

31. QA, SALP, Mine Recruiting File.

32. QA, SALP, Mine Recruiting File (Natal); Greenberg and Giliomee (1983), Greenberg (1987).

33. QA, SALP, Foreign Labour File.

34. *Rand Daily Mail*, 1 May 1984.

35. QA, SALP, Foreign Labour File.

36. Ibid.

37. Ibid.

38. "Reprieve for Up to 30,000 Mozambicans," *Business Day*, 16 January 1987; Centro de Estudos Africanos (1987b), Leger (1987a).

39. "Mine Labour," *Financial Mail*, 23 June 1978.

40. QA, SALP, Foreign Labour File.

41. James (1988), Hirschsohn (1988).

42. TEBA Official, Interview with Jonathan Crush, Johannesburg, February 1986.

43. Thabane and Guy (1984).

44. Anglo American Official, Interview with Jonathan Crush, Johannesburg, August 1988.

45. *Rand Daily Mail*, 1 May 1984.

46. de Vletter (1987).

47. Centro de Estudos Africanos (1987a).

48. McNamara (1988).

49. Jochelson, Mothibeli, and Leger (1988). Rates of HIV positivity (at 3.8 percent) were low among most groups of migrants except Malawians. Random testing showed that Malawian HIV prevalence was at 10 percent by early 1988.

50. United Nations Economic and Social Council (1978a); "Towards a Labour Opec," *Financial Mail*, 17 October 1980.

51. United Nations Economic and Social Council (1978b).

52. Stahl and Böhning (1981).

53. Parsons and Mashaba (1980).

54. de Vletter (1985b).

55. Southern Africa Labour Commission, Report of the Sixth Meeting, Maputo, 18-19 October 1984, Speech by Rui Baltazar, Minister of Finance, People's Republic of Mozambique.

56. "Chamber Scotches Claims of Bias Against Lesotho," *Citizen*, 11 January 1980; and Cobbe (1986).

57. de Vletter (1985b).

Chapter 6

1. NRC Natal, Togela Ferry Reports.

2. Beinart (1978).

3. NRC Natal, Togela Ferry Reports.

4. Wilson (1980).

5. The "unemployment debate" in South Africa is long and involved, centering around issues of measurement and causation. The literature is summarized in Bromberger (1978), Simkins (1981b), and Bell and Padayachee (1984).

6. These figures are from a 1976 sample survey of black mineworkers; see Ault and Rutman (1983, 1985).

7. Wilson and Ramphele (1989: 33–98).

8. Surplus People Project (1983), Freund (1984), Murray (1987), Unterhalter (1987).

9. de Klerk (1984), Lipton (1985: 85–109), Bradford (1988).

10. Yudelman and Jeeves (1986).

11. Thompson designed an aggressive media campaign to change the "image" of mining and was also responsible for the acronym TEBA (The Employment Bureau of Africa) and its new "mining hat" logo. Black miners had referred to the NRC as "Kwateba" for many years, after the corporation's first manager, H. M. Taberer.

12. Chamber of Mines Official, Interview with Jonathan Crush, Johannesburg, February 1984.

13. Much of this section is based on interviews with officials who were involved in this hectic bout of activity. Transcripts of all interviews are in the QA, SALP. Supplementary documentation is lodged in the QA, SALP, Farm Labour File.

14. "The Men on the Mines," *Financial Mail*, 8 October 1976.

15. "Sugar Industry: Topping the Mines," *Financial Mail*, 7 February 1975; "Competing with the Mines," *Financial Mail*, 1 October 1976.

16. A. Fleischer, Interview with David Yudelman, Johannesburg, 1984.

17. TEBA Official, Interview with Jonathan Crush, Ulundi, April 1984.

18. The analysis in this section is based on district-level recruiting figures obtained by the late Jill Nattrass.

19. Southall (1982).

20. TEBA Official, Interview with Jonathan Crush, Pietermaritzburg, March 1984.

21. Sharp and Spiegel (1985).

22. Cobbett (1986b) estimates.

23. TEBA Official, Interview with Jonathan Crush, Nqutu, April 1984.

24. Lacey (1981: 130–180).

25. Wilson, Kooy, and Hendrie (1977), Simkins (1984).

26. Lipton (1985: 97).

27. Platzky and Walker (1985: 122–123).

28. Bekker and Humphries (1986).

29. Chamber of Mines Official, Interview with Jonathan Crush, Johannesburg, February 1984.

30. QA, SALP, Mine Recruiting File.

31. The account of farm and urban recruiting that follows is based upon interviews with participants and material collected for this project. Supporting documentation is lodged with the QA, SALP, Urban and Farm Labour files.

32. *Natal Witness*, 13 September 1975.

33. "Recruits for the Mines," *Natal Mercury*, 18 February 1975.

34. TEBA Official, Interview with Jonathan Crush, Pietermaritzburg, March 1984.

35. QA, SALP, Farm Labour File.

36. TEBA Official, Interview with Jonathan Crush, Pietermaritzburg, March 1984.

37. Bank (1984).

38. Haysom and Thompson (1986).

39. South African Agricultural Union Annual Report 1983/4.

40. For details of controls on farm workers in the 1980s, see Haysom and Thompson (1986) and Farm Labour Project (1982).

41. Worker Interview No. 39, conducted by Zamankosi Mpanza (with Jonathan Crush), May 1984. Transcripts of all interviews with black workers are lodged at Queen's University. To preserve the anonymity of workers all interviews are referred to simply by number.

42. "Urban Blacks: The Mines Beckon," *Financial Mail*, 17 January 1975.

43. Chamber of Mines Official, Interview with Jonathan Crush, Johannesburg, February 1984.

44. Stahl and Böhning (1981: 166).

45. Parsons and Mashaba (1980: 50).

46. TEBA Official, Interview with Jonathan Crush, Durban, March 1984.

47. Ibid.

48. "Bad News for Foreign Miners," *Financial Mail*, 10 June 1977.

49. Møller and Schlemmer (1977).

50. TEBA Official, Interview with Jonathan Crush, Durban, March 1984.

51. For details of the ERPM experiment, see *Business Day*, 26 November 1985; *Sowetan*, 26 November 1985; and *South African Mining*, February 1985; QA, SALP, Urban Labour File.

52. Chamber of Mines Official, Interview with Jonathan Crush, Johannesburg, February 1986.

Chapter 7

1. Information from interviews conducted by Jonathan Crush, Natal, March 1984.

2. See Kruger and Rundle (1981), Packard (1988, 1989), Moodie (forthcoming).

3. Napier (1980).

4. Gunther and de Vries (1978), Lawrence (1979), Parsons (1982).

5. McAllister (1979), Laburn and McNamara (1980), Peart (1982).

6. These included the Centre of Applied Social Sciences (under Lawrence Schlemmer) at the University of Natal; the Institute of Social and Economic Research (under Philip Mayer) at Rhodes University; and two American economists at Southern Illinois University.

7. The Employment Bureau of Africa (TEBA), TEBA Five Year Plan, 1978–1983.

8. The history of reengagement policy is considered in Crush (1989c).

9. TEBA Official, Interview with Jonathan Crush, Johannesburg, February 1986.

10. Worker Interview No. 7.

11. Quoted in Thabane and Guy (1984: 13).

12. TEBA Official, Interview with Jonathan Crush, Nqutu, April 1984.

13. Worker Interview No. 3.

14. Quoted in Thabane and Guy (1984: 19).

15. TEBA Official, Interview with Jonathan Crush, Ulundi, April 1984.

16. For further details, see Crush (1987b).

17. Bush, Cliffe, and Jansen (1987).

18. See, for example, Martin and Beittel (1987), May, Nattrass, and Peters (1985), Sharp and Spiegel (1985), Muller (1986).

19. Market Research Africa (1986).

20. First (1983).

21. QA, SALP, Mine Recruiting File.

22. TEBA Official, Interview with Jonathan Crush, Pietermaritzburg, March 1984.

23. Worker Interview No. 25.

24. Worker Interview No. 16.

25. Worker Interview No. 36.

26. Worker Interview No. 37.

27. QA, SALP, Mine Recruiting File (Ciskei).

28. Quoted in Agency for Industrial Mission (1985: 7).

29. Worker Interview No. 60.

30. *Citizen*, 15 September 1984.

31. Worker Interview No. 41.

32. QA, SALP, Mine Recruiting File.

33. Greenberg and Giliomee (1983), Greenberg (1987).

34. TEBA Official, Interview with Jonathan Crush, Ulundi, April 1984.

35. Spiegel (1980).

36. Murray (1987: 239).

37. TEBA Official, Interview with Jonathan Crush, Johannesburg, March 1984.

38. Thompson (1967).

39. For a discussion of the establishment and role of the Industrial Court, see Friedman (1987).

40. QA, SALP, Commissions File, Du Randt Commission, 1975.

41. Lipton (1980).

42. "Making Do with Migrants," *Financial Mail*, 15 August 1980; "Tightening the Screws," *Financial Mail*, 12 June 1981.

43. See, for example, "South African Mining and Migrant Labour," *Mining Survey*, 2 (1986), 37–43.

44. QA, SALP, Mine Recruiting File, Memorandum by A. Fleischer, 1978; and A. Fleischer, Interview with David Yudelman, Johannesburg, 1984.

45. QA, SALP, Commissions File, Du Randt Commission, 1975.

46. Ibid.

47. QA, SALP, Foreign Labour File.

48. Crush (1989a).

49. QA, SALP, Foreign Labour File.

50. Hindson (1985), Cobbett (1986a).

51. Market Research Africa (1986).

52. "Family Housing for Miners," *Business Day*, 22 September 1987.

53. Anglo American Official, Interview with Jonathan Crush, January 1988.

54. "R700-m Plan for Housing in OFS," *The Star*, 23 April 1987.

55. "Other Mine Groups Plan Houses Like Anglo," *Business Day*, 23 September 1987.

56. For a critical review of current policy, see Crush and James (1991).

57. Crankshaw and Hart (1988).

Chapter 8

1. Moodie (1986).

2. See McNamara (1978: 29–49), Moodie (1980).

3. McNamara (1985: 81).

4. Murray (1981).

5. Friedman (1987).

6. "After the Shooting," *Financial Mail*, 14 September 1973; Leys (1975).

7. Horner and Kooy (1980).

8. McNamara (1985: 367).

9. Unpublished Report of the Inter-Departmental Committee of Inquiry into Riots on the Mines in the Republic of South Africa, 1976, 7–8 (as cited in *South African Labour Bulletin*, hereafter referred to as *SALB*), 4(5), 1978, 51.

10. "Behind the Violence," *Financial Mail*, 8 March 1974.

11. McNamara (1985: 98).

12. Kirkwood (1974), Horner and Kooy (1976), McNamara (1988); "The Mine Workers' Struggle," *SALB*, 1(8), 1975; "At the Crossroads: Violence on the Mines has become Endemic," *Financial Mail*, 17 January 1975.

13. McNamara (1985: 209–221).
14. Ibid.; Horner and Kooy (1980: 40–41).
15. McNamara (1988: 26–28).
16. McNamara (1985: 343–344). On the Russians, see Guy and Thabane (1987).
17. McNamara (1985: 306).
18. Cited in Hirschsohn (1988: 51).
19. The findings of the enquiry were extensively summarized in Hemson and Morris (1978) and in *SALB*, 4(5), 1978, 49-65.
20. QA, SALP, Commissions File, Du Randt Commission.
21. "The Moment of Truth," *Financial Mail*, 30 August 1974. From 1975, the Chamber of Mines research division administered some 20,000 "attitudinal surveys" of black miners in order to provide management with information on "the attitudes, beliefs and opinions of its employees on a routine, continuous basis"; see Robertson (1983: 271).
22. Moodie (1983).
23. Lipton (1980: 133).
24. Friedman (1987: 152–153).
25. Cited in Hirschsohn (1988: 51).
26. Chamber of Mines, Statement of Evidence to the Commission of Inquiry into Labour Legislation, n.d. We are grateful to Wilmot James for providing us with a copy of this document. See also Wiehahn (1982).
27. Pycroft and Munslow (1988); see also *SALB*, 7(1–3), 1981, on the recognition issue.
28. Friedman (1987: 358).
29. On the industrial holdings of Anglo American, see Innes (1984: 142–228). Two prominent Anglo executives, Dennis Etheredge and Zac de Beer both moved from Zambia to South Africa in 1974.
30. A. Fleischer, Interview with David Yudelman, Johannesburg, 1984.
31. Leger and van Niekerk (1986: 72).
32. Thompson (1984).
33. McNamara (1988: 31–32).
34. McNamara (1985: 311).
35. "Daunting Challenge Facing Industry, Says Liebenberg," *S.A. Mining*, February 1987, 5–57.
36. Thompson (1984: 157–158).
37. Leger and van Niekerk (1986).
38. SAIRR, *Race Relations Survey, 1984*, Johannesburg, 1985, 332.
39. Hirschsohn (1988: 48–51). Anglo American recognized the NUM's right to bargain in any job category once union membership reached 33 percent of that category. At Gencor, the equivalent figure was 40–45 percent; at the others it was 50 percent plus one worker.
40. Cited in Hirschsohn (1988: 48).
41. *Industrial Law Journal*, 7, 1986, 379.
42. Thompson (1984: 158–159).
43. National Union of Mineworkers, "Collective Bargaining at Anglo American Mines," unpublished report, 1988.

44. Thompson (1984: 159–160); Ramaphosa (1985).

45. Leger (1987b).

46. Leger, Maller, and Myers (1986: 81).

47. "Kinross Day of Mourning," *SALB*, 12(1), 1986, 15–17.

48. Leger (1987b).

49. Leger and Mothibeli (1988).

50. Southall (1983), Crush (1989b).

51. M. Golding, Interview with David Yudelman, Johannesburg, 1986.

52. Golding (1985a).

53. McNamara (1988: 33).

54. Research on the compounds during the 1987 strike currently being undertaken by Wilmot James of the University of Cape Town should add considerably to our knowledge and understanding of these struggles.

55. NUM v. Western Areas Gold Mining Co. Ltd, *Industrial Law Journal*, 6(2), 1985, 380–387.

56. Leger and van Niekerk (1986: 76).

57. Quoted in *SALB*, 10(7), 1985; and B. Godsell, Interview with David Yudelman, Johannesburg, January 1986.

58. *Weekly Mail*, 14 August 1987.

59. B. Godsell quoted in Markham and Mothibeli (1987: 62).

60. National Union of Mineworkers, "Collective Bargaining at Anglo American Mines," unpublished report, 1988.

61. *Business Day*, 3 March 1987.

62. NUM v. Kloof Gold Mining Co Ltd, *Industrial Law Journal*, 7(2), 1986, 379.

63. *Business Day*, 3 March 1987.

Chapter 9

1. "Gold Mining: Will Smaller Mean Stronger?" cover story, *Financial Mail*, 18 January 1991.

2. Yudelman (1983: 144).

3. *Financial Mail*, 18 January 1991, 22.

4. Wilson (1972).

5. "How Fast Is Gold Mining's Sun Setting?" cover story, *Financial Mail*, 11 May 1990, 28.

Statistical Appendix

Table A.1 South African Gold Mines: Production and Employment

	Gold Production (1985)			Black Work Force	
	Total (Kg)	Grade (g/ton milled)	Total Profit (Rands mil)	No. of Workers (Jan.1986)	No. of Recognized NUM Members (July 1988)
Anglo American					
Vaal Reefs	80,367	7.40	1,082.0	40,336	18,762
Free State Cons. (N)	53,365	5.02	1,255.5	48,023	24,232
Free State Cons. (S)	53,124	4.53	48.9	49,605	32,653
Western Deep Levels	37,200	6.73	593.1	23,921	8,332
Elandsrand	11,836	6.25	194.1	7,336	5,498
Subtotal	235,892	5.80	3,173.6	169,321	84,477
JCI					
Randfontein	27,059	4.12	359.7	13,635	1,739
Western Areas	16,074	4.10	75.6	12,530	
Subtotal	43,133	4.11	435.3	26,165	1,739
Gencor					
Buffelsfontein	35,112	7.16	353.7	23,514	5,102
Winkelhaak	13,761	5.81	239.2	10,180	4,313
Kinross	12,355	6.06	201.1	7,219	5,194
St Helena	9,743	4.41	110.7	11,006	4,218
Unisel	9,407	6.88	174.3	3,976	
Stilfontein	8,556	5.05	42.2	9,971	4,361
Grootvlei	5,735	3.22	48.9	5,981	5,007
West Rand Cons.	3,893	1.90	6.8	4,979	
Leslie	3,493	2.49	27.7	4,389	2,530
Bracken	3,070	3.26	32.6	3,357	2,403
Marievale	1,006	2.88	4.4	1,579	725
Subtotal	106,131	5.03	1,241.6	86,151	33,853

(continues)

Table A.1   *(continued)*

Rand Mines

Harmony	28,730	3.43	240.9	27,228	
Blyvooruitzicht	13,238	5.94	159.3	10,649	900
ERPM	9,223	3.40	-0.3	18,796	
Durban Deep	7,483	3.14	23.6	10,478	
Subtotal	58,314	3.72	423.5	67,151	900

Goldfields

Driefontein	59,766	10.48	1,200.2	30,469	5,685
Kloof	28,841	13.50	605.4	15,370	
Libanon	8,932	5.13	116.3	7,989	5,717
Doornfontein	8,661	5.92	89.0	10,517	4,356
Deelkraal	7,588	5.06	101.3	7,056	3,244
Venterspost	5,903	3.78	37.0	8,186	
Subtotal	119,691	8.49	2,149.2	79,587	19,002

Anglovaal

Hartebeestfontein	30,912	9.80	580.1	15,981	
Loraine	8,734	5.59	92.1	9,087	
Subtotal	39,646	8.40	672.2	25,068	
TOTAL	602,807	5.60	8,095.4	453,443	139,971

Source: Compiled from Chamber of Mines of South Africa, *Annual Reports* (Johannesburg, 1985, 1988) and unpublished data from Chamber of Mines of South Africa.

Table A.2 Gold Mine Minimum Monthly Wage by Job Grade[a] and Mining Group, 1986 (Rands)

Job Grade[b]	Chamber	Anglo	JCI	Gencor	Rand Mines	Goldfields
Underground Workers						
1	229	268	269	244	n/a	229
2	278	313	311	281	n/a	278
3	323	366	364	339	n/a	344
4	377	433	427	396	n/a	416
5	436	547	542	483	n/a	547
6	508	591	588	576	n/a	n/a
7	588	691	691	695	n/a	650
8	725	807	811	846	n/a	812
Surface Workers						
1	195	325	325	205	226	195
2	237	270	271	238	264	249
3	280	316	316	288	300	313
4	326	374	375	343	355	389
5	377	436	438	413	407	477
6	441	520	516	495	490	n/a
7	515	615	605	608	588	580
8	647	723	712	762	751	702

[a]Minimum Industry Rates set by Chamber of Mines of South Africa.
[b]1, least skilled; 8, most skilled.
Source: Unpublished data from Chamber of Mines of South Africa.

Table A.3 Sources of Mine Labor, Black Workers Received by Mines, 1920-1989

	South Africa		HCT/BLS		S. Mozam.		Tropical		Total	
	No.	%	No.	%	No.	%	No.	%	No.	%[a]
1920	107,503	51	27,965	13	76,370	36	0	0	211,838	100
1921	110,978	51	41,319	19	65,747	30	0	0	218,044	100
1922	108,185	55	34,081	17	53,297	27	0	0	195,563	100
1923	122,887	54	33,092	15	71,350	31	0	0	227,329	100
1924	119,547	57	36,460	17	55,504	26	0	0	211,511	100
1925	101,020	54	25,395	14	61,097	33	0	0	187,512	100
1926	109,980	54	39,050	19	54,358	27	0	0	203,388	100
1927	105,572	50	28,959	14	75,866	36	0	0	210,397	100
1928	104,584	52	29,524	15	66,094	33	0	0	200,202	100
1929	102,808	51	36,065	18	60,831	30	0	0	199,704	100
1930	125,598	54	48,873	21	56,258	24	163	0	230,892	100
1931	123,216	55	46,083	21	54,077	24	56	0	223,432	100
1932	127,417	61	43,766	21	39,129	19	29	0	210,341	100
1933	133,727	61	42,894	20	41,398	19	28	0	218,047	100
1934	143,589	59	46,667	19	50,665	21	2,291	1	243,212	100
1935	157,047	58	54,015	20	58,923	22	530	0	270,515	100
1936	167,646	54	67,680	22	70,092	23	3,442	1	308,860	100
1937	154,449	53	63,637	22	64,365	22	10,540	4	292,991	100
1938	177,194	51	81,873	24	73,617	21	15,464	4	348,148	100
1939	174,031	50	78,408	23	73,921	21	19,668	6	346,028	100
1940	200,191	52	90,242	24	71,129	19	22,365	6	383,927	100
1941	196,113	52	76,634	20	78,880	21	26,067	7	377,694	100
1942	154,739	50	59,504	19	74,507	24	21,656	7	310,406	100
1943	138,543	44	65,299	21	84,479	27	23,213	7	311,534	100
1944	131,669	45	53,989	19	78,950	27	26,770	9	291,378	100
1945	150,764	47	59,721	19	78,806	25	30,856	10	320,147	100
1946	133,133	45	58,674	20	74,117	25	31,307	11	297,231	100
1947	121,843	41	55,874	19	78,308	27	39,461	13	295,486	100
1948	110,774	39	54,441	19	76,800	27	41,570	15	283,585	100
1949	131,542	40	71,810	22	82,636	25	42,054	13	328,042	100
1950	137,933	43	61,687	19	78,365	25	39,921	13	317,906	100
1951	132,325	41	68,957	21	89,243	27	35,309	11	325,834	100
1952	133,679	42	70,008	22	80,299	25	31,015	10	315,001	100
1953	129,318	41	63,448	20	81,203	26	39,111	12	313,080	100

Year									
1954	146,647	42	71,335	20	86,103	25	45,369	13	349,454	100
1955	145,066	41	81,674	23	78,350	22	45,520	13	350,610	100
1956	146,031	40	80,995	22	81,003	22	53,509	15	361,538	100
1957	143,592	40	80,177	22	80,743	22	55,402	15	359,914	100
1958	159,669	40	91,537	23	82,391	21	62,038	16	395,635	100
1959	175,705	41	100,175	24	81,673	19	67,825	16	425,378	100
1960	174,287	41	97,781	23	79,065	19	75,000	18	426,133	100
1961	170,151	40	92,480	22	85,387	20	78,933	18	426,951	100
1962	162,721	42	89,522	23	78,118	20	60,256	15	390,617	100
1963	149,446	42	73,360	21	67,679	19	63,279	18	353,764	100
1964	132,050	39	72,158	21	79,920	23	58,120	17	342,248	100
1965	128,311	37	86,151	25	78,168	22	57,752	16	350,382	100
1966	126,221	37	87,471	26	84,911	25	41,234	12	339,837	100
1967	124,062	38	77,498	24	79,493	24	44,414	14	325,467	100
1968	130,029	38	86,499	25	81,583	24	43,254	13	341,365	100
1969	116,373	36	83,056	26	74,648	23	47,099	15	321,176	100
1970	98,917	28	96,917	27	93,773	26	68,365	19	357,972	100
1971	81,806	26	86,429	27	75,365	24	71,699	23	315,299	100
1972	86,399	25	100,457	29	73,936	21	83,976	24	344,768	100
1973	94,653	27	103,488	29	74,759	21	79,462	23	352,362	100
1974	103,966	32	95,979	30	86,324	27	33,705	11	319,974	100
1975	189,165	42	134,451	30	113,488	25	14,410	3	451,514	100
1976	288,344	55	160,210	31	32,648	6	38,979	7	520,181	100
1977	366,255	63	131,293	23	36,447	6	43,481	8	577,476	100
1978	311,380	63	117,966	24	37,905	8	29,482	6	496,733	100
1979	265,790	63	106,462	25	25,090	6	26,378	6	423,720	100
1980	248,333	62	98,592	25	37,734	9	16,586	4	401,245	100
1981	250,226	63	98,307	25	33,928	9	14,831	4	397,292	100
1982	239,943	62	95,881	25	35,732	9	14,997	4	386,553	100
1983	232,550	62	93,795	25	37,157	10	13,713	4	377,215	100
1984	262,478	61	106,540	25	42,294	10	16,060	4	427,372	100
1985	270,872	59	115,044	25	52,410	12	17,613	4	455,939	100
1986	272,083	59	125,528	27	44,258	10	19,046	4	460,915	100
1987	252,727	57	136,666	31	39,599	9	18,592	4	447,584	100
1988	239,969	59	133,197	33	33,805	8	3,490	1	410,461	100
1989	217,474	56	129,869	33	44,015	11	17	0	391,375	100

aPercentages do not always add up to 100 owing to rounding errors.

Note: HCT/BLS, Lesotho, Botswana, Swaziland; S.Mozam., Southern Mozambique: Tropical, Territories situated north of 22° south latitude.

Source: Adapted from Witwatersrand Native Labour Association, *Annual Reports* (Johannesburg, 1920-1984).

Table A.4 Sources of Mine Labor, Average Number of Black Workers Employed, 1920-1989

	RSA	Mozambique	Malawi	Zimbabwe	Zambia	Tanzania	Angola	Botswana	Lesotho	Swaziland	Other	TOTAL
1920	74,452	77,921	354	179	12			2,112	10,439	3,449	5,484	174,402
1921	67,301	77,545	281	159	9			2,403	15,445	3,103	4,684	170,930
1922	66,092	71,465	256	135	13			2,997	14,366	3,965	9	159,298
1923	83,266	70,968	157	100	6			2,710	14,494	4,266	9	175,976
1924	79,099	74,464	131	73	4			2,926	15,731	4,290	11	176,729
1925	78,884	73,210	136	68	4			2,547	14,256	3,999	14	173,118
1926	81,078	75,947	128	58	3			2,720	15,938	4,425	10	180,307
1927	80,129	82,275	141	58	4			1,856	16,898	4,052	8	185,421
1928	83,191	90,914	220	55	9			1,862	15,363	3,541	6	195,161
1929	82,266	85,854	246	46	7			2,463	17,300	3,939	6	192,127
1930	92,772	77,828		44		183		3,151	22,306	4,345	5	200,634
1931	103,679	66,941		42		142		3,149	29,662	4,738	6	208,359
1932	118,114	58,891		38		125		4,304	29,949	4,945	6	216,372
1933	135,615	48,521		29	767	99		5,150	32,494	6,131	6	228,045
1934	146,486	51,437		32	570	101		6,475	33,626	6,227	8	245,159
1935	152,902	62,576	49	27	201	109		7,505	34,788	6,865	8	265,400
1936	167,753	67,622	629	216	1,132			7,799	39,637	7,356	9	291,213
1937	155,868	81,165	1,735	2,336	2,011			8,964	39,666	6,874	8	297,748
1938	156,706	80,844	3,691	6,277	2,402			11,365	43,759	7,062	208	311,923
1939	160,636	75,676	6,563	6,959	2,725			12,038	45,575	6,791	120	316,760
1940	179,708	74,693	8,037	8,112	3,294		698	14,427	52,044	7,152	70	347,766
1941	192,730	80,369	3,621	8,459	2,783		2,949	13,731	50,950	7,749	56	363,908
1942	176,726	89,350	8,145	9,378	1,367	59	3,337	11,544	47,514	6,195	55	355,086
1943	147,413	79,910	2,438	9,767		314	4,555	9,948	39,066	5,694	1,397	301,869
1944	133,802	84,163	4,829	8,534	46	641	6,088	8,657	36,483	5,716	4,034	292,993
1945	143,370	78,588	4,973	8,301	27	1,461	8,711	10,102	36,414	5,688	4,732	302,337
1946	136,768	78,002	7,521	6,763	680	2,605	9,248	9,681	37,317	6,036	4,270	298,891
1947	124,489	81,691	8,304	5,583	4,104	2,497	8,461	10,850	34,210	6,331	2,437	288,957
1948	107,043	80,234	9,403	4,778	3,479	4,449	10,517	10,723	30,330	6,298	4,145	271,399
1949	108,669	85,975	9,196	4,638	3,468	5,609	10,032	11,905	35,275	6,614	4,695	286,076
1950	121,609	86,246	7,831	2,073	3,102	5,495	9,767	12,390	34,467	6,619	4,826	294,425
1951	113,092	91,978	7,717	654	3,108	6,542	8,467	12,246	31,448	6,322	5,114	286,688
1952	110,654	95,485	6,971	380	3,327	6,484	7,485	13,071	32,777	5,866	3,829	286,329
1953	110,718	91,637	5,456	207	3,013	6,869	7,232	12,135	30,843	5,988	3,229	278,327

Year												
1954	116,189	102,974	8,595	136	3,427	7,961	8,279	13,268	31,705	6,631	2,133	301,298
1955	121,364	99,449	12,407	162	3,849	8,758	8,801	14,195	36,332	6,682	2,299	314,298
1956	122,649	99,189	14,035	392	3,689	12,138	9,083	14,727	39,037	6,400	2,175	323,514
1957	117,855	103,008	14,227	482	4,147	13,178	9,727	15,749	38,586	6,507	1,115	324,581
1958	120,671	99,277	16,129	483	4,535	13,396	9,932	17,067	41,222	6,405	799	329,951
1959	138,075	103,125	20,314	596	5,929	14,601	11,566	19,219	48,896	6,766	939	370,026
1960	141,806	101,733	21,934	747	5,292	14,025	12,364	21,404	48,842	6,623	844	375,614
1961	146,605	100,678	30,002	900	7,078	13,856	11,825	20,218	49,050	6,784	1,351	388,345
1962	150,804	101,092	24,425	917	6,720	6,147	12,893	20,044	51,169	7,179	2,104	383,494
1963	150,049	89,694	25,517	887	6,116	3,035	17,010	19,947	52,279	6,688	2,736	373,958
1964	144,684	87,418	35,658	565	5,650	2,165	14,806	21,277	53,292	5,862	3,078	364,455
1965	136,551	89,191	38,580	653	5,898	404	11,169	23,630	54,819	5,580	2,686	369,161
1966	128,810	88,949	39,014	758	6,038	9	9,922	25,175	56,558	4,880	3,119	363,232
1967	126,862	91,797	38,182	76	2,140		6,732	21,507	57,853	4,800	3,249	353,198
1968	129,167	90,580	47,446	3	17		5,282	21,353	59,325	5,183	3,276	361,632
1969	122,319	88,117	53,315	4			4,335	19,571	59,661	5,586	1,906	354,814
1970	105,169	93,203	78,492	3			4,125	20,461	63,988	6,269	972	370,312
1971	86,868	95,431	92,782	3			4,136	21,539	65,639	5,840	1,134	370,547
1972	78,742	82,487	111,768	3			3,444	21,407	69,167	5,015	1,087	361,595
1973	81,375	86,696	119,141	2			2,600	22,799	78,995	5,301	148	378,826
1974	77,350	85,489	108,431	3			2,792	19,406	74,606	5,811	8	349,985
1975	101,553	97,216	27,904	2,485			3,431	20,291	78,114	8,391	12	321,846
1976	143,509	73,863	571	16,778			2,910	23,765	84,873	10,835	475	342,507
1977	189,106	36,922	3,495	18,653			1,043	20,257	92,026	9,335	2,650	373,487
1978	204,318	35,234	17,910	11,984			189	17,647	91,278	8,269	1,965	388,794
1979	215,577	38,995	15,033	7,643			23	17,645	94,379	7,926	1,852	399,123
1980	233,088	39,539	13,569	5,770			5	17,763	96,309	8,090	1,404	415,537
1981	240,082	40,094	12,937	2,968			2	17,539	98,288	8,872	1,334	422,116
1982	239,065	42,544	13,565	112			2	16,659	95,731	9,294	1,215	418,187
1983	245,718	42,473	14,287	1			2	17,225	96,409	10,624	1,264	428,003
1984	253,548	44,195	15,120	2			1	17,257	95,675	10,833	218	436,849
1985	256,377	50,126	16,849				1	18,079	97,639	12,365	4	451,440
1986	266,150	56,237	17,923					19,106	103,742	14,239	1	477,398
1987	273,422	45,917	17,620					17,939	105,506	15,743		476,147
1988	265,268	44,084	13,090					17,061	100,951	16,171		456,625
1989	243,556	42,807	2,212					16,051	100,529	16,730		421,885

Source: Unpublished data from Chamber of Mines of South Africa.

Table A.5 Mine Labor Recruits by Source Area, 1973-1985[a]

	1973	1974	1975	1976	1977	1978	1979	1980	1981	1982	1983	1984	1985
South African Sources													
Transkei	51,402	53,951	85,345	119,777	167,271	144,610	124,583	119,186	133,377	133,428	120,450	128,650	137,339
Ciskei[b]	9,334	11,137	22,794	35,239	43,616	27,237	23,269	24,144	23,179	20,373	19,556	17,872	18,543
Orange Free State[c]	4,042	4,506	6,059	9,412	15,014	20,936	18,331	17,032	17,588	20,344	15,685	19,441	21,565
Bophuthatswana	6,743	7,274	13,988	26,201	39,556	32,531	26,877	31,485	29,647	23,403	28,824	42,331	41,737
Other Transvaal	730	668	1,377	1,679	18,974	14,871	10,992	11,987	10,941	12,023	12,182	12,114	13,492
Kwazulu	1,582	1,648	4,016	8,029	13,281	12,374	13,076	15,364	16,497	18,797	16,495	16,136	14,917
Other Natal	2,590	3,392	9,041	18,738	23,255	17,012	13,134	13,275	12,747	12,715	9,550	10,522	9,966
Depots[d]	230	1,977	8,857	13,465	9,077	4,306	2,211	3,790	3,762	6,307	9,076	11,890	14,070
Subtotal	76,653	84,553	151,477	232,540	330,044	273,877	232,473	236,263	247,738	247,390	231,818	258,956	271,629

Proximate Foreign Sources

Lesotho	61,888	62,162	80,730	98,952	92,075	84,245	75,065	71,213	71,196	73,040	66,323	75,558	84,185
Southern Botswana	18,748	14,796	22,193	24,758	27,166	18,850	17,563	17,005	15,486	18,640	16,549	17,279	17,298
Swaziland	7,795	9,109	16,149	25,961	16,104	14,765	13,863	11,661	12,509	14,593	14,429	14,088	14,665
Subtotal	88,431	86,067	119,072	149,671	135,345	117,860	106,491	99,879	99,191	106,273	97,301	106,925	116,148

Other Foreign Sources

Northern Botswana	4,171	2,122	5,886	6,846	4,585	3,162	2,026	3,248	2,627	2,634	1,493	1,306	1,191
Malawi	79,462	29,951	86	149	17,908	16,382	17,845	11,510	13,115	13,996	13,159	16,082	17,600
Mozambique	73,599	87,456	110,901	29,654	35,898	23,725	25,226	38,503	34,114	37,098	37,714	42,192	52,392
Zimbabwe			8,599	32,475	18,436	9,389	7,715	3,973	681				
Subtotal	157,232	119,529	125,472	69,124	76,827	52,658	52,812	57,234	50,537	53,728	52,366	59,580	71,183
Total	322,316	290,149	396,021	451,335	544,216	444,395	391,776	393,376	397,466	407,391	381,485	425,461	458,960

[a]Includes novices, experienced mineworkers and VRG holders.
[b]Includes urban centers in the Eastern Cape.
[c]Includes Thaba Nchu and Qwa Qwa.
[d]TEBA Depots at Johannesburg, Carletonville and Klerksdorp.
Source: Compiled from unpublished recruiting data of the Employment Bureau of Africa (TEBA).

Bibliography

Agency for Industrial Mission (1976). *Another Blanket: Report on an Investigation into the Migrant Situation, June 1976*. Horizon, AIM.

———— (1985). "With Dirty Shoes." Draft report, Johannesburg.

Alverson, H. (1978). *Mind in the Heart of Darkness: Value and Self-Identity among the Tswana of Southern Africa*. New Haven, CT, Yale University Press.

Association of Mine Managers of South Africa (1971). "Report on Mine Labour Organisations." Unpublished report, Johannesburg.

Ault, D., and G. Rutman (1983). "Economic Factors Affecting the Amount of Labour Supplied by Rural Africans to the Gold Mining Industry, 1976–80." Unpublished report, Johannesburg, Chamber of Mines.

———— (1985). "The Rural African and Gold Mining in Southern Africa, 1976–1980." *South African Journal of Economics*, 53, 1–23.

Bank, L. (1984). "Finding a Job in QwaQwa." Carnegie Conference Paper, No. 282, University of Cape Town.

Beinart, W. (1978). "South Africa's Internal Labour Supply with Special Reference to Transkei and Bophuthatswana." Paper presented at the Conference on Migratory Labour in Southern Africa, Lusaka.

———— (1982). *The Political Economy of Pondoland, 1860-1930*. Cambridge, Cambridge University Press.

———— (1986). "Decline or Stasis: A Return to Transkeian Statistics." Paper presented at the African Studies Association Meeting, New Orleans.

———— (1987). "Worker Consciousness, Ethnic Particularism and Nationalism: The Experiences of a South African Migrant, 1930–1960." In S. Marks and S. Trapido, eds., *The Politics of Race, Class and Nationalism in Twentieth-Century South Africa*. London, Longman, 286–309.

———— (1988). "Agrarian Historiography and Agrarian Reconstruction." In J. Lonsdale, ed., *South Africa in Question*. London, James Currey, 134–153.

Beinart, W., and C. Bundy (1987). *Hidden Struggles in Rural South Africa: Politics and Popular Movements in the Transkei and Eastern Cape, 1890-1930*. London, James Currey.

Bekker, S., and R. Humphries (1986). *From Control to Confusion: The Changing Role of Administration Boards in South Africa, 1971-83*. Johannesburg, Shuter and Shuter.

Bell, T., and V. Padayachee (1984). "Unemployment in South Africa: Trends, Causes and Cures." Carnegie Conference Paper, No. 119, University of Cape Town.

Booth, A. (1987). "Capitalism and the Competition for Swazi Labour, 1945–60." *Journal of Southern African Studies,* 13, 125–150.

Bradford, H. (1988). "Reformulating Resettlement: A Review of *The Surplus People.*" *Social Dynamics,* 14, 67–74.

Brett, E. (1983). *International Money and Capitalist Crisis: The Anatomy of Global Disintegration.* London, Heinemann.

Bromberger, N. (1978). "Unemployment in South Africa: A Survey of Research." *Social Dynamics,* 4, 12–28.

Brookes, E. (1951). "New Outlook on Mine Native Housing at Welkom." *Optima,* 1, 5–7.

Brown, B. (1983). "The Impact of Male Labour Migration on Women in Botswana." *African Affairs,* 82, 367–388.

Bundy, C. (1979). *The Rise and Fall of the South African Peasantry.* Berkeley, University of California Press.

Bush, R., L. Cliffe, and V. Jansen (1987). "The Crisis in the Reproduction of Migrant Labour in Southern Africa." In P. Lawrence, ed., *World Recession and the Food Crisis in Africa.* London, James Currey, 283–299.

Cartwright, A. (1967). *Gold Paved the Way.* London, Macmillan.

———— (1968). *The Golden Age.* Cape Town, Purnell.

Centro de Estudos Africanos (1987a). "The South African Mining Industry and Mozambican Migrant Labour in the 1980s." International Labour Organization, International Migration for Employment Working Paper No. 29.

———— (1987b). "Mozambican Migrant Workers in South Africa: The Impact of the Expulsion Order." International Labour Organization, International Migration for Employment Working Paper No. 37.

Chanock, M. (1977). *Unconsummated Union: Britain, Rhodesia and South Africa, 1900–45.* Manchester, Manchester University Press.

Christiansen, R., and J. Kydd (1983). "The Return of Malawian Labour from South Africa and Zimbabwe." *Journal of Modern African Studies,* 21, 311–326.

Clarke, D. (1976). "Contract Labour From Rhodesia to the South African Gold-mines." Southern Africa Labour and Development Research Unit, University of Cape Town, Working Paper No. 6.

———— (1977a). "The South African Chamber of Mines: Policy and Strategy with Reference to Foreign African Labour Supply." Development Studies Research Group Working Paper No. 2, University of Natal, Pietermaritzburg.

———— (1977b). "Foreign Migrant Labour in Southern Africa: Studies on Accumulation in the Labour Reserves, Demand Determinants and Supply Relationships." International Labour Organization, Migration for Employment Project Working Paper No. 16.

Cobbe, J. (1986). "Consequences for Lesotho of Changing South African Labour Demand." *African Affairs,* 85, 23–48.

Cobbett, W. (1986a). " 'Orderly Urbanisation': Continuity and Change in Influx Control." *South African Labour Bulletin,* 11(8), 106–121.

———— (1986b). "A Test Case for 'Planned Urbanisation.' " *Work in Progress,* 42, 25–30.

Coplan, D. (1987). "The Power of Oral Poetry: Narrative Songs of the Basotho Migrants." *Research in African Literatures,* 18, 1–35.

Crankshaw, O., and T. Hart (1988). "Factors Affecting the Urbanisation of Migrant Labour." Unpublished report, National Institute for Personnel Research, Johannesburg.

Crush, J. (1984). "Uneven Labour Migration in Southern Africa: Conceptions and Misconceptions." *South African Geographical Journal*, 66, 115–132.

_____ (1986). "The Extrusion of Foreign Labour from the South African Gold Mining Industry." *Geoforum*, 17, 161–172.

_____ (1987a). *The Struggle for Swazi Labour, 1890–1920*. Montreal/Kingston, McGill-Queen's University Press.

_____ (1987b). "Restructuring Migrant Labour on the Gold Mines." In G. Moss and I. Obery, eds., *South African Review: Volume 4*. Johannesburg, Ravan Press, 283–291.

_____ (1989a). "Accommodating Black Miners: Home-Ownership on the Mines." In G. Moss and I. Obery, eds., *South African Review: Volume 5*. Johannesburg, Ravan Press, 335–347.

_____ (1989b). "Migrancy and Militance: The Case of the National Union of Mineworkers of South Africa." *African Affairs*, 88, 5–24.

_____ (1989c). "Flexible Migrancy and Labour Control on the South African Gold Mines." Unpublished paper, Queen's University, Kingston, Canada.

Crush, J., and W. James (1991). "Depopulating the Compounds: Migrant Labour and Mine Housing in South Africa." *World Development*, 19, 301–316

Davies, R. (1979). *Capital State and White Labour in South Africa: An Historical Materialist Analysis of Class Formation and Class Relations, 1900–1960*. Atlantic Highlands, NJ, Humanities Press.

de Klerk, M. (1984). "Seasons That Will Never Return: The Impact of Farm Mechanization on Employment, Incomes and Population Distribution in the Western Transvaal." *Journal of Southern African Studies*, 11, 84–105.

Delius, P. (1983). *The Land Belongs to Us: The Pedi Polity, the Boers and the British in the Nineteenth Century Transvaal*. Johannesburg, Ravan Press.

de Vletter, F. (1985a). "Recent Trends and Prospects of Black Migration to South Africa." *Journal of Modern African Studies*, 23, 667–702.

_____ (1985b). "The Rights and Welfare of Migrant Workers: Scope and Limits of Joint Action by Southern African Migrant-Sending Countries." International Labour Organization, International Migration for Employment Working Paper No. 23.

_____ (1987). "Foreign Labour on the South African Gold Mines: New Insights on an Old Problem." *International Labour Review*, 126, 199–218.

de Vries, P., and E. Ackerman (1980). "The Use, Understanding and Administration of Valid Re-engagement Guarantees on Gold Mines." *Human Resources Monitoring Report*, 4(2), 1–16.

Farm Labour Project (1982). "Submission to the Manpower Commission on Farm Labour." Unpublished report, Johannesburg.

First, R. (1983). *Black Gold: The Mozambican Miner, Proletarian and Peasant*. New York, St. Martin's Press.

Fraser, M., and A. Jeeves, eds. (1977). *All That Glittered: Selected Correspondence of Lionel Phillips, 1890–1924*. Cape Town, Oxford University Press.

Freund, W. (1984). "Forced Resettlement and the Political Economy of South Africa." *Review of African Political Economy*, 29, 49–63.

―――― (1988). "South African Gold Mining in Crisis and Transformation." Paper presented at the Annual Meeting of Canadian Association of African Studies, Queen's University, Kingston, Canada.

Friedman, S. (1987). *Building Tomorrow Today: African Workers in Trade Unions, 1970-1984*. Johannesburg, Ravan Press.

Gemmill, J. A. (1961). "Native Labour on the Gold Mines." In *Transactions of the 7th Commonwealth Mining and Metallurgical Congress. Volume 1: Papers and Discussion*. Johannesburg, 290–306.

Gemmill, W. (1930). "A Short Description of the Operations of the Organizations through which the Native Labour Employed by the Witwatersrand Gold Mines is Obtained." In *Proceedings of the Third Empire Mining and Metallurgical Congress*. Johannesburg, 1–16.

―――― (1947). "Statement on Migrant Native Labour." In Transvaal Chamber of Mines, *Statements of Evidence Submitted to the Native Laws Commission of Enquiry*. Johannesburg, 67–77.

―――― (1952). "The Growing Reservoir of Native Labour for the Mines." *Optima*, 2, 15–19.

Golding, M. (1985a). "Mass Dismissals on the Mines: The Workers' Story." *South African Labour Bulletin*, 10(7), 97–118.

―――― (1985b). "Mass Struggles on the Mines." *South African Labour Bulletin*, 10(6), 101–122.

Gowa, J. (1983). *Closing the Gold Window: Domestic Politics and the End of Bretton Woods*. London, Cornell University Press.

Greenberg, S. (1980). *Race and State in Capitalist Development: Comparative Perspectives*. New Haven, CT, Yale University Press.

―――― (1987). *Legitimating the Illegitimate: State, Markets and Resistance in South Africa*. Berkeley, University of California Press.

Greenberg, S., and H. Giliomee (1983). "Labour Bureaucracies and the African Reserves." *South African Labour Bulletin*, 8(4), 37–53.

Gregory, T. (1962). *Ernest Oppenheimer and the Economic Development of Southern Africa*. Cape Town, Oxford University Press.

Gunther, K., and P. de Vries (1978). "Will Mining Be Able to Retain its Novices?" *Human Resources Monitoring Report*, 2(4), 1–6.

Guy, J., and M. Thabane (1987). "The Ma-Rashea: A Participant's Perspective." In B. Bozzoli, ed., *Class, Community and Conflict: South African Perspectives*. Johannesburg, Ravan Press, 436–456.

―――― (1988). "Technology, Ethnicity and Ideology: Basotho Miners and Shaft-Sinking on the South African Gold Mines." *Journal of Southern African Studies*, 14, 257–278.

Hailey, Lord (1957). *An African Survey*, 2nd ed. London, Oxford University Press.

Harries, P. (1983). "Labour Migration from Mozambique to South Africa." Unpublished Ph.D. thesis, University of London.

―――― (1986). "Capital, State, and Labour on the 19th Century Witwatersrand: A Reassessment." *South African Historical Journal*, 18, 25–45.

Haysom, N., and C. Thompson (1986). "Labouring Under the Law: South African Farm Workers." *Industrial Law Journal*, 7, 218–240.

Hemson, D., and J. Morris (1978). "Black Working Class Resistance on South African Mines." Paper presented at the Conference on Migratory Labour in Southern Africa, Lusaka.

Hindson, D. (1985). "Orderly Urbanization and Influx Control: From Territorial Apartheid to Regional Spacial Ordering in South Africa." *Cahiers d'Etudes Africaines*, 99, 401–432.

────── (1987). *Pass Controls and the Urban African Proletariat*. Johannesburg, Ravan Press.

Hirschsohn, P. (1988). "Management Ideology and Environmental Turbulence: Understanding Labour Policies in the South African Gold Mining Industry." Unpublished M.Sc. thesis, Oxford University.

Horner, D., and A. Kooy (1976). "Conflict on South African Mines, 1972–1976." Southern African Labour and Development Research Unit, University of Cape Town, Working Paper No. 5.

────── (1980). "Conflict on South African Mines, 1972–1979." Southern African Labour and Development Research Unit, University of Cape Town, Working Paper No. 29.

Horrell, M., compiler (1978). *Laws Affecting Race Relations in South Africa*. Johannesburg, South African Institute of Race Relations.

Horwitz, R. (1967). *The Political Economy of South Africa*. London, Weidenfeld and Nicolson.

Hyam, R. (1987). "The Geopolitical Origins of the Central African Federation: Britain, Rhodesia and South Africa, 1948–1953." *Historical Journal*, 30, 145–172.

Innes, D. (1984). *Anglo: Anglo American and the Rise of Modern South Africa*. Johannesburg, Ravan Press.

Isaacman, A. (1987). "Mozambique and the Regional Conflict in Southern Africa." *Current History*, 87, 213–216, 230–234.

James, W. (1987). "Grounds for a Strike: South African Gold Mining in the 1940s." *African Economic History*, 16, 1–22.

────── (1988). "African Labour Allocation in South Africa's Gold Industry." Paper presented at the Canadian Association of African Studies Annual Meeting, Queen's University, Kingston, Canada.

James, W., and J. Lever (1987a). "Towards a Deracialized Labour Force: Industrial Relations and the Abolition of the Colour Bar on the South African Gold Mines." Research Unit for the Sociology of Development, University of Stellenbosch.

────── (1987b). "Exit the Colour Bar. But Will It Still Haunt the Mine Shafts?" *Weekly Mail*, 31 July, 17.

Jeeves, A. (1985). *Migrant Labour in South Africa's Mining Economy: The Struggle for the Gold Mines' Labour Supply, 1890–1920*. Kingston/Montreal and Johannesburg, McGill-Queen's University Press and Witwatersrand University Press.

────── (1986). "Migrant Labour and South African Expansion, 1920–50." *South African Historical Journal*, 18, 73–92.

Jochelson, K., M. Mothibeli, and J. Leger (1988). "HIV and Migrant Labour in Southern Africa." Unpublished paper, Department of Sociology, University of Witwatersrand.

Johnstone, F. (1976). *Class, Race and Gold: A Study of Class Relations and Racial Discrimination in South Africa*. London, Routledge and Kegan Paul.

——— (1989). "Rand and Kolyma: Afro-Siberian Hamlet." *South African Sociological Review*, 1(2), 1–45.

Katzen, L. (1964). *Gold and the South African Economy*. Cape Town, A. A. Balkema.

Kirkwood, M. (1974). "Conflict on the Mines, 1974." *South African Labour Bulletin*, 1(7), 35–42.

Keegan, T. (1987). *Rural Transformations in Industrializing South Africa: The Southern Highveld to 1914*. London, Macmillan.

Kimble, J. (1985). " 'Clinging to the Chiefs': Some Contradictions of Colonial Rule in Basutoland, c.1890–1930." In H. Bernstein and B. Campbell, eds., *Contradictions of Accumulation in Africa: Studies in Economy and State*. Beverly Hills, Sage, 25–69.

Knight, J. (1977). "Is South Africa Running Out of Unskilled Labour?" In F. Wilson, A. Kooy, and D. Hendrie, eds., *Farm Labour in South Africa*. Cape Town, David Philip, 31–50.

Kruger H., and G. Rundle (1981). "A Report on the Problems Associated with Excessive Drinking Amongst Black Mineworkers." In Association of Mine Managers of South Africa, *Papers and Discussions, 1978-1979*. Johannesburg, Chamber of Mines.

Kydd, J. (1984). "Malawi in the 1970s: Development Policies and Economic Change." In *Malawi: An Alternative Pattern of Development*. Edinburgh, Centre for African Studies, University of Edinburgh, 295–380.

Laburn, C., and K. McNamara (1980). "Black Migrant Mineworkers' Contact with Home." *Human Resources Monitoring Report*, 4(5), 1–7.

Lacey, M. (1981). *Working for Boroko: The Origins of a Coercive Labour System in South Africa*. Johannesburg, Ravan Press.

——— (1984). "Feudalism in the Age of Computers: An Analysis of Recruitment Strategies to Reserve and Allocate Labour." *Black Sash*, 26, 7–13.

Lawrence, A. (1979). "The Novice Migrant Mineworker." *Human Resources Monitoring Report*, 3(3), 1–15.

Legassick, M. (1977). "Gold, Agriculture and Secondary Industry in South Africa, 1885–1970: From Periphery to Sub-Metropole as a Forced Labour System." In R. Palmer and N. Parsons, eds., *The Roots of Rural Poverty in Central and Southern Africa*. London, Heinemann, 175–200.

Leger, J. (1986). "Safety and the Organisation of Work in South African Gold Mines: A Crisis of Control." *International Labour Review*, 125, 591–603.

——— (1987a). "The Mozambican Miners' Reprieve." *South African Labour Bulletin*, 12(2), 29–32.

——— (1987b). "From Hlobane to Kinross: Disasters and the Struggle for Health and Safety on the Mines." In G. Moss and I. Obery, eds., *South African Review: Volume 4*. Johannesburg, Ravan Press, 292–304.

——— (1987c). "South African Gold Miners' Perceptions of Safety, 1984 to 1987." Paper presented at the Mine Safety and Health Congress, Johannesburg.

Leger, J., J. Maller, and J. Myers (1986). "Trade Union Initiatives in Health and Safety." In South African Research Service, ed., *South African Review: Volume 3*. Johannesburg, Ravan Press, 79–96.

Leger, J., and P. van Niekerk (1986). "Organizing on the Mines: The NUM Phenomenon." In South African Research Service, ed., *South African Review: Volume 3*. Johannesburg, Ravan Press, 68–78.

Leger, J., and M. Mothibeli (1988). "Talking Rocks: Pit Sense Amongst South African Miners." *Labour, Capital and Society*, 21, 222–237.

Lemon, A. (1982). "Migrant Labour and Frontier Commuters: Reorganizing South Africa's Black Labour Supply." In D. Smith, ed., *Living Under Apartheid*. London, George Allen & Unwin, 64–89.

——— (1984). "State Control over the Labor Market in South Africa." *International Political Science Review*, 5, 189–208.

Lever, J. (1988). "Established Trade Unions and Industrial Relations on the Gold Mines in the 1980s." *Industrial Relations Journal of South Africa*, 8, 1–14.

Leys, R. (1975). "South African Gold Mining in 1974." *African Affairs*, 74, 196–208.

Lipton, M. (1977). "South Africa: Two Agricultures?" In F. Wilson, A. Kooy, and D. Hendrie, eds., *Farm Labour in South Africa*. Cape Town, David Philip, 72–86.

——— (1980). "Men of Two Worlds: Migrant Labour in South Africa." *Optima*, 29, 72–201.

——— (1985). *Capitalism and Apartheid: South Africa, 1910–84*. Totowa, NJ, Wildwood House.

Low, A. (1986). *Agricultural Development in Southern Africa*. London, James Currey.

Mabin, A. (1989). "Struggle for the City: Urbanisation and the Political Strategies of the South African State." *Social Dynamics*, 15, 1–28.

Malunga, M. (1988). "My Life as a Miner." *Weekly Mail*, 29 July–25 August.

Market Research Africa (1986). "Accommodation Study Management Report," 2 vols. Johannesburg.

Markham, C., and M. Mothibeli (1987). "The 1987 Mineworkers Strike." *South African Labour Bulletin*, 13(1), 58–75.

Marks, S., and N. Andersson (1987). "Issues in the Political Economy of Health in South Africa." *Journal of Southern African Studies*, 13, 177–186.

Marks, S., and S. Trapido (1979). "Lord Milner and the South African State." *History Workshop*, 8, 50–80.

Martin W., and M. Beittel (1987). "The Hidden Abode of Reproduction: Conceptualizing Households in Southern Africa." *Development and Change*, 18, 215–234.

May, J., J. Nattrass, and A. Peters (1985). "Migrant Labour, Subsistence Production and Income Levels in Rural Kwazulu: A Quantitative Overview." Development Studies Unit, University of Natal, Durban.

McAllister, P. (1974). "Socio-Economic Survey of Malawi." Unpublished report, Johannesburg, Native Recruiting Corporation.

——— (1979). "The Influence of Non-Economic Factors on the Work Cycles of Oscillating Labour Migrants in Southern Africa." Unpublished report, Johannesburg, Chamber of Mines.

McNamara, K. (1978). "Social Life, Ethnicity and Conflict in a Gold Mine Hostel." Unpublished M.A. thesis, University of the Witwatersrand, Johannesburg.

———— (1979). "Some Underlying Causes of Industrial Conflict in the Mining Industry." *Human Resources Monitoring Report*, 3(4), 1–10.

———— (1985). "Black Worker Conflicts on South African Gold Mines: 1973–1982." Unpublished Ph.D. thesis, University of Witwatersrand, Johannesburg.

———— (1988). "Inter-Group Violence among Black Employees on the South African Gold Mines, 1974–86." *South African Sociological Review*, 1, 23–38.

Møller, V., and L. Schlemmer (1987). "Images of Mine Work Among Non-Mining Migrants in Durban." Unpublished report, Centre for Applied Social Sciences, University of Natal, Durban.

Moodie, D. (1980). "The Formal and Informal Social Structure of a South African Gold Mine." *Human Relations*, 33, 555–574.

———— (1983). "Mine Culture and Miners' Identity on the South African Gold Mines." In B. Bozzoli, ed., *Town and Countryside in the Transvaal: Capitalist Penetration and Popular Response*. Johannesburg, Ravan Press, 176–197.

———— (1986). "The Moral Economy of the Black Miners' Strike of 1946." *Journal of Southern African Studies*, 13, 1–35.

———— (1988a). "Migrancy and Sexuality on the South African Gold Mines." *Journal of Southern African Studies*, 14, 228–256.

———— (1988b). "The South African State and Industrial Conflict in the 1940s." *International Journal of African Historical Studies*, 21, 21–61.

———— (forthcoming). "Alcohol and Resistance on the South African Gold Mines." In J. Crush and C. Ambler, eds., *Drinking in Africa*. Athens, Ohio University Press.

Moroney, S. (1982). "Mine Married Quarters: The Differential Stabilisation of the Witwatersrand Workforce, 1900–1920." In S. Marks and R. Rathbone, eds., *Industrialisation and Social Change in South Africa*. London, Longman, 259–269.

Morrell, R. (1988). "The Disintegration of the Gold and Maize Alliance in South Africa in the 1920s." *International Journal of African Historical Studies*, 21, 619–635.

Muller, N. (1986). "Behind the Bolted Door: Rural Poverty and Social Relations in the Transkei Bantustan." Africa Seminar paper, Centre for African Studies, University of Cape Town.

Murray, C. (1980). "Migrant Labour and Changing Family Structure in the Rural Periphery of Southern Africa." *Journal of Southern African Studies*, 6, 141–156.

———— (1981). *Families Divided: The Impact of Migrant Labour in Lesotho*. Cambridge, Cambridge University Press.

———— (1987). "Displaced Urbanization: South Africa's Rural Slums." *African Affairs*, 86, 311–329.

Napier, J. (1980). "Gold Mine Planning." Unpublished Ph.D. thesis, University of the Witwatersrand, Johannesburg.

National Union of Mineworkers (1988). "Collective Bargaining at Anglo American Mines." Johannesburg.

Nattrass, J. (1981). *The South African Economy: Its Growth and Change*. Cape Town, Oxford University Press.

Obery, I., S. Singh, and D. Niddrie (1987). "Disciplined Mine Strike a Test of Strength." *Work in Progress*, 49, 34–37.

O'Meara, D. (1978). "Analysing Afrikaner Nationalism: The 'Christian-National' Assault on White Trade Unionism in South Africa, 1934–1948." *African Affairs*, 77, 45–72.

——— (1982). "The 1946 African Mine Workers' Strike and the Political Economy of South Africa." In M. Murray, ed., *South African Capitalism and Black Political Opposition*. Cambridge, MA, Schenkman, 361–396.

Owen, K. (1963). "Summary of the Report of the Findings of the Froneman Committee." Johannesburg, South Africa Institute of Race Relations.

Packard, R. (1987). "Tuberculosis and the Development of Industrial Health Policies on the Witwatersrand, 1902–32." *Journal of Southern African Studies*, 13, 187–209.

——— (1988). "Labour Supplies and Health in the South African Gold Mines." Paper presented at the Canadian Association of African Studies Meeting, Queen's University, Kingston, Canada.

——— (1989). "Labor Stabilization and the Risk of Tuberculosis on the South African Gold Mines, 1977–1985." Paper presented at African Studies Association Meeting, Atlanta.

——— (1989). *White Plague, Black Labor: Tuberculosis amd the Political Economy of Health and Disease in South Africa*. Los Angeles, University of California Press.

Parson, J. (1984). *Botswana: Liberal Democracy and the Labor Reserve in Southern Africa*. Boulder, Westview.

Parsons, J. (1982). "Novices in Gold Mining." Unpublished paper, Johannesburg.

Parsons, J., and W. Mashaba (1980). "Report on the Recruitment of Black Workers for the South African Gold Mines in the 1970s and 1980s." Unpublished report, Johannesburg, Chamber of Mines.

Peart, C. (1982). "Implications of Demographic Change in the Black Labour Force for Conditions of Service in the Mining Industry." Unpublished report, Johannesburg, Chamber of Mines.

Pillay, P. (1987). "Future Developments in the Demand for Labour by the South African Mining Industry." International Labour Organization, International Migration for Employment Working Paper No. 34.

Platzky, L., and C. Walker (1985). *The Surplus People: Forced Removals in South Africa*. Johannesburg, Ravan Press.

Price, R., and C. Rosberg, eds. (1980). *The Apartheid Regime: Political Power and Racial Domination*. Berkeley, University of California Press.

Prior, F., and C. Chipeta (1990). "Economic Development through Estate Agriculture: The Case of Malawi." *Canadian Journal of African Studies*, 24.

Pycroft, C., and B. Munslow (1988). "Black Mine Workers in South Africa: Strategies of Co-option and Resistance." *Journal of Asian and African Studies*, 23, 156–179.

Rafel, R. (1987). "Job Reservation on the Mines." In G. Moss and I. Obery, eds., *South African Review: Volume 4*. Johannesburg, Ravan Press, 265–282.

Ramaphosa, C. (1985). "Organising on the Mines." South African Institute of Race Relations, Opinion Paper.

_____ (1986). *Evidence to the South African Parliamentary Standing Committee on Minerals and Energy Affairs.*

Rheinallt Jones, R. D. (1953). "Industrial Relations in South Africa." *International Affairs,* 29, 43–51.

Robertson, N. (1983). "Monitoring of Mineworkers' Attitudes, Beliefs, and Opinions." *Journal of Social Psychology,* 121, 271–272.

Sharp J., and A. Spiegel (1985). "Vulnerability to Impoverishment in South African Rural Areas: The Erosion of Kinship and Neighbourhood as Social Resources." *Africa,* 55, 133–151.

Simkins, C. (1981a). "Agricultural Production in the African Reserves of South Africa, 1918–1969." *Journal of Southern African Studies,* 7, 256–283.

_____ (1981b). "The Demographic Demand and Institutional Context of African Unemployment in South Africa, 1960–80." Southern African Labour and Development Research Unit, University of Cape Town, Working Paper No. 39, University of Cape Town.

_____ (1984). "African Population, Employment and Incomes on Farms Outside the Reserves, 1923–69." Carnegie Conference Paper No. 25, University of Cape Town.

Simons, J., and R. Simons (1978). "Changing Conditions of Labour in South African Mining." Paper presented at the Conference on Migratory Labour in Southern Africa, Lusaka.

_____ (1983). *Class and Colour in South Africa, 1850–1950,* 2nd ed. London, International Defence and Aid Fund.

_____ (1987). "One Hundred Years of Job Reservation on the South African Mines." International Labour Organization, International Migration for Employment Working Paper No. 31.

Sitas, A. (1979). "Rebels without a Pause: The M.W.U. and the Defence of the Colour Bar." *South African Labour Bulletin,* 5(3), 30–58.

South African Labour Bulletin (1978). "Extracts from the Report of the Inter-Departmental Committee of Inquiry into Riots on the Mines in the Republic of South Africa." *SALB,* 4(5), 49–65.

Southall, R. (1982). *South Africa's Transkei: The Political Economy of an "Independent" Bantustan.* London, Heinemann.

_____ (1983). "Labour Migrancy and Independent Unions in South Africa." Institute for International Development and Co-operation, University of Ottawa.

Spiegel, A. (1980). "Changing Patterns of Migrant Labour and Rural Differentiation in Lesotho." *Social Dynamics,* 6, 1–13.

_____ (1982). "Spinning Off the Developmental Cycle: Comments on the Utility of a Concept in the Light of Data from Matatiele Transkei." *Social Dynamics,* 8, 30–45.

Stahl, C., and W. Böhning (1981). "Reducing Dependence on Migration in Southern Africa." In W. Böhning, ed., *Black Migration to South Africa: A Selection of Policy-Oriented Research.* Geneva, International Labour Organization, 147–184.

Stein, M. (1978). "Max Gordon and African Trade Unionism on the Witwatersrand, 1935–1940." In E. Webster, ed., *Southern African Labour History.* Johannesburg, Ravan Press, 143–157.

Stichter, S. (1985). *Migrant Laborers*. Cambridge, Cambridge University Press.

Surplus People Project (1983). *Forced Removals in South Africa*, 5 vols., 2nd impression. Cape Town, Citadel Press.

Taylor, J. "The Pattern and Consequences of Declining Mine Labour Recruitment in Botswana." Geneva, International Labour Organization, 1986.

Thabane, M., and J. Guy (1984). "Unemployment and Casual Labour in Maseru: The Impact of Changing Employment Strategies on Migrant Labourers in Lesotho." Carnegie Conference Paper No. 124, University of Cape Town.

Thompson, C. (1984). "Black Trade Unions on the Mines." In *South African Review: Volume 2*. Johannesburg, Ravan Press, 156–164.

Thompson, E. P. (1967). "Time, Work-Discipline and Industrial Capitalism." *Past and Present*, 38, 56–97.

Turrell, R. (1987). *Capital and Labour on the Kimberley Diamond Fields, 1871–1890*. Cambridge, Cambridge University Press.

United Nations Economic and Social Council (1978a). "Report of the Conference on Migratory Labour in Southern Africa: Lusaka," Executive Committee Meeting of ECA, 4–8 April.

_____ (1987b). "Resolutions and Charter of Rights for Migrant Workers in Southern Africa, para. 1.2," Lusaka.

Unterhalter, E. (1987). *Forced Removal: The Division, Segregation and Control of the People of South Africa*. London, International Defence and Aid Fund.

Vail, L., and L. White (1980). *Capitalism and Colonialism in Mozambique: A Study of Quelimane District*. London, Heinemann.

Van Onselen, C. (1976). *Chibaro: African Mine Labour in Southern Rhodesia, 1900–1933*. London, Pluto Press.

Wagner, H. (1986). "The Challenge of Deep-Level Mining in South Africa." *Journal of the South African Institute of Mining and Metallurgy*, 86, 377–392.

Watson, V. (1986). "South African Urbanisation Policy: Past and Future." *South African Labour Bulletin*, 11(8), 77–90.

Webster, E. (1988). "The Rise of Social-Movement Unionism: The Two Faces of the Black Trade Union Movement in South Africa." In P. Frankel, N. Pines, and M. Swilling, eds., *State, Resistance and Change in South Africa*. London, Croom Helm, 174–196.

Wiehahn, N. (1982). *The Complete Wiehahn Report: With Notes by Prof. N.E. Wiehahn*. Johannesburg and Cape Town, Lex-Patria Publishers.

Wilson, F. (1972). *Labour in the South African Gold Mines, 1911–1969*. Cambridge, Cambridge University Press.

_____ (1975). "The Political Implications for Blacks of Economic Changes Now Taking Place in South Africa." In L. Thompson and J. Butler, eds., *Change in Contemporary South Africa*. Berkeley, University of California Press, 168–200.

_____ (1980). "Current Labor Issues in South Africa." In R. Price and C. Rosberg, eds., *The Apartheid Regime: Political Power and Racial Domination*. Berkeley, University of California Press, 152–173.

Wilson, F., A. Kooy, and D. Hendrie, eds. (1977). *Farm Labour in South Africa*. Cape Town, David Philip.

Wilson, F., and M. Ramphele (1989). *Uprooting Poverty: The South African Challenge.* Cape Town, David Philip.

Wolpe, H. (1972). "Capitalism and Cheap Labour-power in South Africa: From Segregation to Apartheid." *Economy and Society,* 1, 425–458.

Worger, W. (1987). *South Africa's City of Diamonds: Mine Workers and Monopoly Capitalism in Kimberley, 1867–1895.* New Haven, CT, Yale University Press.

Yudelman, D. (1983). *The Emergence of Modern South Africa: State, Capital and the Incorporation of Organized Labor on the South African Gold Fields, 1902–39.* Westport, CT, Greenwood.

—————— (1987). "State and Capital in Contemporary South Africa." In J. Butler, R. Elphick, and D. Welsh, eds., *Democratic Liberalism in South Africa: Its History and Prospect.* Middletown, CT, Wesleyan University Press, 250–270.

Yudelman, D., and A. Jeeves (1986). "New Labour Frontiers for Old: Black Migrants to the South African Gold Mines, 1920–85." *Journal of Southern African Studies,* 13, 101–124.

About the Book
and Authors

For over a century, South Africa has been the world's largest supplier of gold. South African gold mines recruit hundreds of thousands of low-paid, largely unskilled, black migrants from rural areas throughout southern Africa to mine the ore. Without them, South Africa's gold would have remained in the ground. Consequently, the black mineworker has been an essential player in the emergence of South Africa as a modern industrial state and has borne a significant part of the burden of labor controls and exploitation commonly associated with the system of apartheid. Barred from access to skilled jobs, prevented by law from forming unions until 1982, and subjected to the harsh and unrelenting environment of single-sex compounds and deep-level mining, black mineworkers have seen little of the enormous wealth they helped to create.

South Africa's Labor Empire charts the expansion and transformation of this unique system of labor mobilization since 1920, showing how the mining industry, in its search for unlimited supplies of cheap labor, constructed a vast subcontinental labor empire and how periodic challenges to this system were resisted. Ultimately, the book illuminates the crucial link between apartheid and the expansion of the mining labor system to all sectors of the economy.

Focusing especially on the dramatic changes of the past two decades, the authors offer the first systematic analysis of the emergence of the National Union of Mineworkers and the significance of the 1987 strike that brought the industry to a standstill for three weeks. Basing their work on archival sources, contemporary evidence, and interviews with workers and management, the authors evaluate the complex interplay of forces fueling the transformation of the gold mining industry and its labor systems; they show how fluctuations in the international gold price brought fundamental change in the cost structure of mining, how the mines switched from an overwhelmingly foreign to a predominantly domestic labor force in less than a decade, and how black mineworkers formed unions and began to fight for basic rights. Although the migrant labor and compound systems remain intact, Crush, Jeeves, and Yudelman argue that there are fundamental forces at work eroding this coercive system of control. They contend that changes in the gold mining industry cannot be divorced from the broader struggle for a post-apartheid South Africa.

Jonathan Crush, Alan Jeeves, and David Yudelman have written extensively on the South African gold mining industry and its labor systems. Their recent books include Dr. Crush's *The Struggle for Swazi Labour* (1987), winner of the first Joel Gregory Prize, awarded by the Canadian African Studies Association in 1989; Dr. Jeeves's *Migrant Labour in South Africa's Mining Economy* (1985); and Dr. Yudelman's *The Emergence of Modern South Africa* (1983). Jonathan Crush is a Canada Research Fellow and associate professor of geography at Queen's University in Kingston, Ontario, where Alan Jeeves is professor of history. David Yudelman, formerly a research associate at the Centre for Resource Studies at Queen's University, is senior strategic projects officer at the head office of Ontario Hydro, Toronto, Ontario.

Index